COMPUTER NETWORKING

Zeeshan Qaiser

Toronto Academic Press

Computer Networking

Zeeshan Qaiser

Toronto Academic Press
224 Shoreacres Road
Burlington, ON L7L 2H2
Canada
www.tap-books.com
Email: orders@arclereducation.com

ISBN: 978-1-77469-755-9

ABOUT THE AUTHOR

Zeeshan Qaiser is a dynamic and accomplished professional with over 15 years of experience in the fields of IT, project management, and business development. He is currently serving as the CEO of Axondevs, a leading software development company based in Islamabad, Pakistan. Zeeshan's passion for technology and entrepreneurship led him to co-found Axondevs in 2013, which has since grown into a highly respected and sought-after firm in the software industry. Under his leadership, the company has successfully completed numerous projects for clients in Pakistan, the Middle East, Europe, and the United States. Prior to founding Axondevs, Zeeshan worked as a project manager and IT consultant for several prestigious organizations in Pakistan and the United States. He holds a bachelor's degree in computer science from the University of Central Punjab and a master's degree in business administration from the University of Illinois at Urbana-Champaign. Zeeshan is a forward-thinking and results-driven leader who is constantly seeking new opportunities to innovate and grow. His expertise in software development, project management, and business development, combined with his exceptional communication and leadership skills, make him an invaluable asset to any organization.

Contents

Preface xvii
List of Figures ix
List of Tables xi
List of Abbreviations xiii

1 Basics of Computer Networking 1

Unit Introduction 1
1.1. Computer Networks 3
1.1.1. Properties of Computer Network 3
1.1.2. Significance of Networks 4
1.1.3. Network Technologies 4
1.2. History of Computer Networking 7
1.3. Connecting to the Internet 9
1.4. The Web Concepts 10
1.4.1. Web Page 10
1.4.2. Website 11
1.4.3. The Web Terms 11
1.4.4. Search Engine 12
1.4.5. Internet Protocols 12
1.4.6. Web Server 13
1.4.7. Client 14
1.4.8. Web Browsers 14
1.4.9. Web Operations 14
1.4.10. Site Structure 15
1.4.11. Hyperlinks 16
1.4.12. Display of Web Pages 17
1.4.13. Kinds of Websites 17
1.4.14. Website Design Problems 18
1.4.15. E-mail (Electronic Mail) 19
1.4.16. FTP (File Transfer Protocol) 20
1.4.17. Telnet (Remote Computing) 21
1.5. World Wide Web (WWW) 22
1.5.1. Newsgroup/Usenet Newsgroups New 23
1.5.2. Hierarchies 23
1.5.3. Web Conferencing/Video Conferencing 24
1.5.4. Internet Chat 26
1.6. Ways of Connecting to the Networks 28
1.6.1. Broad Band Internet Connection 28
1.6.2. Dial-Up Connection 31
1.6.3. Satellite Internet 33
1.7. Summary 33
Review Questions 34
Multiple Choice Questions 34
References 36

2 Protocols and Standards of Computer Networks 43

Unit Introduction 43
2.1. Computer Networks Ecosystem 45
2.2. Data Link Protocol 46
2.2.1. IEEE 802.15.4 46
2.2.2. IEEE 802.11 AH 48
2.2.3. Wireless HART 49

2.2.4. Z-Wave 50
2.2.5. Bluetooth Low Energy 50
2.2.6. Zigbee Smart Energy 50
2.3. Limited Data Protocols 51
2.3.1. DASH7 51
2.3.2. Home Plug 51
2.3.3. G.9959 52
2.3.4. LTE-A 52
2.3.5. LoRaWAN 53
2.3.6. Weightless 54
2.3.7. DECT/ULE 54
2.4. Network Layer Routing Protocols 54
2.4.1. RPL 54
2.4.2. CORPL 55
2.4.3. CARP 55
2.5. Network Layer Encapsulation Protocols 56
2.5.1. 6LoWPAN 56
2.5.2. 6TiSCH 56
2.5.3. 6Lo 57
2.5.4. IPv6 Over G.9959 57
2.5.5. IPv6 over Bluetooth Low Energy 57
2.6. Session Layer Protocols 58
2.6.1. MQTT 58
2.6.2. SMQTT 59
2.6.3. AMQP 59
2.6.4. CoAP 60
2.6.5. XMPP 61
2.6.6. DDS 61
2.7. Management Protocols 63
2.7.1. Interconnection of Heterogeneous Datalinks 63
2.7.2. Smart Transducer Interface 64
2.8. Security In Computer Networks Protocols 64
2.8.1. MAC 64
2.8.2. 6LoWPAN 65
2.8.3. RPL 65
2.8.4. Application Layer 65
2.9. Summary 66
Review Questions 66
Multiple Choice Questions 66
References 67

3 Hardware and Software used in Computer Networks 73

Unit Introduction 73
3.1. Hardware Components 76
3.2. Processing and Memory Devices: Power, Speed, and Capacity 76
3.2.1. Processing Characteristics and Functions 77
3.2.2. Memory Characteristics and Functions 78
3.2.3. Multiprocessing 80
3.3. Secondary Storage, Input, and Output Devices 83
3.3.1. Secondary Storage Devices 84
3.3.2. Input Devices 88
3.3.3. Output Devices 93
3.4. Overview of Software 97
3.5. Systems Software 97
3.5.1. Operating Systems 98
3.5.2. Current Operating Systems 103
3.6. Utility Programs 106
3.7. Application Software 106
3.7.1. Types and Functions of Application Software 107
3.7.2. Personal Application Software 109
3.7.3. Mobile Application Software 112
3.8. Summary 114
Review Questions 114
Multiple Choice Questions 115
References 116

4 Understanding Computer Network Security 125

Unit Introduction 125
4.1. Understanding Computer Network Security 127
4.1.1. Computer Security 127
4.1.2. Network Security 128

4.2. Network Security 128
4.3. Difference Between Data Security and Network Security 130
4.4. Vulnerable Security Aspects in Internet Architecture 131
4.5. Attacks Through IPV4 and Security Issues IN IPV6 132
4.5.1. Common Internet Attack Methods 132
4.5.2. Internet Security Technologies 133
4.6. Security in Computer Network 135
4.6.1. Securing the Computer Network 135
4.6.2. Hardware 136
4.6.3. Software 136
4.7. Forms of Protection 136
4.7.1. Access Control 136
4.7.2. Authentication 138
4.7.3. Confidentiality 140
4.7.4. Integrity 141
4.8. Future Scope of Network Security 141
4.9. Summary 143
Review Questions 143
Multiple Choice Questions 143
References 144

5 Wireless Networking 149

Unit Introduction 149
5.1. Wireless Links 151
5.1.1. Terrestrial Microwave 151
5.1.2. Cellular and PCS systems 151
5.1.3. Radio and Spread Spectrum Technologies 151
5.1.4. Free-Space Optical Communication 152
5.2. Types of Wireless Networks 152
5.2.1. Wireless PAN 153
5.2.2. Wireless LAN 154
5.2.3. Wireless WAN 154
5.2.4. Cellular Network 155
5.2.5. Global Area Network 156
5.2.6. Space Network 156
5.3. WLAN Standards 157
5.3.1. DSSS 157
5.3.2. OFDM 157
5.3.3. 802.11 b 157
5.3.4. 802.11 a 158
5.3.5. 802.11 g 158
5.4. Different Uses of Wireless Networks 159
5.4.1. General 159
5.4.2. Performance 160
5.4.3. Space 160
5.4.4. Home 161
5.4.5. Time Savings 161
5.4.6. Flexibility and Quality of Work 161
5.5. Electromagnetic Interference (EMI) in Wireless Networks 162
5.5.1. Absorption and Reflection 162
5.5.2. Multipath Fading 162
5.5.3. Hidden Node Problem 163
5.5.4. Shared Resource Problem 163
5.5.5. Network 163
5.5.6. Safety 163
5.5.7. Security Concerns 164
5.5.8. Economic Impact 165
5.6. Summary 166
Review Questions 166
Multiple Choice Questions 166
References 168

6 Emerging Networking Applications 173

Unit Introduction 173
6.1. Functionality and Requirements 175
6.2. General Characteristics 175
6.3. Caches and Memory Access Patterns in Web Caching 176
6.3.1. Caching Architectures 177
6.3.2. Cache Resolution/Routing 178
6.3.3. Prefetching 179
6.3.4. Cache Placement/ Replacement 179
6.3.5. Cache Coherency 180
6.4. Parallelism 180

6.4.1. Layer Parallelism 181
6.4.2. Connection Level Parallelism 181
6.4.3. Functional Parallelism 181
6.4.4. Data Level Parallelism 182
6.4.5. Packet Level Parallelism 182
6.5. Bottlenecks 182
6.6. Case Study: Distributed Video Streaming Over The Internet 183
6.6.1. Receiver Side: Rate Allocation Algorithm 183
6.6.2. Sender Side: Packet Partition Algorithm 183
6.7. Processor Architectures 184
6.8. Summary 185
Review Questions 185
Multiple Choice Questions 185
References 186

7 Network Performance and Optimization 191

Unit Introduction 191
7.1. Factors Affecting the Performance of Network 193
7.1.1. Throughput and Bandwidth 193
7.1.2. Jitter and Latency 193
7.1.3. Error Rates and Packet Loss 194
7.1.4. Queuing and Congestion 194
7.2. Measuring the Performance of Network 195
7.2.1. Tools for Measuring the Performance of a Network 196
7.2.2. Analyzing Network Performance Data 196
7.3. Network Optimization Techniques 197
7.3.1. Quality of Service (QoS) 197
7.3.2. Policing and Traffic Shaping 198
7.3.3. Traffic Routing and Load Balancing 198
7.3.4. Network Caching 198
7.3.5. Deduplication and Compression 198
7.4. Performance Troubleshooting and Tuning 199
7.5. Network Security Considerations 201
7.5.1. Balancing Security and Performance 201
7.5.2. Strategies for Securing a High-Performance Network 201
7.5.3. Common Network Security Vulnerabilities and Threats 202
7.6. Future Directions In Network Optimization and Performance 203
7.6.1. Emerging Trends and Technologies 203
7.6.2. Challenges in Network Optimization and Performance 204
7.6.3. Research Directions and Open Problems in the Field 204
7.7. Summary 206
Review Questions 206
Multiple Choice Questions 206
References 207

8 Future of Computer Networking 211

Unit Introduction 211
8.1. Edge Computing 213
8.2. Cloud Networking 214
8.2.1. Infrastructure as a Service (IaaS) 215
8.2.2. Platform as a Service (PaaS) 216
8.2.3. Software as a Service (SaaS) 216
8.3. Software Defined Wan (SD-WAN) 217
8.4. Software Defined Networking (SDN) 218
8.4.1. SDN-Architecture 219
8.4.2. Adaptive SDN 220
8.5. Cloud Automation and Orchestration 220
8.6. Intent-Based Networking 223
8.7. 5G And Its Applications 224
8.8. 4D Network 225
8.8.1. Data Plane 226
8.8.2. Discovery Plane 226
8.8.3. Dissemination Plane 226
8.8.4. Decision Plane 227
8.9. Summary 228
Review Questions 228
Multiple Choice Questions 228
References 229

Index 233

List of Figures

Figure 1.1. The internet is the global system of interconnected computer networks

Figure 1.2. Illustration of different network topologies

Figure 1.3. Diagram representing local area networks (LANs)

Figure 1.4. Schematic of HTML and its components

Figure 1.5. Uniform resource locator

Figure 1.6. Explanation of the client server

Figure 1.7. Illustration of the web architecture

Figure 1.8. Web server design

Figure 1.9. Diagram representing the website root

Figure 1.10. How browsers display web pages

Figure 1.11. Illustration of the telnet (remote computing)

Figure 1.12. Diagram representing video conferencing

Figure 1.13. Image demonstrating internet chats and various communication methods

Figure 1.14. Explanation of a gateway access

Figure 1.15. Schematic description of a leased connection

Figure 1.16. Illustration of a dial-up connection

Figure 2.1. Image of machine-to-machine (M2M) communication

Figure 2.2. Illustration of computer networks ecosystem

Figure 2.3. Diagram of protocols for computer networks

Figure 2.4. Schematic of components of wireless HART

Figure 2.5. Image of LTE-A framework

Figure 2.6. Schematic of mechanism of MQTT architecture

Figure 2.7. Schematic of mechanism of AMQP architecture

Figure 2.8. Diagram of CoAP messages

Figure 2.9. Schematic of IEEE 1905.1 protocol configuration

Figure 3.1. The input-process-output concept

Figure 3.2. Illustration of the memory vs. storage

Figure 3.3. Schematic of the central processing unit (CPU)

Figure 3.4. Architecture of the multiprocessor microprocessor

Figure 3.5. Illustration of the parallel computing

Figure 3.6. Schematic of the grid computing

Figure 3.7. Schematic of the hard disk and its components

Figure 3.8. Illustration of the storage area network (SAN)

Figure 3.9. Image of an optical disk drive

Figure 3.10. Image of a USB flash drive

Figure 3.11. Schematic of the personal computer input devices

Figure 3.12. Illustration of the various types of digital cameras
Figure 3.13. Image of display monitor
Figure 3.14. Illustration of system software
Figure 3.15. Schematic of networking capabilities
Figure 3.16. Picture of window vista
Figure 3.17. Illustration of components of utility programs
Figure 3.18. Schematic of software as a service (SaaS)
Figure 3.19. Floe diagram of word processing
Figure 4.1. Network and data link in OSI model
Figure 4.2. Visual representation of IPsec implementation
Figure 4.3. Illustration of the viruses attack on computers
Figure 4.4. Schematic of the firewall internet security
Figure 4.5. Illustration of the access control methods
Figure 4.6. Authentication as a form of protection
Figure 4.7. Illustration of the scope of future computer networks security
Figure 5.1. Illustration of the terrestrial microwave technology
Figure 5.2. Illustration of the WPANs communication
Figure 5.3. Schematic of the wireless WAN
Figure 5.4. Illustration of the working of a GSM network
Figure 5.5. Illustration of the use of wireless networking in space
Figure 5.6. Example diagram showing electromagnetic interference to highlight inductive, conductive, capacitive, and radiative EMI in a system
Figure 5.7. Schematic of the wired equivalent privacy
Figure 6.1. Illustration of the web caching
Figure 6.2. Illustration of the network latency
Figure 6.3. Graphs of the bimodal distribution
Figure 6.4. Schematic of the functional parallelism
Figure 7.1. Illustration of throughput and bandwidth in performance of network
Figure 7.2. Graph showing the jitter and latency in network performance
Figure 7.3. Quality of service and its factors
Figure 7.4. Illustration of the duplication and compression of data
Figure 7.5. Illustration of the distributed denial-of-service (DDoS) and denial-of-service (DoS) attacks
Figure 8.1. Schematic of the edge computing architecture
Figure 8.2. Illustration of the cloud computing
Figure 8.3. Components and architecture of SDN
Figure 8.4. Illustration of the cloud automation vs. cloud orchestration
Figure 8.5. Schematic of the internet-based networking

List of Tables

Table 2.1. Tabular data about computer networks transport layer protocols contrast

Table 3.1. Comparison for various forms of data storage

Table 8.1. Parameter values

List of Abbreviations

AI	Artificial Intelligence
ALM	Application Lifecycle Management
ALME	Abstraction Layer Management Entity
AP	Access Point
API	Application Program Interface
ARPA	Advanced Research Projects Agency
ARPANET	Advanced Research Projects Agency Network
ASP	Active Server Pages
ASP	Application Service Provider
AWS	Amazon Web Services
CAGR	Compound Annual Growth Rate
CCK	Complementary Code Keying
CCTV	Closed Circuit Television
CD-R	CD-Recordable
CD-ROM	Compact Disc Read-Only Memory
CD-RW	CD-Rewritable
CIX	Commercial Internet Exchange
CMDU	Control Message Data Units
CPU	Central Processing Unit
CRC	Cyclic Redundancy Check
CU	Control Unit
DAO	Destination Advertisement Object

DDoS	Distributed Denial-of-Service
DIS	DODAG Information Solicitation
DMZs	Demilitarized Zones
DODAG	Destination-Oriented Directed Acyclic Graph
DoS	Denial-of-Service
DRM	Digital Rights Management
DSL	Digital Subscriber Line
DVD	Digital Video Disc
EMI	Electromagnetic Interference
EPROM	Erasable Programmable Read-Only Memory
FTP	File Transfer Protocol
GAN	Global Area Network
GPS	Global Positioning System
GSM	Global System for Mobile Communications
GUI	Graphical User Interface
HPA	Health Protection Agency
HTML	Hyper Text Markup Language
IDS	Intrusion Detection Systems
IEEE	Institute of Electrical and Electronics Engineers
IETF	Internet Engineering Task Force
IoT	Internet of Things
IP	Internet Protocol
IPS	Intrusion Prevention Systems
ISM	Industrial Scientific Medical
ITU	International Telecommunication Union
JSP	Java Server Pages
LAN	Local Area Network
M2M	Machine-to-Machine
MAC	Medium Access Control
MANs	Metropolitan Area Networks
Mbps	Megabits per Second
MICR	Magnetic Ink Character Recognition
MIT	Massachusetts Institute of Technology
ML	Machine Learning
MPLS	Multiprotocol Label Switching
MR	Magnetic Resonance

NCP	National Control Protocol
NI	Network Interface
NIC	Network Interface Card
OCR	Optical Character Recognition
OFDM	Orthogonal Frequency Division Multiplexing
OFDMA	Orthogonal Frequency Division Numerous Access
OLED	Organic Light-Emitting Diode
OMG	Object Management Group
OS	Operating System
OSI	Open System Interconnection
PANs	Personal Area Networks
PBCC	Packet Binary Convolution Coding
PCS	Personal Communications Service
PIMs	Personal Information Managers
POA	Point of Access
REST	Representational State Transfer
RF	Radio Frequency
RFID	Radio Frequency Identification
RIA	Rich Internet Application
ROM	Read-Only Memory
SaaS	Software as a Service
SAN	Storage Area Network
SDN	Software Defined Network
SD-WAN	Software-Defined Wide Area Network
SIG	Special Interest Group
SMBs	Small to Medium-Sized Businesses
SOA	Services-Oriented Architecture
SSD	Solid-State Storage
TCP	Transmission Control Protocol
TDMA	Time Division Multiple Access
TSCH	Time-Slotted Channel Hopping
UIL	User-in-the-Loop
ULE	Ultra Low Energy
URI	Uniform Resource Identifier
VMs	Virtual Machines
VoIP	Voice Over Internet Protocol

VPN	Virtual Private Networks
WAN	Wide Area Network
WEP	Wired Equivalent Privacy
WLAN	Wireless Local Area Networks
WMAN	Wireless Metropolitan Area Networks
WPAN	Wireless Personal Area Networks
WWW	World Wide Web

PREFACE

Computer networking refers to the practice of connecting multiple devices, such as computers, servers, and mobile devices, to communicate and share resources. It enables the sharing of information, data, and resources between devices, regardless of their physical location. Computer networking has revolutionized the way we live and work, facilitating instant communication, global information access, and seamless resource sharing. With the increasing importance of digital connectivity in our lives, computer networking has become an essential part of our daily routine and is critical to the functioning of businesses, organizations, and governments worldwide.

Chapter 1 provides an introduction to computer networking, explaining the fundamental concepts and terminology used in the field. The chapter also covers the history of computer networking, including its evolution over time.

Chapter 2 focuses on network protocols and standards, providing an in-depth understanding of the various communication protocols used in computer networking. The chapter discusses the OSI model, TCP/IP protocol suite, and other commonly used network protocols. Chapter 3 delves into network devices and hardware, providing an overview of the various components that make up a computer network. The chapter covers switches, routers, firewalls, and other network devices, as well as their features and functions.

Chapter 4 is all about network security, covering the various threats that computer networks face, including malware, hacking, and phishing. The chapter discusses the various security measures that can be taken to protect a network from these threats. Chapter 5 focuses on wireless networking, providing an in-depth understanding of the various wireless technologies and standards used in computer networking. The chapter covers Wi-Fi, Bluetooth, and cellular networks, as well as their features and functions.

Chapter 6 explores network applications and services, providing an overview of the various applications and services that are available on computer networks. The chapter covers e-mail, web browsing, file sharing, and other commonly used network applications. Chapter 7 is all about network performance and optimization, discussing the various factors that can affect the performance of a computer network. The chapter covers bandwidth, latency, packet loss, and other performance-related metrics, as well as strategies for optimizing network performance. Finally, Chapter 8 explores the future of computer networking, discussing emerging technologies, such as the internet of things (IoT) and software-defined networking (SDN), that are likely to shape the future of the field.

This book is intended for anyone who wants to gain a comprehensive understanding of computer networking, including students, professionals, and enthusiasts. It provides a valuable resource for learning and reference, covering all the essential topics in computer networking.

—***Author***

CHAPTER 1

BASICS OF COMPUTER NETWORKING

UNIT INTRODUCTION

The basic Internet protocol suite (commonly referred to as Transmission Control Protocol/ Internet Protocol (TCP/IP), though not all applications utilize TCP) is used by the Internet, a system of networked computers that serves billions of people globally (Greenstein, 2020).

The Web is a group of computers that are located all over the world and are linked to one another by a high-speed connection. The primary means of transmitting knowledge and sharing cultures is now the Internet. Millions of personal, public, educational, corporate, and government networks, ranging from local to worldwide, are connected by a wide range of electronic, optical, and wireless networking technologies to form this network of networks. The World Wide Web (WWW) and e-mail architecture are only two examples of the wide variety of services and information available on the Internet (Comer, 2018) (Figure 1.1).

All computers and systems that are linked exchange data and use multiple services. As a result, the Internet is not the WWW. Despite being the most commonly utilized service, the WWW is simply one of the services provided by the Internet. The Internet is a worldwide network of networked computers. The Internet provides infinite information and services, including interconnected web documents and Web services, electronic mail, telecommunications, and document sharing (Xingmei et al., 2013).

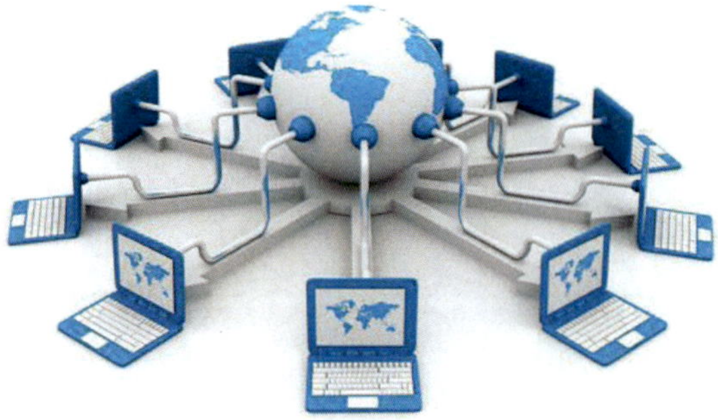

Figure 1.1. The internet is the global system of interconnected computer networks.

Source: Sutori, Creative Commons License.

Learning Objectives

At the end of this chapter, readers will be able to learn the following:

- The concept of computer networks;
- History of the computer networking;
- Various types of connections to the internet;
- The concept and usage of Web and World Wide Web;
- Different ways of connecting to the internet including Broad Band and Dial-up connection.

Key Terms

- Broad band internet
- Communication
- Computer networks
- Data
- Dial-up connection
- E-mail
- Internet technologies
- Private network
- Satellite internet
- Web
- Web conferencing
- Web services
- World wide web

1.1. COMPUTER NETWORKS

A computer network is an architecture that enables two or even more computers (referred to as hosts) to interact with one another (Madakam et al., 2015).

Following are the common definitions of computer networks:

i. A network is a collection of interconnected computers and other equipment that can transfer information. – Every device on the network is considered a node, and every node has a specific address.

ii. A computer network, sometimes known as a network, is a set of hardware devices and computers joined by channels of communication that enable the exchange of resources and data.

The network accomplishes this by offering a set of guidelines for communication, known as protocols, which all contributing sites must follow. A communication standard is a set of guidelines governing data exchange through a network. The necessity of a protocol must be self-evident: it enables computers from various manufacturers with varying operating features to communicate in the same language (Leiner et al., 2009).

KEYWORD

A **network** is a collection of computers, servers, mainframes, network devices, peripherals, or other devices connected to allow data sharing.

1.1.1. Properties of Computer Network

Following are the properties of computer networks:

1. **Ease Communications:** E-mail, messaging service, chat rooms, the telephone, virtual telephone conversations, and video conferencing are just a few of the ways that individuals may interact quickly and easily thanks to the use of a network.
2. **Allow Sharing of Files, Information, and Other Kinds of Data:** Data and information saved on other computers that are part of a network are accessible to users who have been granted permission to do so in a distributed system. The capacity of several networks to give users access to the data and information stored on devices that several users maintain is a significant aspect.
3. **Share Network and Computing Resources:** Each computer connected to a network can access and utilize the resources made available by networked devices, like printing a file on a mutual network printer. Distributed

computing takes advantage of computational resources across the network to accomplish projects.

4. **Might be Insecure:** Computer hackers might exploit a network to infect linked devices with malware attacks or to prohibit these machines from connecting to the network correctly.
5. **It Might be Problematic to Set Up:** Setting up a complicated computer network could be challenging. Setting up an efficient computer network in a large corporation or organization might also be expensive.

1.1.2. Significance of Networks

The following are some reasons why networks are necessary:

1. **Load Sharing:** The software and information are sent to a remote server to distribute the load amongst the two sites.
2. **Message Service:** Interpersonal message exchanges can be handled by a network. This solution is also suitable for educational purposes and seminar events. Consequently, it is not a compelling reason for establishing a system of scientific computers.
3. **Information Sharing:** The application is transmitted to a remote host that contains a vast database. This technique will be incredibly beneficial when data sets are too enormous to replicate affordably (Lane et al., 1993).
4. **Program Sharing:** Program sharing is a key feature of network computing that enables more efficient, cost-effective, and collaborative use of software applications in a networked environment.
5. **Remote Service:** Remote service is a key feature of network computing that enables more efficient and flexible management and support of devices and computers.

KEYWORD

Devices are objects or systems that have a specific purpose or intention, like electronic communication devices like cell phones.

1.1.3. Network Technologies

Following are various network terminologies:

1. **Intranet:** It is a collection of networks controlled by one administrative authority and utilizing the Internet Standard and IP-based tools like web browsers and data transfer apps. This administrative organization restricts intranet

access to approved users only. Typically, an intranet is a firm's internal network. Usually, a substantial intranet will have 1 web server at minimum to deliver corporate information to consumers (Sallai, 2013).

2. **Extranet:** It is a network of computers utilized outside of the intranet. An extranet is a network technology that permits regulated connectivity from the outside for corporate or academic reasons. In some business-to-business settings, an extranet can be considered an expansion of a firm's intranet that is provided to external users, typically partners, suppliers, and distributors, in independence from other Internet users.
3. **Local Area Network (LAN):** It is a system that links computers and other devices inside a constrained physical space, like a home, school, office block, or set of facilities close to one another. A node is any computer or other equipment connected to a network.
4. **Wide Area Network (WAN):** It is an abbreviation for wide area network, which refers to a kind of computer network spanning a massive area, including a city, nation, or even intercontinental ranges, by utilizing a communication system that incorporates many different kinds of media like telephone lines, wires, and airwaves. A wide area network (WAN) will frequently use the broadcasting facilities offered by common carriers like phone companies.
5. **Enterprise Private Network:** It is a network created by an organization to link several firm locations, such as manufacturing facilities, corporate headquarters, outlying offices, and retail locations, to share system resources (Mattern & Floerkemeier, 2010).
6. **Virtual Private Network (VPN):** It is a type of network where some interconnections amongst nodes are handled by open connections or electronic circuits in a wider network rather than physical cables. When this occurs, the virtual network's data link layer standards are thought to be routed through the wider network. A secure connection over the public Internet is one common application, but a VPN does not need to contain specific security features like identification or data encryption. VPNs, for instance, can isolate the traffic of distinct user communities across a secure network infrastructure (Powers, 1997).

KEYWORD

A **communi cations system** or communi cation system is a collection of individual telecommunications networks systems, relay stations, tributary stations, and terminal equipment usually capable of interconnection and interoperation to form an integrated whole.

7. **Network Topology:** It is the arrangement of the nodes' connections in a computer system. Network topology describes how computer networks see their functional connections with each other. The significance of the phrase logical cannot be overstated. That is, the topology of the network is irrespective of the network's physical layout. Even though connected computers are practically arranged in a linear configuration, if they are interconnected via a gateway, the network's topology is a Star instead of a bus. In this aspect, a network's visual and functional properties are diverse; the logical and physical architecture isn't always the same. Digital networks are two types of networks that can be categorized based on the mode of data transmission utilized (Batinić, 2015).

Following are the typical layouts of networks (Whitacre, 2010) (Figure 1.2):

- **Bus Network:** Along this network, all nodes are linked to one common medium.
- **A star Network:** Each node is linked to a unique central node.
- **A Ring Network:** Each node is linked to its right and left neighbors, making all nodes interconnected and able to be reached by moving through nodes to the left or right.
- **A Mesh Network:** Each node has an unlimited number of neighbors linked to it, allowing for one traversal as a minimum between every pair of nodes.
- **A Fully Connected Network:** Every node in this network is linked to every node.

Figure 1.2. Illustration of different network topologies.

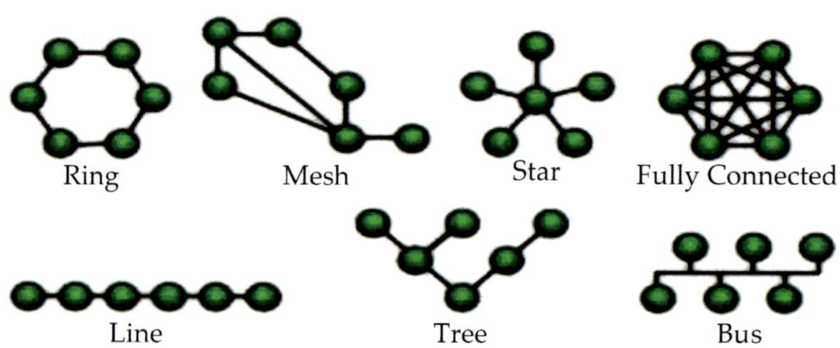

Source: Malyszkz, Creative Commons License.

1.2. HISTORY OF COMPUTER NETWORKING

The ARPA (Advanced Research Projects Agency) was established in the U.S. ARPA and private enterprise contractors engaged with officials from the Department of Defense in 1967 to consider possible methods for information exchange via computers. In 1969, the United States Defense Department supported a study to create a bomb-resistant network. The basic aim was to create a robust security network that could function even following a nuclear assault. The Advanced Research Projects Agency Network (ARPANET) was the name given to this project. The envisioned network was not expected to have centralized control—an apparent target. It linked 4 facilities at the University of Utah, the University of California at Santa Barbara, the University of California at Los Angeles, and the Stanford Research Institute (Piccoli et al., 2001). All through the 1970s, studies concentrated on inventing standards for managing networks, transporting messages throughout a structure of networks, and enabling remote network connectivity. When the first mail was sent in 1972, there were roughly 2 dozen sites with linked computers, but the number of places and messages swiftly exploded. In 1975, there were 63 sites (Piccoli et al., 2001).

Did you Know?

In the late 1950s, the main objective of developing information systems was to withstand a nuclear attack.

Local Area Ethernet Networks were built after 10 years of research, and computers were created to link to LANs. These workstations and local area networks were then linked to the ARPANET. The recent growth of the ARPANET was aided by its autonomous characteristics during the following decade (Wu et al., 2019) (Figure 1.3).

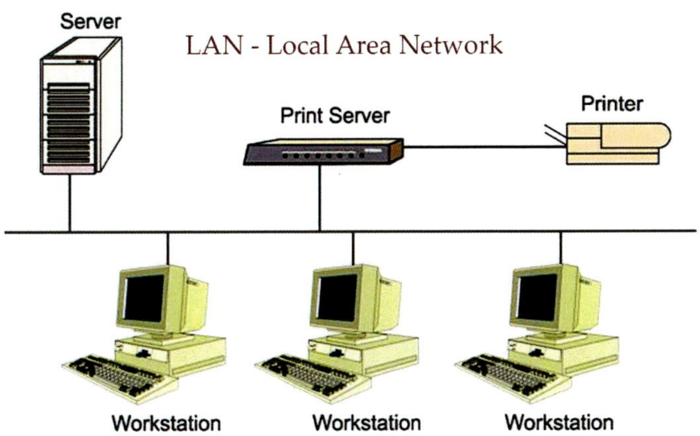

Figure 1.3. Diagram representing local area networks (LANs).

Source: Techno Pedia, Creative Commons License.

ARPANET-connected computers communicated with one another according to a protocol or regulation. The ARPANET-compatible standard is termed as National Control Protocol (NCP). A network word known as a protocol describes the standard a network uses for communication. However, as time passed and information systems changed quickly, NCP was stifled, and Transmission Control Protocol/Internet Protocol entered the networking field (Gyrard et al., 2016). At the source, TCP "transform instructions into streams of packets, and at the endpoint, they are reconstructed back into messages." IP dispatches these packets. It takes care of the routing and ensures that a packet gets to its target over several nodes and networks using different standards. The ability of TCP/IP to manage various networks using various protocols promotes other networks to join ARPANET. The ARPANET gradually expanded into a vast network of networks, and today it is regarded as the Internet (Yue et al., 2015).

The telecommunications and computer industries have been completely upended due to the advent of the Internet. This great unification of capacities was made possible by the introduction of the telegraph, telephony, radio, and computer, which laid the ground for this incorporation. The Internet is simultaneously a facility for worldwide dissemination, a method for the diffusion of information, and a medium for cooperation and communication amongst people and their computers regardless of physical location. The Internet is among the most notable advantages that may be gained from making consistent investments and maintaining a dedication to the research and innovation of information systems (Tate et al., 2001).

Did you Know?

In the 1970s and 1980s, internet users posted advertisements for furniture and automobiles they wished to sell.

- **Commercial Development:** In 1963, during the initial stages of computers and six years before the creation of ARPANET, Massachusetts Institute of Technology (MIT) students created the first video game, Space War. This game foretold the industrialization of the Internet 20 years before the TCP/IP protocol promoted the establishment of numerous networks and roughly 30 years before the U.S. government opened the Web to private corporations in 1991.

When the CIX (commercial internet exchange) was established in 1991, the genie could not be put back in the bottle despite heated debates over whether this was a suitable utilization of the Internet's latest research tool (Hodge et al., 2017).

Since its start, corporate contractors have contributed to the growth of ARPANET. As Tang and Teflon originated as space program discoveries and evolved into everyday consumer products, so have mail, internet research, and online purchasing. It has been 10 years since the first corporate relay was established between a private corporation and the Internet. Since then, innovations that have fueled the expansion of private corporations on the Internet have evolved. Gopher, a program that allows academics to obtain relevant data from eight locations, was developed in 1992 at the University of Minnesota by Paul Linder and Mark McCahill. The following year, Netscape creator Marc Andreesen created Mosaic, a web browser, the World Wide Web (WWW) became publicly available, and Intel debuted the Pentium chip to accelerate the entire process (Schoech, 2017). The Internet became simpler to use as technology evolved, and WWW pages became more complicated and enticing. Shopping centers first appeared on the Internet in 1994. One might order pizza from Domino's Pizza online or finance at the first cyberbank, First Electronic Bank. The gains had a drawback. When Vladimir Levin of Russia used the Internet to illegally transfer money to his bank, he was the first known Web bank robber. In 1995, several cutting-edge technologies were introduced, including JAVA and JAVAscript, and RealAudio, which improved the type of product details that customers might provide (Lodder, 2013). In light of the 2 to 1 commercial user to research and educational user ratio, Bill Gates decided to reposition Microsoft as a Web corporation. Nowadays, one may purchase books, meals, wine, trips, and rental properties online. Purchasing securities and bonds, financing, and planning for retirement are further commercial operations. In 1997, there were over 9 billion dollars in online sales. The U.S. Commerce Department will start researching how internet purchasing affects overall retail business in light of this development (Feizollahi et al., 2014).

TIPS

Although online consumer expenditure receives a lot of attention, business-to-business interaction is also expanding.

1.3. CONNECTING TO THE INTERNET

- **Internet Service Provider:** It gives an internet connection and the software required to navigate.
- **The Telecommunications Line:** It is needed to establish a connection between, the user, and the internet service provider.
- **Modem:** It takes a digital signal acquired from a computer and changes it into an analog form that can be transmitted over regular telephone lines. On the other side, it turns the signal to its digital form.

- **Web Browser:** It is a piece of software that allows users to browse and download numerous kinds of files, including text, images, and video, as well as web pages. Internet Explorer, Mozilla Firefox, and Google Chrome are a few instances of alternative browsers (Cerf, 2004).

1.4. THE WEB CONCEPTS

The WWW was designed to be a repository of human traditions and practices, enabling faraway participants to share their thoughts and all parts of a shared endeavor (Musa et al., 2021).

The WWW comprises many documents and data saved on such computers and structured in some HTML (hypertext markup language) that instructs browsers on presenting the content. The machines that keep the files are referred to as servers since they may simultaneously fulfill queries from several users. The browser software accesses these HTML documents and other files (Patel et al., 2016) (Figure 1.4).

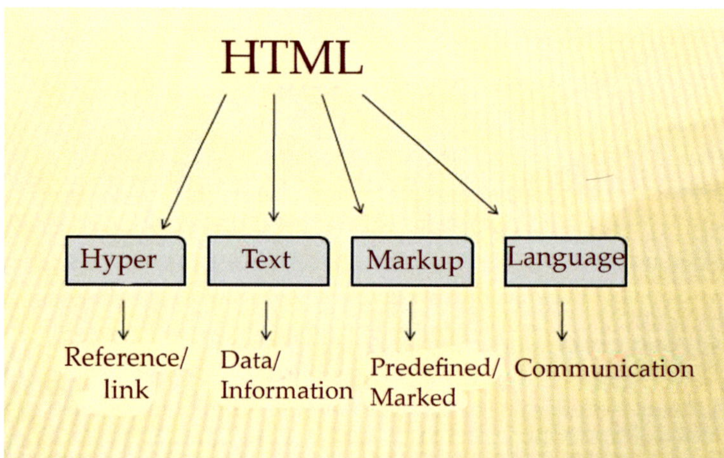

Figure 1.4. Schematic of HTML and its components.

Source: Freelancing Design, Creative Commons License.

The key Web notions are as in subsections (Sharma et al., 2019).

1.4.1. Web Page

A Web page is an Internet space that contains data about a specific person, enterprise, institution, or cause.

i. The Web is made up of files known as Web pages.
ii. It contains links to online sources (text, photos, audio recordings, videos, and other information).

1.4.2. Website

A website is a set of web pages arranged in groups and frequently related in different ways, normally referred to as a website or just a site. Typically, the website provides details about a specific individual, company, group, or purpose.

There are primarily two sorts of website designs: dynamic and static websites (Lin & Shi, 2014):

i. A static website stores its web pages on the server exactly as the visitor will see them.
ii. A dynamic website does not keep its web pages on the server in the same format that users will see. Instead, a set of parameters is used to determine how often and dynamically the content of web page updates. A dynamic website might have two different meanings. The first is that web page code is created piece by piece and arbitrarily. The second is that different content of web pages is shown depending on specific parameters. The standards might be predetermined laws or might depend on flexible user input.

1.4.3. The Web Terms

It is the complete domain of a WWW page and is made up of 3 parts that determine where the web page can be found on the Web. These components are the protocol, the website name, and the exact path to the content or resource (Figure 1.5).

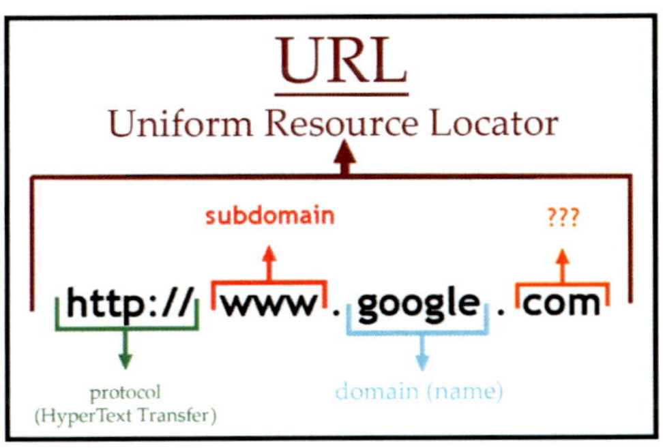

Figure 1.5. Uniform resource locator.

Source: Code Bridge Plus, Creative Commons License.

- Protocol name "HTTP://" is the first function of the URL is to specify the standard that will be utilized for this specific transaction. The characters HTTP instruct the server to utilize Hypertext Transfer Protocol and enter internet mode.
- Domain name/hostname, for instance, www.example.com, the domain name specifies the site in the following elements of the URL. The domain name, in this case, is example.com. The "www." portion at the start of the domain is the specific hostname. Additionally, there may be growth. example.com, customers.example.com, etc.

After creating a website, it must be stored in a location accessible to users. This is why Web hosting companies are utilized. They possess web servers capable of storing data (Navani et al., 2017).

1.4.4. Search Engine

Remember

Websites are typically dedicated to a particular topic or purpose, such as news, education, commerce, entertainment or social networking.

Search engines enable users to search the Web for data, photos, and other sorts of items located in various locations accessible all through the network. Search engines utilize algorithms to display appropriate, desired search terms to users. Initially, information from multiple websites is gathered and stored before being processed and saved in a database for subsequent use. When a person enters a query into the web browser, an index organizes the database and presents the visitor with outcomes that best fit the provided search words. As a result, it is critical to recognize that utilizing a search engine doesn't search the entire Web but rather the search engine's database (Botta et al., 2016). As an outcome, we may receive different outcomes when we utilize different internet engines.

1.4.5. Internet Protocols

Following are some internet protocols (Figure 1.6):

1. **TCP/IP Protocol:** This protocol is the primary Internet communication standard. It specifies the guidelines that computers must follow to interact with one another over a network.
2. **HTTP:** It is a network standard that facilitates the transfer of nearly all web resources. Files, webpages, photos, and search results are referred to as resources. It is the language used by web browsers to make queries. The HTTPs variant is also a protected, encrypted form of HTTP interaction.

3. **FTP (File Transfer Protocol):** It is used to upload or retrieve files between the customer and server or between two Internet-connected machines. This protocol is accountable for online file transfer.
4. **Internet Service Provider:** This company offers Internet access and associated services, like e-mail, to consumers and other businesses (Fathima et al., 2017).
5. **Client-Server Model:** Client-server topology is utilized by computers connected to the Internet. This indicates that the system acting as the remote server offers the user's local customer machine documents and other services (Gyrard et al., 2017).

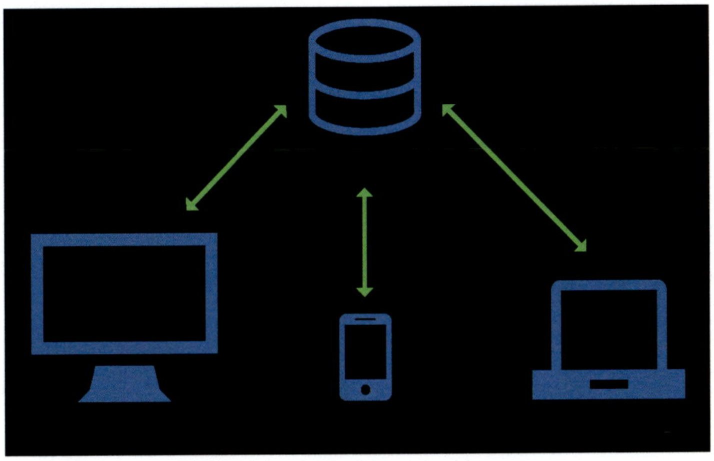

Figure 1.6. Explanation of the client server.

Source: Tech Terms, Creative Commons License.

1.4.6. Web Server

A machine designed to run specialized distributing software is called a web server. When a user, typically a Web browser, requests them, that software provides the HTML pages the customer queries along with any files that go with them. If a user is on the same system as the Web Server, they might be able to store the data straight onto the Web Server machine (Al-Fuqaha et al., 2015). However, the computer is protected, so only authenticated users can connect it to make modifications. Server-side:

- JSP (Java Server Pages);
- ASP (Active Server Pages);
- ASP.NET;

- PHP;
- Python.

1.4.7. Client

The client or customer side of the Internet often relates to the user's computer's Web browser. It might also relate to plug-ins and assistance apps that improve the browser's capability to handle specific site services. The phrase can apply to a full-user machine or a mobile device that allows Internet access (Abdel-Basset et al., 2019).

i. HTML/XHTML;
ii. CSS;
iii. JavaScript.

1.4.8. Web Browsers

A software tool or program used to retrieve, present, and navigate online information on the WWW. A URI (Uniform Resource Identifier) identifies a data resource: a website, picture, video, or another component (Kamssu et al., 2004) (Figure 1.7).

Figure 1.7. Illustration of the web architecture.

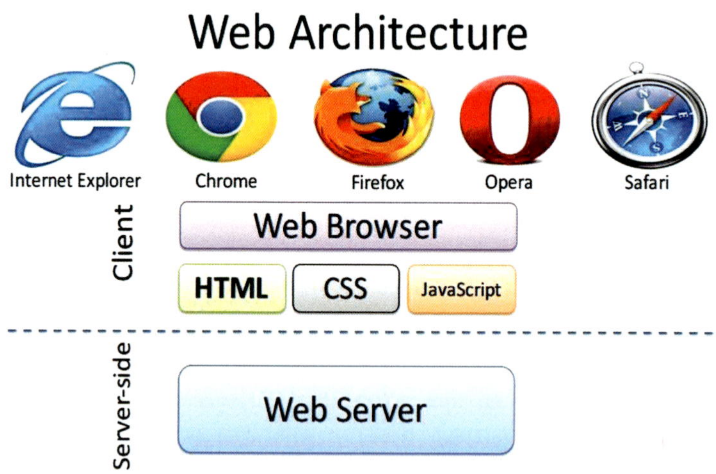

Source: Tutorials Point, Creative Commons License.

1.4.9. Web Operations

The Web operates on a client-server model. The steps below illustrate how the internet works (Zhu et al., 2017) (Figure 1.8):

- The user inputs the web page's URL (for example, http://www.learningpoint.com) in the address bar of a web browser.
- The browser then seeks the IP address belonging to www.learningpoint.com from the Domain Name Server.
- After acquiring an IP address, the browser transmits a message for the web page to a web server via the HTTP standard, which describes how the internet browser and web server interact.
- The web server then gets an HTTP message and performs a lookup for the specified web page. If the URL is discovered, the server responds to the internet browser and closes the HTTP session.
- Now that the web browser has received the website, it understands it and displays its information in its window.

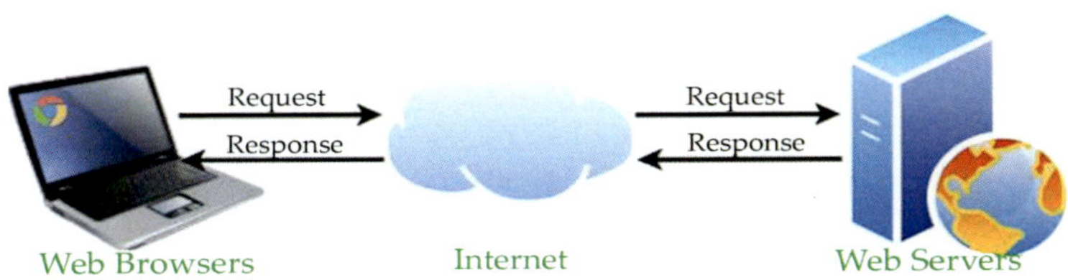

Figure 1.8. Web server design.

Source: Nanduri Balajee, Creative Commons License.

1.4.10. Site Structure

Every website must have what is known as a site structure, an institution that is uniform and straightforward and developed using an inherited structure. A website comprises several files, including HTML files, scripts, and images, all stored in a single master folder. One can store their documents and subdirectories in a way that is comprehensible not only to themself but also to other members of division who might need to make changes to the material in a way that is well-organized within this master folder (Keshav & Kesahv, 1997).

As a result, it is suggested that the following components be included in the architecture of the webpage (Sunyaev, 2020) (Figure 1.9):

- A root (master) folder that encompasses the website.
- The root folder contains a website with the name index.htm that serves as the site's standard home page.

- The visuals, graphics, images, and pictures used throughout the Web pages might be found in the images folder.
- Extra folders for managing the content.

Figure 1.9. Diagram representing the website root.

Source: Tutorials Point, Creative Commons License.

1.4.11. Hyperlinks

The primary way to move between webpages and sites is through hyperlinks. Links can direct users to certain other web pages, sites, images, documents, audio files, e-mail accounts, and other areas of the same website page. Typically, text that serves as a hyperlink is underscored and has a different color. Links come in four different varieties (Li et al., 2021):

- **Text Hyperlink:** Visitors are directed to another website, file, or page using a phrase or term.
- **Image Hyperlink:** A picture redirects visitors to another website, file, or page.

- **Bookmark Hyperlink:** Utilizes text or a picture to direct readers to another website section.
- **E-mail Hyperlink:** Allows audiences to write an e-mail to the e-mail address presented.

1.4.12. Display of Web Pages

When user access the webpage in an internet browser, the web browser reads and translates the HTML file and prepares it for presentation. External files, like photos or multimedia, are retrieved from the server and shown in the browser tab if referenced. It is vital to understand that Html documents are text files that carry links to external files; these documents are not embedded inside the Web page (Shi & Hou, 2013) (Figure 1.10).

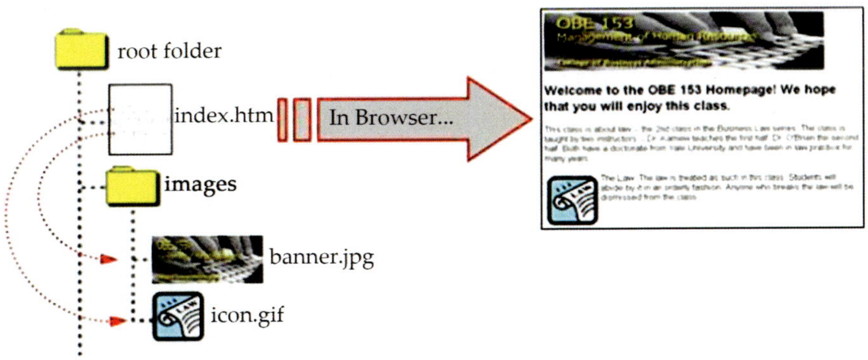

Figure 1.10. How browsers display web pages.

Source: Tutorials Point, Creative Commons License.

1.4.13. Kinds of Websites

There are multiple websites, each appealing to a specific content or function (Pool, 1993). Consequently, some exemplary but not comprehensive examples are provided below:

- **Blog:** A website typically utilized for online diaries that might also contain discussion boards
- **Social Networking Site:** A website where visitors may chat with each other and share content like photos, videos, songs, and blogs. These might contain Web applications and games.
- **Wiki Site:** Cooperatively edited by the site's users (like Wikipedia).

- **Web Portal:** A website that serves as a launching point or gateway to additional online sources.
- **Search Engine Site:** A website that gives basic information and is meant as a gateway or search engine for other websites such as Google, and Yahoo
- **Education Site:** A website where instructors, students, and administration can submit information about recent school functions.

1.4.14. Website Design Problems

There are numerous considerations when developing a website. These factors, which are outlined below, make a site useful and readily available to customers (Chaqfeh & Mohamed, 2012):

- **Information Availability:** All information that assists a user in making educated judgments must be available on the website. A great site must provide 80% to 90% of what a visitor seeks, according to the rule of thumb.
- **Page Design:** How the information is shown on the page — The page must be laid out so that teams can quickly locate appropriate stuff. Else they lose interest and leave the site. Page should be simple to enhance the usability of the page.
- **Colors:** These must be utilized because they can impact a site's usability. For instance, it is best to stick with the traditional link colors of blue for hyperlinks, violet for viewed links, and red for related benefits to avoid upsetting visitors.
- **Web Accessibility:** It refers to the ability of all users, including those with impairments (such as those affecting their ability to see, hear, move, or speak), to engage with or participate in the Web. Individuals with disabilities must be better able to utilize and participate on the Internet as more and more adaptive Websites and applications become accessible.
- **User-Friendly Website:** A website must be created considering the audience's needs.
- **Download Speed:** A web designer cannot predict the download speed. Making smaller web pages, eliminating nested tables, and compressing the graphics (pictures no more than 10 kb) are a few things to consider.
- **Internet-based Services**

KEYWORD

A **hyperlink** is a text or an icon that you can click on to get to another website.

But what is the Web's purpose? Mail, discussion forums, long-distance computation, and data transfer are 4 potential examples. Internet mail (e-mail) is significantly faster than traditional postal mail. Additionally, one can transfer software and specific buffered digital image formats as attachments. Internet users can join news channels or discussion forums for multiple kinds of debate, conversation, and news exchange.

Remember

Long-distance computation was the original motivation for the creation of ARPANET, and it continues to offer a valuable service on the Internet.

Programmers can manage credentials on remote, powerful machines and implement applications. The file transfer service enables Web users to obtain programs, data, and text from remote computers.

Programmers can manage credentials on remote, powerful machines and implement applications. The file transfer service enables Web users to obtain programs, data, and text from remote computers.

1.4.15. E-mail (Electronic Mail)

E-mail, often known as electronic mail, is a digital form of communicating with others online, whether one individual at a time or several. E-mail is far quicker than regular mail. E-mail communications typically reach their recipients within a few moments. Whenever, day or night, one could send a message, and it will be sent immediately. Both are waiting for the postal service to open, and worrying about vacations is unnecessary. It operates every day of the week, round the clock.

Additionally, r user will always be able to access a copy of the e-mail he/she has sent, even during the midst of the night. One can include something else with the e-mail, like a file, pictures, or photos. The main benefit of e-mail is its low cost, particularly when sending communications to different states or nations, and its ability to reach many individuals globally (Moro, 2022).

Though e-mail is quicker and less expensive than standard mail, it has some of the same components. It enables user to create a note, obtain the recipient's address, and deliver it. After receiving and reading the e-mail, it can be shared and responded to. One can even save it for subsequent use or remove it. In an e-mail, the sender can also demand delivery and read receipts from the receiver.

Following are the characteristics of e-mail (Tozal, 2016):

- Individual or group communications;
- Instantaneous communications;
- The physical existence of the receiver is not needed;
- Cheapest mail service, available 24/7 available;
- Supports informal communication.
- **Constituents of an E-mail Address:** E-mail is based on the notion of a destination address, much as the traditional postal system is. The e-mail address contains all the data necessary to deliver a message from any part of the globe to the receiver. Think about the e-mail address sam@yahoo.com.

In the preceding instance, "sam" is the local component, the mail address on the target machine where the letter would ultimately be transmitted. Yahoo is the mail server with the mailbox "sam" com, which is the company on the net that operates the mail server (Wellman et al., 1996).

1.4.16. FTP (File Transfer Protocol)

KEYWORD

File Transfer Protocol(FTP) is an application layer protocol that moves files between local and remote file systems

File Transfer Protocol is an Internet tool used to upload and retrieve files. It enables access to folders or files on remote machines and the transmission of software, information, and text files among various computer types. The same Client/Server paradigm underlies how FTP operates. The user can communicate with and download files from remote machines using an FTP Client application that runs on the machine. The FTP client transmits queries for data from the remote server, also referred to as the FTP server, using FTP protocols. It is preferable but not essential to have a login on the FTP server to access external FTP servers (Comer, 2018). When an FTP client connects, the FTP server requests authentication in the form of the FTP client's User Account name and password. A user can still establish a connection using an unidentified login even without a remote FTP server account.

The primary goals of FTP are:

- to provide flexibility and encourage the distribution of computer programs, information, and files

- to transfer information consistently and more competently over a network
- to promote embedded or indirect utilization of remote computers with the help of the Internet
- to protect a user from modifications in file-saving systems between hosts.

The primary phases of an FTP session are (Akinsanmi, 2017):

- Launch your FTP client by entering FTP on your computer's cmd line/'C>' interface.
- Provide an address for the FTP client to link to. This is the location of the FTP server to whom the FTP client will link.
- Give the Login Name to the FTP remote location to identify yourself.
- Set a password for the remote location.
- The remote location will validate the User Name/Password before allowing the FTP entry to its files.
- Search for files in the FTP server's folder.
- Modify Directories as needed
- Choose a transfer mode.
- Obtain the desired file; and
- Quit.

Did you Know?

On March 5, 1973, a Telnet protocol standard was defined at UCLA with the publication of two NIC documents: Telnet Protocol Specification, NIC 15372, and Telnet Option Specifications, NIC 15373.

1.4.17. Telnet (Remote Computing)

Telnet or remote computation is a telecommunication application feature that enables user to become a client on a remote server by utilizing accessible telecommunication facilities. Once user access a particular computer, he/she can use it for the proper application. The TELNET operates in a reasonably sequential manner.

The commands entered on the client machine are transmitted to the local ISP and subsequently from the ISP to the remote server to which access has been granted. Most ISPs allow clients to TELNET into your profile from another city and read the e-mail while traveling or conducting business elsewhere (Kahn et al., 1997) (Figure 1.11).

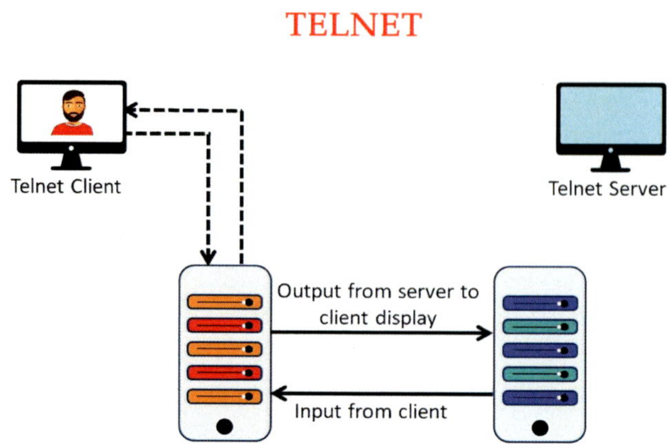

Figure 1.11. Illustration of the telnet (remote computing).

Source: Teachoo, Creative Commons License.

The followings phases are needed for the TELNET session (Hart et al., 1992)

- Start up the TELNET program.
- Give the TELNET program an address to connect to (some nifty TELNET packages allow you to combine steps 1 and 2 into one simple step!).
- Make a note of what the "escape character" is.
- Log in to the remote computer.
- Set the "terminal emulation."
- Play around on the remote computer.
- Quit.

1.5. WORLD WIDE WEB (WWW)

The World Wide Web (WWW) is known by the abbreviation WWW. It is also frequently referred to as "The Web." We connect to the Web using a system called the WWW. The WWW is a system for data retrieval that employs hypertext to retrieve the numerous kinds of data accessible on different networks around the globe (Abbate, 2017).

One can quickly navigate the Web by exploiting the links in individual files. These papers come in various formats, including text, images, cartoons, sound, and, most recently, video. They might be any of these things combined (Perwej et al., 2019).

The user is provided with all available data on the Internet as a page, more commonly referred to as a Web Page. These websites have links to one another or even to specific parts of other websites. These links are also referred to as hyperlinks (Atzori et al., 2012).

1.5.1. Newsgroup/Usenet Newsgroups New

Newsgroups are similar to classic noticeboard systems' public comment boards. A Usenet newsgroup is a storehouse for material posted by numerous users in various locations, generally inside the Usenet system. Usenet newsgroups are comparable to e-mail conference systems. Still, they are less intrusive to users than list servers because messages are distributed to Usenet sites worldwide rather than displayed in every subscriber's mailbox. The Usenet is a massive collection of communications published to hundreds of thousands of newsgroups worldwide. Millions worldwide read newsgroup postings daily, pursuing their preferred areas of interest. Each day, new newsgroups are introduced, and old ones are removed. Usenet can provide a unique information resource that is not easily accessible through any other source. Newsgroup forums can be helpful if one is seeking anecdotal stories regarding products, particularly computer-related hardware and software, how-to knowledge, sound guidance, or the most recent news headlines.

KEYWORD

Software is a set of computer programs and associated documentation and data.

Generally, the newsgroup is centered around a specific subject of interest. Some newsgroups let the publishing of communications on a wide range of topics, including whatever a member decides to express as on-topic. In contrast, others limit submissions to their specific subject and frown upon off-topic comments. The news administrator determines how long publications are retained on his server till expiration. Diverse servers will have varying retention policies for an identical newsgroup; some will store content for as short as 1–2 weeks, while others will preserve them for several months. Some administrators maintain local or specialized newsgroup articles longer than other newsgroup items. Newsgroups are often either binary or text-in format (Marson, 1997).

1.5.2. Hierarchies

Newsgroups are frequently organized into hierarchies, which should, in theory, make it easier to locate groups that are relevant to one another. The hierarchy specified by the prefix that comes before the first period is referred to as the top-level hierarchy.

The Usenet hierarchy is the one that has the widest spread of public recognition (Kleinrock, 2008). For example, the newsgroup *rec.arts.sf.starwars.games* would fall under the rec.* category at the top level of the Usenet structure. This is because the asterisk (*) is considered a wildcard character. The Big 7 refers to the seven primary hierarchies that existed in the Usenet newsgroups when they were first created:

- *Comp.** – Discussion of computer-related topics.
- *news.** – Discussion of Usenet itself.
- *sci.** – Discussion of scientific subjects.
- *rec.** – Discussion of recreational activities (e.g., games and hobbies).
- *soc.** – Socializing and discussion of social issues.
- *Talk.* * – Discussion of contentious issues such as religion and politics.
- *misc.** – Miscellaneous discussion—anything that does not fit the other hierarchies.

1.5.3. Web Conferencing/Video Conferencing

Numerous firms are finding innovative methods to incorporate Internet activity into their operations. Internet or video conferencing is among the most well-liked methods (Shahin, 2006).

Employing network services to communicate audio and visual data during a conference amongst two or more individuals located at separate locations. Videoconferencing uses a collection of telecommunications technologies to perform a videoconference, enabling two or more places to interact by concurrent two-way audio and video broadcasts. It is also known as visual collaboration and belongs to the groupware category (Said & Masud, 2013) (Figure 1.12).

KEYWORD

Video conferencing is live, visual connection between two or more remote parties over the internet that simulates a face-to-face meeting.

Web conferencing connects people from various locations using video and audio telecommunications. This might be as basic as a chat between persons in office buildings or as complex as communication among several sites in huge rooms at multiple places. In addition to transmitting audio and video of conference activities, associated videoconferencing technology can be employed to share files and visualize data on whiteboards (Campbell-Kelly & Garcia-Swartz, 2013).

Figure 1.12. Diagram representing video conferencing.

Source: VOX-Cpass, Creative Commons License.

Businesses are presently using Web conferencing for staff training, conferences, and conversations. Web conferencing is being used by academic institutions to supplement on-site or distant education sessions. Web/video conferencing is a tool that allows students to share material, ask any questions, receive answers, discuss difficulties, and collaborate. Conferencing facilitates problem-solving by allowing for the dynamic interchange of text, images, and HTML links to articles, sound, and video in a controlled discourse organized by topic. Web conferences can occur in real-time, with all members communicating simultaneously (Li et al., 2017).

1.5.3.1. Components of Video Conferencing

Codec: The essential technology of a videoconferencing solution is the real-time digital reduction of video and audio streams. A codec is a software or hardware that accomplishes compression.

The following additional components are needed for a videoconferencing scheme (Atzori et al., 2012):

- **Video Input:** Video camera or webcam.
- **Video Output:** Computer monitor, television, or projector.
- **Audio Input:** Microphones, CD/DVD player, cassette player, or any other source of PreAmp audio outlet.
- **Audio Output:** Usually loudspeakers associated with the display device or telephone.
- **Data Transfer:** Analog or digital telephone network, LAN or Internet;

- **Computer:** A data processing unit that ties together the other components, does the compressing and decompressing, and initiates and maintains the data linkage via the network.

1.5.3.2. Types of Video Conferencing Systems

Dedicated systems incorporate all essential parts into a single tool, typically a panel with a high-quality, remotely controlled video camera. These cameras may be remotely operated to pan left and right, slant up and down, and zoom in and out. They gained the moniker of PTZ cameras. The panel includes all electrical connections, the controlling computer, and a software- or hardware-based codec. The console has omnidirectional microphones, a TV display with speakers, and a video projector. There are various varieties of videoconferencing equipment (Benslimane et al., 2015):

TIPS

A codec compresses or decompresses media files such as songs or videos. Windows Media Player and other apps use codecs to play and create media files.

- Large group videoconferencing are non-portable, more expensive devices used for large rooms and auditoriums.
- Small group videoconferencing are non-portable or portable, smaller, less expensive devices used for small meeting rooms.
- Individual videoconferencing devices are usually portable for single users and have fixed cameras, microphones, and loudspeakers integrated into the console.

Desktop systems are extensions that may be attached to regular personal computers to turn them into conferencing equipment. The board, which has the required codec and transmitting interfaces, is compatible with various mics and cameras. These can be connected to the panel using the interfaces. E-meetings are another name for videoconferences conducted over many personal computers (Choi, 2016).

1.5.4. Internet Chat

In addition to personal e-mail, forums, and e-mail lists, real-time dialogs between two or more individuals are also included in the definition of communication on the Web. IRC, also known as Internet Relay Chat, allows for online chat. There are tens of thousands of conversation channels, each featuring a separate subject and users from around the globe.

1.5.4.1. Chat Rooms

The word chat room is commonly used in public to designate concurrent and sometimes asynchronous conferencing. As a result, the phrase can refer to any tool, from real-time internet chat to messaging apps and internet forums to completely immersive graphical social situations (Finkelstein et al., 2001) (Figure 1.13).

Figure 1.13. Image demonstrating internet chats and various communication methods.

Source: Alamy, Creative Commons License.

1.5.4.2. Chat Based on Text

Web chat is a real-time communication method that involves transferring text messages to individuals within the same chat room. Several chat rooms, like Yahoo!, utilize voice and text at the same time. Text-based discussion forums are the most traditional type of chat room (Montgomery & Smith, 2009).

1.5.4.3. Graphical Multi-User Environments

Graphical chat rooms enhance the chat perspective by incorporating graphics in either 2D or 3D. These are characterized by using a graphic representation of the user (Avatar (virtualing elements such as games) in particular massively multiplayer online games) and educational material most often developed by individual site owners, who in general are simply more advanced users of the systems. Users may also design their rooms in the most famous environments.

Some graphical chat rooms also include audio and videoconferencing communications, allowing users to view and hear one another (Katerattanakul, 2002).

The fundamental aim of a chat group is to exchange textual information with a community of participants. Chat rooms are distinguished from online messaging initiatives, primarily created for one-on-one communication, by the capacity to engage in simultaneous conversations with various persons. A common interest or other relation typically links the participants in a specific chat room, with numerous rooms devoted to various topics. Some initiatives can now include data transfer and video cameras due to technological advances.

KEYWORD

Data transfer refers to the collection, replication, and transmission of large datasets from one organization or business unit to another.

1.6. WAYS OF CONNECTING TO THE NETWORKS

There are numerous types of Internet connections available. They may all be divided into the following classification (Wang et al., 2002).

1.6.1. Broad Band Internet Connection

Definition: Broadband is the data transmission method that transmits multiple data streams over a single wire (Guinard et al., 2011).

- **Gateway Access:** It is referred to as a Level-One linkage. It is an Internet connection from a network that is not connected to the Web. The gateway enables the two different kinds of networks to talk to one another. However, Gateway Web users have restricted Internet access. They may be unable to use all the tools offered by the Internet. The local ISP typically defines this restriction (Dahan & Srinivasan, 2000) (Figure 1.14).

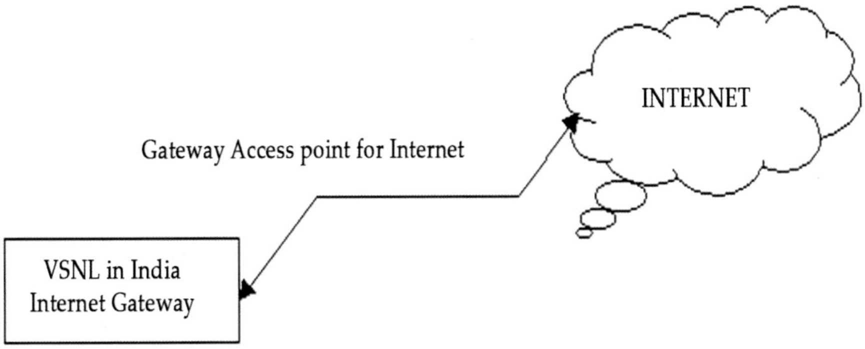

Figure 1.14. Explanation of a gateway access

Source: CUTM Courseware, Creative Commons License.

- **Leased Connection:** Direct web access and level-three connections are other names for it. It is the costliest, most reliable level of Internet access. When user has a leased linkage, his/her computer is explicitly and exclusively linked to the Internet through high-speed transmission lines. It is accessible online every day of the week, around-the-clock. Multinational businesses and universities that might pay the price are the only ones who can use leased Network connectivity (Khanzode & Sarode, 2016) (Figure 1.15).

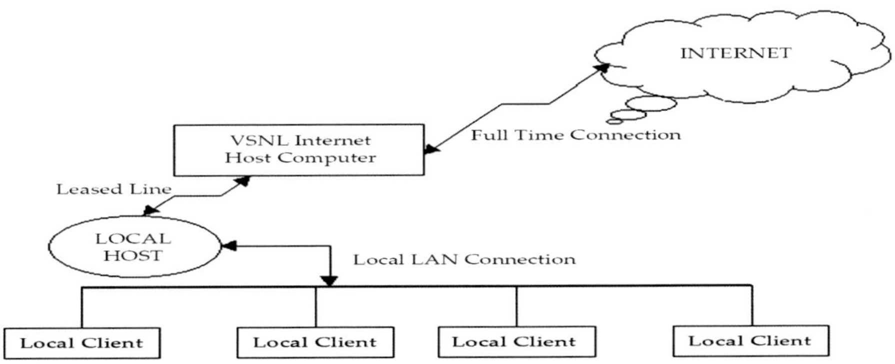

Figure 1.15. Schematic description of a leased connection.

Source: CUTM Courseware, Creative Commons License.

- **T-1 Lines:** Businesses that want to access the internet and ISPs that want to hook up to the backbone of the internet frequently utilize this type of leased line alternative. It is a fixed telephone connection that can support data transfer rates of up to 1.544 Mbps. In reality, a T-1 line comprises 24 separate channels, each capable of transmitting 64 kilobits of data every second. Data or voice traffic can be carried over every channel with a capacity of 64 kilobits each second. The majority of providers of telecommunications services enable customers to buy only one or a few of these separate channels. This connectivity type is called fractional T-1 (Szilagyi & Wira, 2016).

- **Bonded T-1:** These lines are comprised of two or even more T-1 lines bonded together to enhance bandwidth. Compared to the 1.5 Mbps that a single T-1 offers, 2 bonded T1s offer three Mbps or forty-six channels for data or voice. Two bonded T-1s enable client to utilize the maximum bandwidth of three Mbps, whereas 2 individual T-1s only utilize 1.5 Mbps simultaneously. To be bonded, the T-1 should terminate at the same router, connecting to the identical ISP (Berthold et al., 2000).
  - T-1 Lines provides speeds of around 1.544 Mbps.
  - Fractional T-1 speeds are 64 Kbps for each channel, reliant on several leased channels.
  - Normal Bonded T-1 speed is nearly three Mbps.
- **Digital Subscriber Line (DSL):** It is the most current Internet access method. Utilizing the same phone connection that runs from the town's telephone pole, DSL links the residence or place of business to the Web. A single landline is used by DSL service to mix distinct speech and data channels. In DSL, data occupies the top end of the frequency band, while voice occupies the low end. Like ISDN, DSL allows users to link to the Web and make and receive calls at the same time (Chu et al., 2007).

Remember

In an interface that has a number of parallel channels the channels are usually separately dedicated to the passing of a single type of information, e.g. data or control information.

Conversely, the range from the supplier's presence point that one may be using DSL service is constrained. One will require a DSL modem, a NIC (Network Interface Card), and a landline to utilize DSL. DSL is a similarly recent innovation now being made available in several locations. Hardware developers are collaborating with service suppliers to lower the price of the services for users. The service should be more broadly accessible and reasonably priced over time (Arlitt & Williamson, 1997).

- **Cable Connection:** A cable modem provides broadband Internet access that is meant to be used via cable TV lines. Cable Internet operates by transmitting data via TV channel slots, with specific channels utilized for downstream distribution and others for upstream transmission. Since coaxial cable utilized by cable TV has substantially more bandwidth than telephone lines, a modem router might provide extraordinarily rapid access. Cable connection speeds vary from 512 Kbps-20 Mbps (Guinard et al., 2011).

Cable lines provide very high-speed Internet connectivity. It splits the connection into many bands and transforms the information in the bands into signals that may be transmitted across cable lines. Cable modems convert these signals into Ip datagrams that your machine can interpret. To use cable modems, one will require a cable divider, a cable modem, and a cable provider service (Du et al., 2009).

- **Wireless Internet Connections:** Wireless internet, often known as wireless broadband, is among the latest kinds of Internet connections. Rather than using phone or cable connections to connect to the Internet, you employ radio frequency bands. Wireless Internet delivers always-on connectivity accessible from everywhere, so long as user is inside the network's service area. In some regions, it might be challenging to locate a wireless supplier due to the novelty of wireless connection. It is often more costly and primarily offered in urban areas (Turner & Brackbill, 2011).

1.6.2. Dial-Up Connection

- **Definition:** Using dial-up communications technology, computers, and other networked devices can connect to a LAN or WAN.

Level Two connection is another name for a dial-up connection. With this, one can access the Internet using a dial-up interface connection. By calling a phone number supplied by the ISP, the consumer's machine links to the Web by connecting to the ISP machine that gives users access and links to the network. The machine that connects to the Internet is referred to as the Host, while the machine that obtains access is referred to as the Client or Terminal (Gunawan et al., 2019). The client computer seems to be a terminal linked directly to the Host when communicating with it through the modem (Figure 1.16).

KEYWORD

The World Wide **Web**, commonly known as the Web, is an information system enabling documents and other web resources to be accessed over the Internet according to specific rules, the Hypertext Transfer Protocol.

Figure 1.16. Illustration of a dial-up connection.

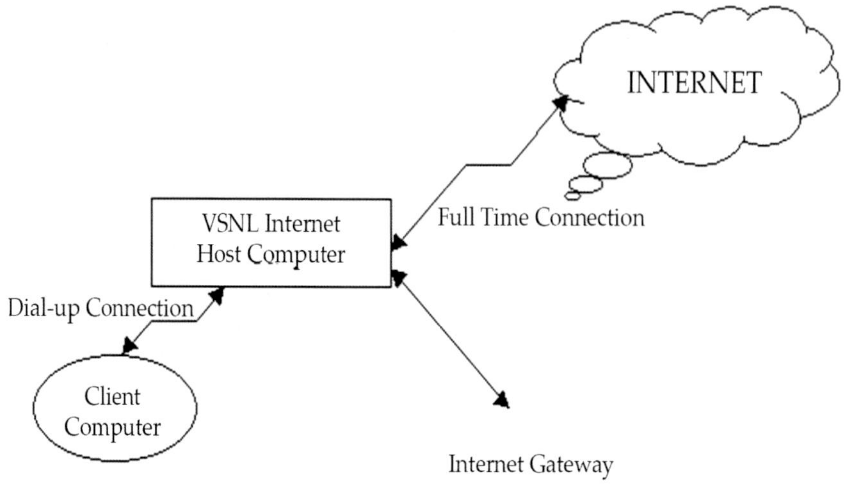

Source: CUTM Courseware, Creative Commons License.

The Host handles all of the commands that are entered on a client system and send them onto the Web when using a dial-up connection to access the Web. In addition, it obtains the material or data from the Web on the client's account and then transmits it to the latter. The client machine is nothing more than a dumb terminal that is linked to the remote computer (Arlitt & Williamson, 1996).

Since data is transmitted over an analog telephone network, dial-up access is considered to be an analog connection. The modem is responsible for converting any analog data obtained into its digital equivalent and vice versa. Since dial-up access uses regular phone lines, the network's reliability is not guaranteed to be high, and the data speeds it can support are restricted.

Three distinct subtypes of connections can be created using this method (Brin, 1998):

- **Shell Connection:** This Internet connection provides the user with merely the text information of a website. This network doesn't enable the viewing of graphics. Conversely, the user will have a connection to the Web, FTP, and e-mail. Before the Web came into the world of visuals and became more user-friendly, Shell Accounts were the only means of Internet connectivity accessible for several years.
- **TCP/IP Connection:** Today's visual WWW browsers make it much easier to acquire multimedia content such as sound and images. The primary distinction between a Shell and a TCP/IP account is that a Shell account can only present

text and doesn't support images, while a TCP/IP account can exhibit both. As a result, it is a more standard online connection. Shell accounts are gradually disappearing from the Internet landscape.

- **ISDN:** It is a global communications protocol for transmitting audio, video, and information across analog or digital phone lines. It provides Internet access through digital telephone lines at rates of around 128 Kbps. Phone providers have offered dial-up services like ISDN for a long time. This line integrates 2 64 Kbps channels to provide a 128 Kbps frequency bandwidth divided into 3 bands: one for data and one for the device's ringing signal (Dean & Henzinger, 1999).

ACTIVITY 1.1.

How conventional business such as textile industry, agriculture, medicine etc. can benefit from the state-of-the-art internet technologies? Discuss in detail.

1.6.3. Satellite Internet

One Internet service that operates at a very high speed is known as satellite Internet. Consumers who use satellite Internet connections have their Internet access provided by satellite systems placed in orbit around the Earth. Web over Satellite, also known as IoS, is a technology that allows users to connect to the internet through a satellite that circles the Earth. A satellite is stationed in a predetermined location in space, typically high above the planet's surface. IoS connections are noticeably more sluggish than high-speed terrestrial links using copper or fiber optic cables. This is due to the large distances' signals travel from the Earth to the satellites and back again.

Internet access through Satellite is possible in some locations where DSL and cable connections are not accessible. Compared to DSL and cable, satellite Internet has a lower bandwidth capacity. The usual connection speeds for Internet access through Satellite (for regular IP services) range from 492–512 kilobits per second (Kbps) (Berners-Lee et al., 1994).

1.7. SUMMARY

Internet Technologies is a term used to describe the systems and protocols that enable different computer networks, devices, and services to communicate and interact. Some of the most common Internet technologies include computer networks, the WWW, e-mail, Web conferencing, broadband internet, dial-up connection, and satellite internet. Computer networks are physical networks of computers that are interconnected. These networks can be used to share files and can also be used for data transmission and communication. The most common computer networks are Local Area Networks (LANs), Wide Area Networks (WANs), and Metropolitan Area Networks (MANs). The WWW is a system of interlinked documents and other resources accessed through the internet. These documents, known as web pages, are written in HTML and are accessed using web browsers such as Google Chrome, Mozilla Firefox, and Microsoft Internet Explorer. E-mail is a service that allows users to send and receive messages over the internet. It is one of the most commonly used Internet technologies for personal and business communications. Web conferencing is a technology that allows users to communicate and collaborate over the internet in a virtual.

REVIEW QUESTIONS

1. What are the basic objectives of FTP?
2. What is the difference between a Leased connection and a Dial-up connection?
3. Explain in brief:
   a. TCP/IP connection
   b. Telnet
   c. Gateway Access
   d. Shell connection
4. Explain in brief the working principle of a cable modem connection.
5. How does a search engine get the required information from the Web? Write the names of 2 popular search engines.
6. Explain the following terms:
   a. DSL
   b. ISDN

MULTIPLE CHOICE QUESTIONS

1. What type of connection typically offers higher speeds than a dial-up connection?

a. Broadband internet
b. Satellite internet
c. Web conferencing
d. E-mail

2. What is the main purpose of computer networks?

a. To store data
b. To facilitate communication

c. To provide internet access
d. To process information

3. What was the first web browser?

a. Chrome
b. Mozilla Firefox
c. Safari
d. Mosaic

4. What type of address is used by websites?

a. IP address
b. DNS address
c. URL address
d. Network address

5. What type of technology is used to share documents, presentations, and other files over the internet?

a. Web conferencing
b. Satellite internet
c. Dial-up connection
d. E-mail

6. What type of internet connection requires a satellite dish?

a. Dial-up connection
b. Broadband internet
c. Satellite internet
d. Web conferencing

7. What is the World Wide Web?

a. A collection of websites
b. An online search engine
c. A type of internet connection
d. A network of computers

8. What is the main purpose of the e-mail?

a. To store data
b. To provide internet access
c. To send and receive messages
d. To process information

9. What is the difference between the Internet and the World Wide Web?

a. The Internet is a collection of websites, while the World Wide Web is a network of computers.

b. The Internet is a network of computers, while the World Wide Web is a collection of websites.

c. The Internet is an internet connection, while the World Wide Web is an online search engine.

d. The Internet is an online search engine, while the World Wide Web is an internet connection.

10. What technology is used for online meetings, lectures, and other interactive events?

a. Dial-up connection

b. Web conferencing

c. Broadband internet

d. Satellite internet

Answers to Multiple Choice Questions

1. (a); 2. (b); 3. (d); 4. (c); 5. (d); 6. (c); 7. (a); 8. (c); 9. (b); 10. (b)

REFERENCES

1. Abbate, J., (2017). What and where is the Internet? (Re)defining Internet histories. *Internet Histories, 1*(1, 2), 8–14.
2. Abdel-Basset, M., Manogaran, G., Mohamed, M., & Rushdy, E., (2019). Internet of things in smart education environment: Supportive framework in the decision-making process. *Concurrency and Computation: Practice and Experience, 31*(10), e4515.
3. Akinsanmi, O., (2017). Internet facilities on global system for mobile communication (GSM) devices. *Journal of Sustainable Development, 2*(2), 9–14.
4. Al-Fuqaha, A., Guizani, M., Mohammadi, M., Aledhari, M., & Ayyash, M., (2015). Internet of things: A survey on enabling technologies, protocols, and applications. *IEEE Communications Surveys & Tutorials, 17*(4), 2347–2376.
5. Arlitt, M. F., & Williamson, C. L., (1996). Web server workload characterization: The search for invariants. *ACM SIGMETRICS Performance Evaluation Review, 24*(1), 126–137.
6. Arlitt, M. F., & Williamson, C. L., (1997). Internet web servers: Workload characterization and performance implications. *IEEE/ACM Transactions on Networking, 5*(5), 631–645.

7. Atzori, L., Iera, A., Morabito, G., & Nitti, M., (2012). The social internet of things (SIoT)–when social networks meet the internet of things: Concept, architecture and network characterization. *Computer Networks, 56*(16), 3594–3608.
8. Batinić, I., (2015). The role and importance of Internet marketing in modern hotel industry. *Journal of Process Management and New Technologies, 3*(3), 34–38.
9. Benslimane, D., Sheng, Q. Z., Barhamgi, M., & Prade, H., (2015). The uncertain web: Concepts, challenges, and current solutions. *ACM Transactions on Internet Technology (TOIT), 16*(1), 1–6.
10. Berners-Lee, T., Cailliau, R., Luotonen, A., Nielsen, H. F., & Secret, A., (1994). The worldwide web. *Communications of the ACM, 37*(8), 76–82.
11. Berthold, O., Federrath, H., & Köhntopp, M., (2000). Project "anonymity and unobservability in the Internet." In: *Proceedings of the Tenth Conference on Computers, Freedom and Privacy: Challenging the Assumptions* (Vol. 1, pp. 57–65).
12. Botta, A., De Donato, W., Persico, V., & Pescapé, A., (2016). Integration of cloud computing and internet of things: A survey. *Future Generation Computer Systems, 56*, 684–700.
13. Brin, S., (1998). Extracting patterns and relations from the world wide web. In: *International Workshop on the World Wide Web and Databases* (Vol. 1, pp. 172–183). Springer, Berlin, Heidelberg.
14. Campbell-Kelly, M., & Garcia-Swartz, D. D., (2013). The history of the Internet: The missing narratives. *Journal of Information Technology, 28*(1), 18–33.
15. Cerf, V. G., (2004). On the evolution of Internet technologies. *Proceedings of the IEEE, 92*(9), 1360–1370.
16. Chaqfeh, M. A., & Mohamed, N., (2012). Challenges in middleware solutions for the internet of things. In: *2012 International Conference on Collaboration Technologies and Systems (CTS)* (Vol. 1, pp. 21–26). IEEE.
17. Choi, M., (2016). A concept analysis of digital citizenship for democratic citizenship education in the Internet age. *Theory & Research in Social Education, 44*(4), 565–607.
18. Chu, S. C., Leung, L. C., Van, H. Y., & Cheung, W., (2007). Evolution of e-commerce websites: A conceptual framework and a longitudinal study. *Information & Management, 44*(2), 154–164.
19. Comer, D. E., (2018). *The Internet Book: Everything You Need to Know About Computer Networking and How the Internet Works* (Vol. 1, pp. 2–9). Chapman and Hall/CRC.
20. Dahan, E., & Srinivasan, V., (2000). The predictive power of Internet-based product concept testing using visual depiction and animation. *Journal of Product Innovation Management: AN International Publication of the Product Development & Management Association, 17*(2), 99–109.
21. Dean, J., & Henzinger, M. R., (1999). Finding related pages in the world wide web. *Computer Networks, 31*(11–16), 1467–1479.

22. Du, T. C., Li, F., & King, I., (2009). Managing knowledge on the web–extracting ontology from HTML web. *Decision Support Systems, 47*(4), 319–331.
23. Fathima, N., Ahammed, A., Banu, R., Parameshachari, B. D., & Naik, N. M., (2017). Optimized neighbor discovery in internet of things (IoT). In: *2017 International Conference on Electrical, Electronics, Communication, Computer, and Optimization Techniques (ICEECCOT)* (Vol. 1, pp. 1–5). IEEE.
24. Feizollahi, S., Shirmohammadi, A., Kahreh, Z. S., & Kaherh, M. S., (2014). Investigation the effect of Internet technology on performance of services organizations with e-commerce orientations. *Procedia-Social and Behavioral Sciences, 109*, 605–609.
25. Finkelstein, L., Gabrilovich, E., Matias, Y., Rivlin, E., Solan, Z., Wolfman, G., & Ruppin, E., (2001). Placing search in context: The concept revisited. In: *Proceedings of the 10th International Conference on World Wide Web* (Vol. 1, pp. 406–414).
26. Greenstein, S., (2020). The basic economics of Internet infrastructure. *Journal of Economic Perspectives, 34*(2), 192–214.
27. Guinard, D., Trifa, V., Mattern, F., & Wilde, E., (2011). From the internet of things to the web of things: Resource-oriented architecture and best practices. In: *Architecting the Internet of Things* (Vol. 1, pp. 97–129). Springer, Berlin, Heidelberg.
28. Gunawan, R., Rahmatulloh, A., Darmawan, I., & Firdaus, F., (2019). Comparison of web scraping techniques: Regular expression, HTML DOM and Xpath. In: *2018 International Conference on Industrial Enterprise and System Engineering (ICoIESE 2018)* (Vol. 1, pp. 283–287). Atlantis Press.
29. Gyrard, A., Patel, P., Datta, S. K., & Ali, M. I., (2017). Semantic web meets internet of things and web of things. In: *Proceedings of the 26th International Conference on World Wide Web Companion* (Vol. 1, pp. 917–920).
30. Gyrard, A., Patel, P., Datta, S., & Ali, M., (2016). Semantic web meets internet of things (IoT) and web of things (WoT). In: *The 15th International Conference on Semantic Web (ISWC)* (Vol. 1, pp. 2–9).
31. Hart, J. A., Reed, R. R., & Bar, F., (1992). The building of the Internet: Implications for the future of broadband networks. *Telecommunications Policy, 16*(8), 666–689.
32. Hodge, H., Carson, D., Carson, D., Newman, L., & Garrett, J., (2017). Using Internet technologies in rural communities to access services: The views of older people and service providers. *Journal of Rural Studies, 54*, 469–478.
33. Kahn, R., Leiner, B. M., Cerf, V. G., Clark, D. D., Kleinrock, L., Lynch, D. C., & Wolff, S., (1997). The evolution of the Internet as a global information system. *The International Information & Library Review, 29*(2), 129–151.
34. Kamssu, A. J., Siekpe, J. S., Ellzy, J. A., & Kamssu, A. J., (2004). Shortcomings to globalization: Using Internet technology and electronic commerce in developing countries. *The Journal of Developing Areas, 1*, 151–169.
35. Katerattanakul, P., (2002). Framework of effective website design for business-to-consumer Internet commerce. *INFOR: Information Systems and Operational Research, 40*(1), 57–70.

36. Keshav, S., & Kesahv, S., (1997). *An Engineering Approach to Computer Networking: ATM Networks, the Internet, and the Telephone Network* (Vol. 116, pp. 3–8). Reading: Addison-Wesley.
37. Khanzode, C. A., & Sarode, R. D., (2016). Evolution of the world wide web: From web 1.0 to 6.0. *International Journal of Digital Library Services, 6*(2), 1–11.
38. Kleinrock, L., (2008). History of the Internet and its flexible future. *IEEE Wireless Communications, 15*(1), 8–18.
39. Lane, E., Summerhill, C., Mallinckrodt, A. J., & McKay, S., (1993). Internet primer for information professionals: A basic guide to Internet networking technology. *Computers in Physics, 7*(5), 543–544.
40. Leiner, B. M., Cerf, V. G., Clark, D. D., Kahn, R. E., Kleinrock, L., Lynch, D. C., & Wolff, S., (2009). A brief history of the Internet. *ACM SIGCOMM Computer Communication Review, 39*(5), 22–31.
41. Li, J. Q., Yu, F. R., Deng, G., Luo, C., Ming, Z., & Yan, Q., (2017). Industrial Internet: A survey on the enabling technologies, applications, and challenges. *IEEE Communications Surveys & Tutorials, 19*(3), 1504–1526.
42. Li, S., Wang, H., Xu, T., & Zhou, G., (2011). Application study on internet of things in environment protection field. In: *Informatics in Control, Automation and Robotics* (Vol. 1, pp. 99–106). Springer, Berlin, Heidelberg.
43. Lin, N., & Shi, W., (2014). The research on Internet of things application architecture based on web. In: *2014 IEEE Workshop on Advanced Research and Technology in Industry Applications (WARTIA)* (Vol. 1, pp. 184–187). IEEE.
44. Lodder, A. R., (2013). Ten commandments of Internet law revisited: Basic principles for Internet lawyers. *Information & Communications Technology Law, 22*(3), 264–276.
45. Madakam, S., Lake, V., Lake, V., & Lake, V., (2015). Internet of things (IoT): A literature review. *Journal of Computer and Communications, 3*(05), 164.
46. Marson, S. M., (1997). A selective history of Internet technology and social work. *Computers in Human Services, 14*(2), 35–49.
47. Mattern, F., & Floerkemeier, C., (2010). From the Internet of computers to the internet of things. In: *From Active Data Management to Event-Based Systems and More* (Vol. 1, pp. 242–259). Springer, Berlin, Heidelberg.
48. Montgomery, A. L., & Smith, M. D., (2009). Prospects for personalization on the Internet. *Journal of Interactive Marketing, 23*(2), 130–137.
49. Moro, V. R., (2022). *From Physical Reality to the Internet and the Metaverse: A Multilayer Network Valuation* (Vol. 1, pp. 4–9). Available at SSRN.
50. Musa, A., Hashim, M. N., Abdullah, N. A. C., & Musa, R. M. A., (2021). Use of computer technology in the Internet using the YouTube in teaching and learning student basic technique dances contemporary University of Malaysia Terengganu. In: *Journal of Physics: Conference Series* (Vol. 1793, No. 1, p. 012032). IOP Publishing.

51. Navani, D., Jain, S., & Nehra, M. S., (2017). The internet of things (IoT): A study of architectural elements. In: *2017 13th International Conference on Signal-Image Technology & Internet-Based Systems (SITIS)* (Vol. 1, pp. 473–478). IEEE.
52. Patel, K. K., Patel, S. M., & Scholar, P., (2016). Internet of things-IoT: Definition, characteristics, architecture, enabling technologies, application & future challenges. *International Journal of Engineering Science and Computing, 6*(5), 1–5.
53. Perwej, Y., AbouGhaly, M. A., Kerim, B., & Harb, H. A. M., (2019). An extended review on internet of things (IoT) and its promising applications. *Communications on Applied Electronics (CAE), ISSN, 5*(1), 2394–4714.
54. Piccoli, G., Ahmad, R., & Ives, B., (2001). Web-based virtual learning environments: A research framework and a preliminary assessment of effectiveness in basic IT skills training. *MIS Quarterly, 1*, 401–426.
55. Pool, R., (1993). Beyond databases and email: In the coming decade, computer networks such as the Internet will link researchers into "electronic communities" that will create new ways of collaborating and sharing information. *Science, 261*(5123), 841–843.
56. Powers, S. M., (1997). Designing an interactive course for the Internet. *Contemporary Education, 68*(3), 194.
57. Said, O., & Masud, M., (2013). Towards internet of things: Survey and future vision. *International Journal of Computer Networks, 5*(1), 1–17.
58. Sallai, G., (2013). Chapters of future Internet research. In: *2013 IEEE 4th International Conference on Cognitive Infocommunications (CogInfoCom)* (Vol. 1, pp. 161–166). IEEE.
59. Schoech, D., (2017). *Human Services Technology: Understanding, Designing, and Implementing Computer and Internet Applications in the Social Services* (Vol. 1, pp. 4–7). CRC Press.
60. Shahin, J., (2006). A European history of the Internet. *Science and Public Policy, 33*(9), 681–693.
61. Sharma, N., Solanki, V. K., & Davim, J. P., (2019). Basics of the internet of things (IoT) and its future. In: *Handbook of IoT and Big Data* (Vol. 1, pp. 165–186). CRC Press.
62. Shi, Y. R., & Hou, T., (2013). Internet of things key technologies and architectures research in information processing. In: *Applied Mechanics and Materials* (Vol. 347, pp. 2511–2515). Trans Tech Publications Ltd.
63. Sunyaev, A., (2020). *Internet Computing: Principles of Distributed Systems and Emerging Internet-Based Technologies* (Vol. 1, pp. 5–9). Springer Nature.
64. Szilagyi, I., & Wira, P., (2016). Ontologies and semantic web for the Internet of things-a survey. In: *IECON 2016–42nd Annual Conference of the IEEE Industrial Electronics Society* (Vol. 1, pp. 6949–6954). IEEE.

65. Tate, D. F., Wing, R. R., & Winett, R. A., (2001). Using Internet technology to deliver a behavioral weight loss program. *JAMA, 285*(9), 1172–1177.
66. Tozal, M. E., (2016). The Internet: A system of interconnected autonomous systems. In: *2016 Annual IEEE Systems Conference (SysCon)* (Vol. 1, pp. 1–8). IEEE.
67. Turner, T. P., & Brackbill, L., (2011). Rising to the top: Evaluating the use of the HTML meta tag to improve retrieval of world wide web documents through Internet search engines. *Library Resources & Technical Services, 42*(4), 258–271.
68. Wang, L., Shen, W., Xie, H., Neelamkavil, J., & Pardasani, A., (2002). Collaborative conceptual design—State of the art and future trends. *Computer-Aided Design, 34*(13), 981–996.
69. Wellman, B., Salaff, J., Dimitrova, D., Garton, L., Gulia, M., & Haythornthwaite, C., (1996). Computer networks as social networks: Collaborative work, telework, and virtual community. *Annual Review of Sociology, 22*(1), 213–238.
70. Whitacre, B. E., (2010). The diffusion of Internet technologies to rural communities: A portrait of broadband supply and demand. *American Behavioral Scientist, 53*(9), 1283–1303.
71. Wu, J., Xiong, F., & Li, C., (2019). Application of internet of things and blockchain technologies to improve accounting information quality. *IEEE Access, 7*, 100090–100098.
72. Xingmei, X., Jing, Z., & He, W., (2013). Research on the basic characteristics, the key technologies, the network architecture and security problems of the Internet of things. In: *Proceedings of 2013 3rd International Conference on Computer Science and Network Technology* (Vol. 1, pp. 825–828). IEEE.
73. Yue, Z., Sun, W., Li, P., Rehman, M. U., & Yang, X., (2015). Internet of things: Architecture, technology and key problems in implementation. In: *2015 8th International Congress on Image and Signal Processing (CISP)* (Vol. 1, pp. 1298–1302). IEEE.
74. Zhu, J., Xie, P., Xuan, P., Zou, J., & Yu, P., (2017). Renewable energy consumption technology under energy Internet environment. In: *2017 IEEE Conference on Energy Internet and Energy System Integration (EI2)* (Vol. 1, pp. 1–5). IEEE.

CHAPTER 2

PROTOCOLS AND STANDARDS OF COMPUTER NETWORKS

UNIT INTRODUCTION

Network protocols are among the subjects that receive the most funding from businesses and academics. Computer networks have been made possible by the rapid development of portable internet, mini-hardware production, micro-computing, and M2M (machine-to-machine) communication. Computer networks are presently at the peak of Gartner's hype cycle, which suggests that the industry is spending a significant amount of funds on it. On Internet-related technologies, supporting technologies, and research, several billions of dollars are now being invested, and in the years to come, considerably more is anticipated (Gartner, 2014) (Figure 2.1).

Figure 2.1. Image of machine-to-machine (M2M) communication.

Source: Business Industry Reports, Creative Commons License.

Computer networks enable non-computer items to respond intelligently and make coordinated choices that help specific applications (Choi et al., 2017). They allow objects to hear, perceive, think, and react by enabling them to cooperate and communicate with each other to make crucial decisions like saving lives or structures. They shift from passive processing and making independent decisions to continuing to interact and cooperate on a single essential decision. The enabling technologies of interconnected devices, embedded devices, and internet protocols enable Computer networks to give value. Yet, they present numerous constraints and necessitate particular guidelines and communication protocols (Salman & Jain, 2017).

This chapter focuses on the Internet protocols that operate at MAC (Medium Access Control), network, and session layers of the underlying network. IETF (Internet Engineering Task Force), IEEE (Institute of Electrical and Electronics Engineers), ITU (International Telecommunication Union), and other standard bodies' protocols are presented. These guidelines were suggested throughout the past five years to suit Computer networks and future requirements.

Learning Objectives

At the end of this chapter, readers will be able to learn the following:

- Computer networks ecosystem;
- Data link protocol in computer networks;
- Network layer routing protocols;
- Network layer Encapsulation protocols;
- Session layer protocols;
- Management protocols;
- Security protocols.

Key Terms

- Computer networks
- Data link standards
- MAC standards
- Management standards
- Network standards
- Routing standards
- Transport layer standards

2.1. COMPUTER NETWORKS ECOSYSTEM

A seven-layer ecosystem paradigm of Computer networks is depicted in Figure 2.1. The marketplace or application area, such as smart grid, linked homes, or intelligent health, is found at the base of the stack. The application is made possible by the sensors in the 2nd layer. Typical sensors include cameras, thermocouples, humidity sensors, and electric utility meters (Salman & Jain, 2019). The 3rd layer comprises an interconnection layer that enables communication of sensor-generated data, typically to a computer center, data center, or cloud. The data is then amalgamated with other well-known data sets, like geographic, demographic, or economic information. The pooled data is then examined using data mining and machine learning methods (Akbar et al., 2022). More up-to-date application-level communication and networking software like SOA (services-oriented architecture), SDN (software-defined networking), etc., are needed to permit such massive dispersed systems. The final layer, the top layer, comprises capabilities that support the market. These services could include the administration of energy and health, teaching, and transportation, among other things. In addition to the seven levels that are constructed on top of one another, there are administration and security applications that are necessary for every one of the layers; these programs are displayed on the side since they are needed for every one of the layers (Beck, 1999; Hansen, 1975) (Figure 2.2).

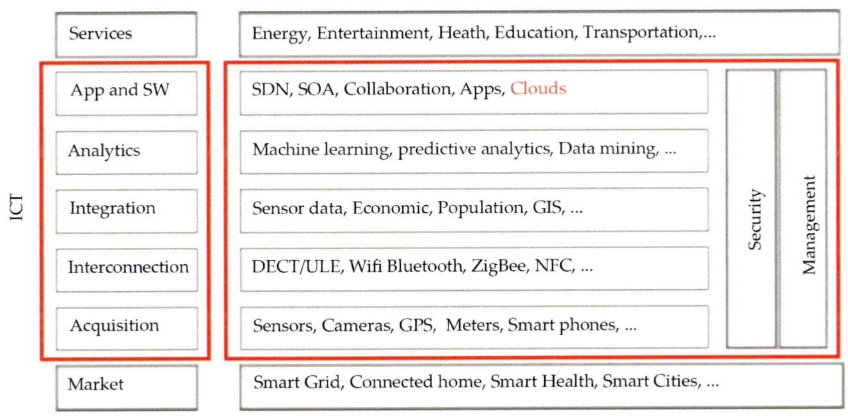

Figure 2.2. Illustration of computer networks ecosystem.

Source: Tara Salman, Creative Commons License.

The focus of this chapter is the connectivity layer. The connectivity layer can be displayed in some multi-layer stacks, as depicted in Figure 2.3. The data link, system, and session/ transport layers have been demonstrated. The data link layer joins

2 computer networks pieces, which are usually two sensors or just one sensor, along with a gateway device that links a collection of devices to the Internet (Aijaz & Aghvami, 2015).

Various sensors must frequently communicate and integrate information before sending it to the internet. As a component of the routing layer, dedicated protocols have been developed for device routing. Protocols at the session layer facilitate communication between various parts of the internet's connectivity subsystem (Standard, 2012). As depicted in the picture, many administration and security guidelines have also been created for computer network.

Figure 2.3. Diagram of protocols for computer networks.

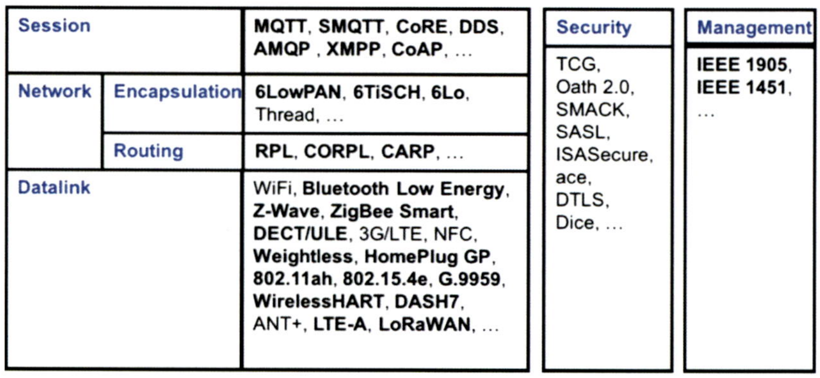

Source: Tara Salman, Creative Commons License.

2.2. DATA LINK PROTOCOL

The protocol specifications of the datalink layer are covered in this section. Most standards integrate physical and MAC layer protocols, which are discussed below.

2.2.1. IEEE 802.15.4

It is the most widely utilized MAC Computer network standard. It specifies a message format, headers that include the destination and source addresses, and how nodes communicate with one another (Cetinkaya & Akan, 2015). Because of their overhead, existing network frame formats aren't suited for low-power multi-hop connectivity in computer networks. IEEE802.15.4e was developed in 2008 to augment IEEE802.15.4 and provide low-power communication. It employs synchronization and channel hopping to achieve high consistency, low price, and meet Computer networks' communications specifications. Its unique MAC characteristics are as follows (Grabia et al., 2017):

1. **Slot Frame Structure:** The frame structure of IEEE 802.15.4e is anticipated for planning and instructing each node. A node can transmit or receive data, sleep, or both. The node caches all the information it needs to communicate at the next available transmission possibility while in sleep mode, which also switches off its radio to conserve power. It transmits its data during transmission and then waits for a response. Before the specified time for the reception, the node activates its radio, gathers data, sends a confirmation, then switches off the radio to transmit the message to the top layers before going back to sleep.
2. **Scheduling:** The standard doesn't specify the scheduling process, but it must be appropriately constructed to account for mobility models. It can be administered by a manager node who is in charge of creating the program, disseminating the plan, and having other nodes adhere to it.
3. **Synchronization:** Keeping nodes connected to their companions and gateways is vital. There are two techniques for synchronization: acknowledgment-based and frame-based. In an acknowledgment-based configuration, the nodes have already entered communication mode and transmit a confirmation to ensure reliability; therefore, it may also be used to preserve connectivity. Because nodes aren't interacting in frame-based configuration, they share a blank frame at predefined intervals.
4. **Channel Hopping:** IEEE802.15.4e adds channel hopping to the wireless links for timed access. Channel hopping is shifting the frequency channel by following a predefined arbitrary sequence. Channel hopping provides frequency variability while reducing crosstalk and multi-path decaying. Sixteen channels are provided, increasing network capacity because two frames can be broadcast simultaneously on separate frequency channels via the same link.
5. **Network Formation:** It has advertising and connecting elements. New equipment must wait for marketing commands and may transmit a mutual application to the marketing device upon obtaining at least one. In centralized exchanges, join requests are moved toward the manager

Remember

Systems that operate with all parts in synchrony are said to be synchronous or in sync—and those that are not are asynchronous.

node and controlled there, but in distributed applications, join requests are handled remotely. Once a gadget joins the network and functions fully, the configuration is disabled and will only be reactivated if some other join request is received.

2.2.2. IEEE 802.11 AH

This edition of the IEEE 802.11 wireless transmission access protocol is a more lightweight variant. This variant has been developed to have lower overhead to accommodate the necessities of Computer network. The IEEE 802.11 protocols are the wireless guidelines that are utilized most frequently. They have gained widespread usage acceptance across all digital platforms and gadgets, including computers, mobile phones, iPods, and digital televisions. On the other hand, because of the frame overhead and energy consumption of the initial Wi-Fi protocols, they are inappropriate for use in applications involving Computer network. As a result, the IEEE 802.11 steering committee decided to establish the 802.11ah task group to design a protocol appropriate for sensors and motes and enables low-cost and energy-friendly communication. The following is a list of the fundamental 802.11ah MAC layer characteristics (Ayoub et al., 2018):

KEYWORD

Network Information is an extension that provides information about your system's connection.

1. **Synchronization Frame:** A station cannot broadcast without appropriate network information that permits it to secure the medium and prevent other stations from exchanging packets. It will know this information if it successfully obtains the time field packet. If it does not acquire it properly, it must wait for a period known as the Probe Delay. In 802.11ah, the points of access can set the Probe Delay and declare it by broadcasting a synchronization message at the start of the period.
2. **Effective Bidirectional Packet Exchange:** By enabling uplink and downlink transmission between the point of access and the sensors and enabling it to go into sleep mode as quickly as the communication is complete, this characteristic allows for the sensor module to save additional power.
3. **Short Mac Frame:** The standard IEEE 802.11 frame is around thirty bytes long, which is insufficient for Computer network applications. IEEE 802.11ah addresses this problem by providing a small MAC frame of about twelve bytes.

4. **Null Data Packet:** Control packets in IEEE 802.11, like Acknowledgement frames, are around fourteen bytes long and contain no information, adding a significant amount of overhead. IEEE 802.11ah addresses this issue by substituting the ACK packet with a preamble, which is a small signal.
5. **Upsurge Sleep Time:** Because 802.11ah is built for devices having low power, it allows for long periods of sleep and just occasional waking up to transfer files.

2.2.3. Wireless HART

It is a data link standard that functions atop IEEE 802.15.4 physically and incorporates TDMA (Time Division Multiple Access) in its MAC. It is a safe and efficient MAC standard that utilizes sophisticated encryption to secure communications and compute consistency to ensure reliability (Pardo-Castellote, 2003). As depicted in Figure 2.4, the design comprises the network administrator, a security administrator, a gateway to link the wireless connection to the wired connections, and wireless field types of equipment, points of access, routers, and adapters. The standard includes methods for end-to-end, per-hop, and peer-to-peer encryption. End-to-end security techniques maintain safety from sources to endpoints, whereas per-hop security controls maintain safety to the next step (Dong et al., 2014).

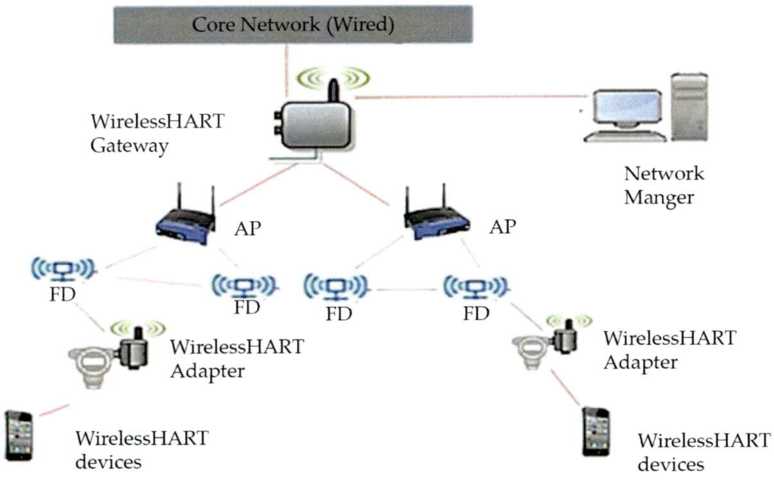

Figure 2.4. Schematic of components of wireless HART.

Source: Tara Salman, Creative Commons License.

2.2.4. Z-Wave

It's a MAC standard built for smart home devices with low power consumption. It has been utilized for connectivity across Computer networks, particularly for smart homes and small business sectors. It was created for usage in home automation. It has a range of around thirty meters for point-to-point connectivity. It is ideal for sending short messages in Computer network applications such as the management of lights, electricity, portable healthcare devices, and other similar applications. It employs CSMA/CA for obstacle detection to guarantee stable transmission, and ACK signals are used. The design is centered on a master-slave association, with the master having authority over the slaves, sending messages to them, and managing the planning for the entire network (Cao et al., 2012).

2.2.5. Bluetooth Low Energy

It is a popular in-vehicle networking standard for short-range communications with physical and MAC layers. Whereas its latency can be increased by 15, its low power can be ten times lower than that of traditional Bluetooth. Its access point (AP) uses a short, low latency, contention-less MAC (Madhyastha et al., 2006). It has a master/slave topology and provides data and advertising frames. Slaves transmit the information frame utilized for identification on one or more channels specifically designated for advertisements. Primary nodes perceive marketing channels to locate and link slaves. The master notifies the slave of its awakening cycle and planning order after connecting. Nodes typically only stay up while communicating. Otherwise, they sleep to conserve power (Madhyastha et al., 2006).

Did you Know?

These stack configurations provide full mesh connectivity and function with a variety of applications, permitting low storage and processing power deployments.

2.2.6. Zigbee Smart Energy

It is intended for many Internet-based applications such as intelligent residences, remote controls, and healthcare organizations. It accommodates a variety of network architectures such as star, peer-to-peer, and cluster tree. A coordinator is a master node in the star network, the root in a tree or cluster configuration, and can be positioned anywhere in a peer-to-peer network. The ZigBee protocol specifies two stack profiles: ZigBee and ZigBee Pro.

ZigBee Pro adds security via symmetric-key transfer, scalability through random address allocation, and improved performance through effective many-to-one routing techniques (Dujovne et al., 2014).

2.3. LIMITED DATA PROTOCOLS

2.3.1. DASH7

It is a wireless transmission standard for RFID that works in the universally accessible ISM (Industrial Scientific Medical) band and is compatible with the needs of Computer networks. It is primarily intended for expandable, long-range outside connectivity with a higher data rate than standard ZigBee. It is a cheap solution that provides IPv6 addressing and protection. It provides a master/slave topology for burst, light, asynchronous, and transitory traffic. The characteristics of its MAC layer can be summed up as follows (Al-Fuqaha et al., 2015):

1. **Filtering:** Three methods are used to screen incoming frames: CRC (cyclic redundancy check) verification, a four-bit subnet mask, and connection quality evaluation. Those frames that satisfy all three tests are subsequently processed.
2. **Addressing:** DASH7 employs two sorts of addresses: the distinct identification, the EUI64 ID, and the dynamic network identification, a sixteen-bit network administrator-specified address.
3. **Format of Frame:** The MAC frame has a configurable overall limit of 255 bytes, which includes addressing, subnets, anticipated transmission power, and other additional elements.

KEYWORD

A **subnet,** or subnetwork, is a segmented piece of a larger network. More specifically, subnets are a logical partition of an IP network into multiple, smaller network segments.

2.3.2. Home Plug

Another MAC standard created by the Home Plug Power line Alliance used throughout home automation systems is Home Plug Green PHY. Three versions of the Home Plug suite—Home Plug-AV, HomePlug-AV2, and Home Plug GP—cover both physical and MAC layers. Home Plug-AV is a fundamental power line communication standard that employs four modulation schemes, OFDM (orthogonal frequency division multiplexing) and the MAC layer standards TDMA and CSMA/CA (Mohammadi et al., 2017). It also facilitates adaptive bit loading, which enables it to alter its rate in response to noise levels. Home Plug is intended for Computer networks generally and particularly for applications related to house automation and the smart grid. Its main goal is to retain Home Plug-interoperability, AV dependability, and range while lowering its price and energy usage. As a result, it utilizes OFDM, similar to Home Plug, but with a single modulation (Lee et al., 2012).

Additionally, to accommodate a lower rate and high consistency communication, Home Plug GP employs Resilient OFDM coding. Whereas Home Plug GP uses both CSMA and TDMA, Home Plug-AV solely utilizes CSMA as the MAC layer method. Additionally, Home Plug GP features a power-saving mode that synchronizes nodes' sleep times and only wakes them up when essential, allowing nodes to sleep far longer than Home Plug (Wong et al., 2012).

TIPS

Select from a broad and affordable portfolio of proven wireless radios for 2.4 GHz, Sub-1 GHz and Wi-Fi connectivity.

2.3.3. G.9959

It is an ITU MAC layer standard for low-bandwidth, cheap, half-duplex dependable wireless connectivity. It is intended for real-time scenarios where time is crucial, dependability is essential, and low energy usage is necessary. The MAC layer features comprise:

- Specific network designations that enable 232 nodes to engage one network;
- Collision prevention processes;
- Back of time in the occurrence of a collision;
- Automatic retransmission to ensure reliability;
- Devoted wakeup sequence that enables nodes to sleep once they are out of connectivity, thus saving power.

Distinctive channel access, packet verification, recognitions, and retransmission are all characteristics of the G9959 MAC layer (Oliveira et al., 2019).

2.3.4. LTE-A

Long-Term Evolution Advanced is a collection of protocols for mobile network applications involving M2M connectivity and Computer network. It is a cost-efficient, flexible protocol when contrasted to other cellular networks. As the MAC layer access technique, LTE-A employs OFDMA (Orthogonal Frequency Division Numerous

Access), which splits the frequency into various bands that can be utilized independently. LTE-A architecture includes a core network, RAN (radio access network), and mobile nodes. The CN is accountable for mobile device management and IP address tracking. The radio access network is responsible for developing the control and data planes, managing wireless capabilities, and controlling radio access. RAN and CN interact through the S1 link (Figure 2.5; Salman & Jain, 2017). RAN comprises of eNBs to which other network elements are wirelessly linked.

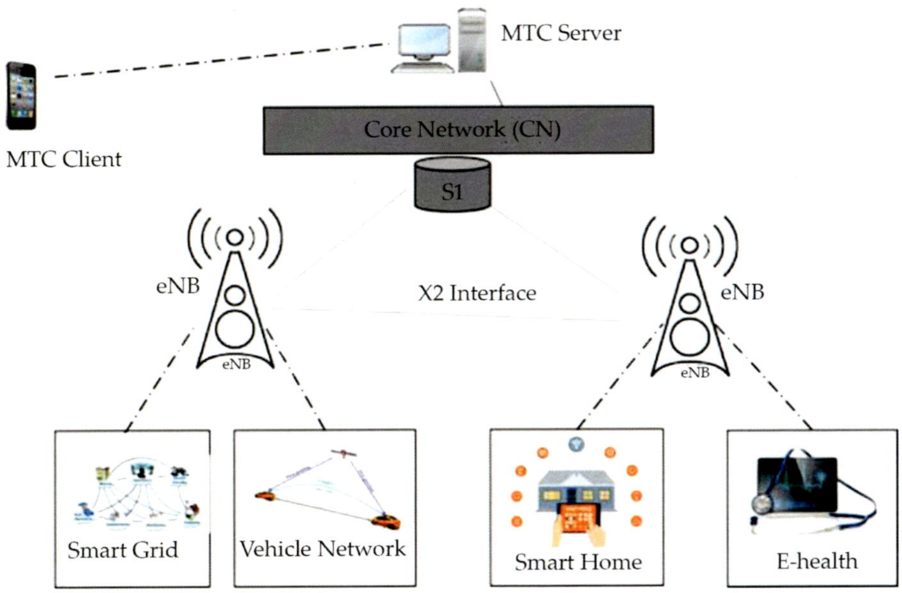

Figure 2.5. Image of LTE-A framework.

Source: Tara Salman, Creative Commons License.

2.3.5. LoRaWAN

It is a comparatively new wireless technology developed for low-power wide area networks (WANs) with the goals of having cheap costs, mobility, safety, and bi-directional connectivity for the applications of computer networks. It is an efficient standard with low energy consumption created for flexible wireless networks that can support numerous devices. It enables redundancy functioning, location-free, cheap, low power, and power harvesting techniques to support the future requirements of Computer networks while also providing portability and simplicity of use characteristics (Rivera & Van der Meulen, 2014).

2.3.6. Weightless

The Weightless SIG (Special Interest Group), an international non-profit group, has again created another wireless WAN solution for Computer networks purposes. Weightless-N and Weightless-W are two types of protocols that apply to it. Weightless-N was initially designed to allow TDMA with frequency hopping to reduce interference at a cheap rate and reduced power M2M connectivity. It operates in the sub-1GHz ISM frequency spectrum using highly narrow bands. Weightless-W, in contrast, offers the same functionality but uses tv band frequencies (Gartner, 2014).

2.3.7. DECT/ULE

It is a European cordless phone protocol. They have defined a low-power and cheap air interface technique that can be utilized for Computer networks in their recent DECT/ULE (Ultra Low Energy). DECT is free of overcrowding and interference because of its exclusive channel assignment. DECT/ULE includes FDMA, TDMA, and time division multiplexing, whereas the initial DECT protocol didn't (Gomez et al., 2012).

TIPS

In encapsulation, it adds the local destination address to the header.

2.4. NETWORK LAYER ROUTING PROTOCOLS

This part describes some conventional and non-standard guidelines employed in Computer network applications for routing. Notably, the network layer is divided into two sublayers: the routing layer, which manages the movement of messages from the sender to the receiver, and the encapsulation layer, which creates packets. Methods of encapsulating will be addressed in the following section.

2.4.1. RPL

The distance-vector standard known as Routing Protocol for Reduced-Power and Lossy Systems can handle several data link standards and those covered in the earlier sections (Ashok & Krishnaiah, 2013). It develops a DODAG (destination-oriented directed acyclic graph) with just one path connecting every leaf node to the root, where all communication from that node will be required. Every node initially transmits a DODAG Information Object announcing its claim to be the root (Hasan et al., 2013). As this signal spreads throughout the network, the entire DODAG is eventually constructed. When a node wants to communicate, it transmits its parents a DAO (destination advertisement object), which is then transferred to the root, which determines where to send it based on the location. The root will respond with a DAO-ACK Acknowledgment confirming the connection when a new node transmits a DIS (DODAG information solicitation) request for joining the system. Stateless RPL nodes are most prevalent; however, stateful nodes are also possible (Görmüş et al., 2018).

2.4.2. CORPL

It is an expansion of RPL that is developed for cognitive systems and employs DODAG architecture generation but with two novel additions to RPL. CORPL forwards the message utilizing opportunistic forwarding, which chooses various forwarders and collaborates between nodes to select the optimum next step to send the message to. DODAG is constructed in the same manner as RPL. Rather than just its parent, each node keeps a forwarding set and notifies its companion with modifications via DIO messages. Every node continuously alters its neighbor preferences based on the latest information to create the forwarder set (Karagiannis et al., 2015).

Remember

The ping command calculates round-trip times and packet loss statistics, and displays a brief summary on completion.

2.4.3. CARP

It is a cooperative routing standard explicitly created for underwater connectivity. Because of its lightweight packets, it could be employed in Computer network. It selects the forwarding nodes depending on the signal strength, which is determined based on previous effective data transfer from surrounding sensors. There are two situations: network setup and data transmission. During the initialization of the network, the sink transmits a Hello message to all other network nodes. In packet transmission, the message is transported hop-by-hop from the device to the sink. Every subsequent jump is individually decided. The primary shortcoming of CARP is that it does not permit the reuse of already obtained data. In other words, CARP information forwarding isn't advantageous for an application that wants device data only when it varies considerably. E-CARP is an improvement of CARP that allows the sink node to store formerly acquired sensory data. When novel data is required, E-CARP transmits a Ping packet to which the devices respond with their data. Therefore, E-CARP dramatically minimizes the network overhead (Kim et al., 2008).

2.5. NETWORK LAYER ENCAPSULATION PROTOCOLS

IPv6 addresses are very long to fit in most data link frames used by Computer networks because those frames are often considerably smaller. This presents a challenge for applications that make use of Computer networks. As an outcome, the IETF is now working on a set of protocols to package IPv6 datagrams in various data link layer packets to be utilized in Computer network applications (Locke, 2010). In this part, these methods will be discussed in-depth.

2.5.1. 6LoWPAN

IPv6 over Reduced power Wireless Personal Area Network is this segment's most frequently utilized protocol. It effectively wraps IPv6 lengthy prefixes in IEEE802.15.4 short packets, which can't surpass 128 bytes. The requirement allows for addresses of varying lengths, low bandwidth, various configurations, such as star and mesh, low energy consumption, cheap, scalable systems, mobility, unpredictability, and extended sleep times. The standard includes header reduction to minimize communication overhead, segmentation to fulfill IEEE802.15.4's maximum packet length of 128 bytes, and multi-hop delivery capability. There are four sorts of headers utilized in 6LoWPAN frames (Park, 2015):

Remember

Bandwidth may be characterized as network bandwidth, data bandwidth, or digital bandwidth.

- No 6LoWPAN header (00);
- Dispatch header (01);
- Mesh header (10);
- Fragmentation header (11).

2.5.2. 6TiSCH

The 6TiSCH working group of the IETF is establishing specifications to permit IPv6 to travel via the TSCH (Time-Slotted Channel Hopping) configuration of IEEE 802.15.4e datalinks. It provides a Channel Distribution utilization matrix with columns of accessible frequencies and rows of timeslots for connectivity scheduling tasks. This matrix is divided into chunks, including time and frequency information. Each piece is widely known to every node within the network (Poole, 2014). Every node within the same interfering area negotiates its planning such that each node can broadcast in a chunk inside its interfering area. Scheduling transforms into an optimization process in which periods are allotted to a collection of surrounding nodes that share the same purpose. To provide for added versatility for diverse Computer networks uses, the standard does not define how planning might be performed and instead leaves that as an application-specific issue. Planning might be centralized or disseminated based on the application, or the architecture employed in the MAC layer (Pongle & Chavan, 2015).

2.5.3. 6Lo

The IETF's IPv6 over Networks of Resource-constrained Nodes working group is creating a collection of guidelines for IPv6 frame distribution over multiple data links. Even though the working groups that created 6LowPAN and 6TiSCH, which address IEEE 802.15.4 and IEEE 802.15.4e, were separate, it soon became apparent that there was a great deal more data links that needed to be addressed, and the 6Lo working group was established. Most 6Lo specs are still in multiple development phases and haven't been completed (Raza & Voigt, 2010).

TIPS

Apps requiring a greater level of protection must implement their own end-to-end strong encryption protocols.

2.5.4. IPv6 Over G.9959

RFC 7428 specifies the message format for IPv6 packet transmission over ITU-T G.9959 systems. G.9959 specifies a 32-bit home router identification issued by the console and an eight-bit host identification assigned to every node. An IPv6 link-local identity should be generated from an eight-bit host identification obtained from the link layer to be compacted in a G.9959 frame. In addition, a similar header compression as 6lowPAN is utilized here to pack an IPv6 packet within G.9959 stands. RFC 7428 additionally offers a level of protection by using a mutual system key for encryption (Montenegro et al., 2007).

2.5.5. IPv6 over Bluetooth Low Energy

Bluetooth Low Energy was launched in Bluetooth V4.0 and further improved in Bluetooth V4.1. Most 6LowPAN data compression is reused in RFC 7668, which describes IPv6 over Bluetooth LE. Conversely, because Bluetooth's Logical Link Control and Adaptation Standard (L2CAP) sublayer typically allows fragmentation and reassembly of bigger payload into 27-byte L2CAP packages, 6LowPAN fragmentation characteristics aren't required. Another critical distinction is that it presently doesn't permit the establishment of multi-hop systems at the connection layer. Instead, a central node serves as a hub for lower-powered periphery nodes (Saint-Andre, 2011).

2.6. SESSION LAYER PROTOCOLS

This part discusses the protocols and guidelines for passing messages in the session layer of Computer networks suggested by various standardizing groups. Most IP applications, such as those for Computer networks, rely on TCP or UDP as their transport protocol of choice (Hui & Thubert, 2011). However, these operations must be executed in a compatible standard manner by various applications that use Computer networks. This is because multiple message distribution operations are similar among many Computer networks programs. The standards that are explained in this part are those that are known as the Session Layer.

2.6.1. MQTT

IBM first presented it in 1999, and OASIS certified it in 2013. It is made to offer an embedded connection between networks and connectivity on the one hand and programs and middleware on the other. The system has a publish/subscribe design and includes three primary parts: publishers, subscribers, and a broker, as depicted in Figure 2.6 (Kim et al., 2012).

Figure 2.6. Schematic of mechanism of MQTT architecture.

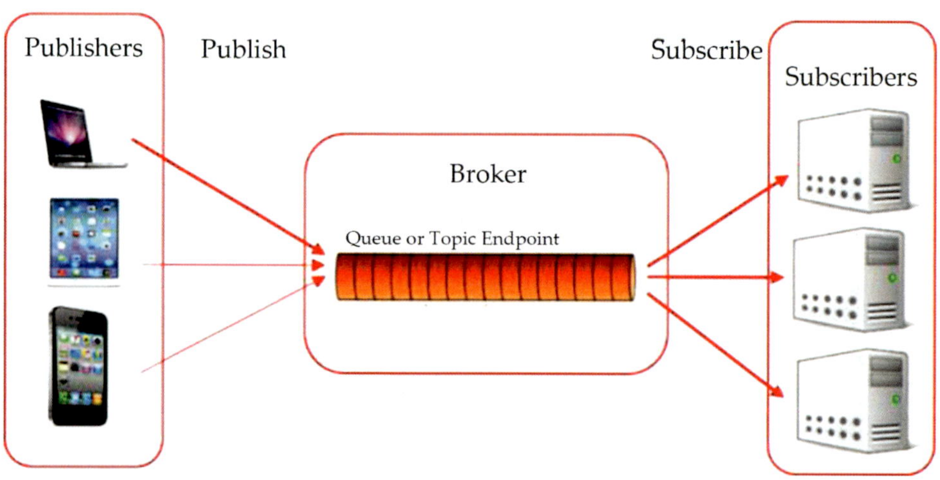

Source: Tara Salman, Creative Commons License.

Publishers are essentially the tiny devices that link to the broker to transmit information and then go to sleep again whenever feasible from the perspective of Computer network. Apps that are concerned with a particular subject or sensory data link to brokers as subscribers to be informed when new information is obtained. Brokers organize sensory data according to subjects and disseminate it to subscribers keen on specific areas (Winter et al., 2012) (Figure 2.6).

2.6.2. SMQTT

Secure MQTT is an MQTT addon that employs encryption centered on insubstantial attribute-based encryption. The key benefit of using such encryption is the broadcasting encryption capability, which encrypts one message and sends it to numerous other nodes, which is prevalent in Computer network applications. Generally, the algorithm is divided into 4 phases setup, encryption, publishing, and decryption. During the setup phase, subscribers and publishers join with the broker and receive a master private key centered on the critical development algorithm chosen by their provider. The data is then encrypted before being provided by the broker, who distributes it to the subscribers, and lastly, decoded by the subscribers who share the same master private key. The algorithms for generating keys and encrypting data aren't consistent. SMQTT is suggested to improve MQTT's security characteristics (Shelby et al., 2014).

KEYWORD

An algorithm is a procedure used for solving a problem or performing a computation.

2.6.3. AMQP

It is another standard intended for the financial company's session layer. It operates over TCP and has a publish/subscribe topology comparable to MQTT. As depicted in Figure 2.7, the broker is split into two main components: exchange and queues. The exchange is accountable for getting publisher notifications and allocating them to buffers according to prescribed criteria and roles. Queues represent the subjects and subscribers who will get sensory information once it becomes accessible in the buffer (Nieminen et al., 2015) (Figure 2.7).

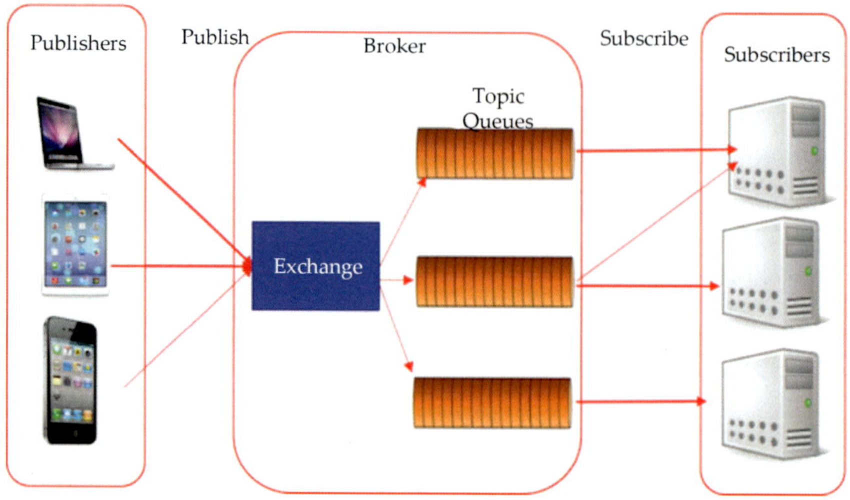

Figure 2.7. Schematic of mechanism of AMQP architecture.

Source: Tara Salman, Creative Commons License.

2.6.4. CoAP

The IETF Constrained RESTful Environment working team formed this additional session layer standard to provide compact RESTful (HTTP) access. The typical HTTP client and server interface is REST (Representational State Transfer). Conversely, REST might outcome in substantial overhead and energy usage for lightweight purposes like Computer network. Low-power sensors might utilize RESTful services using CoAP while still following their power limitations (Patil et al., 2015). Rather than the traditional TCP used in HTTP, it is made atop UDP and comprises a simple way to confirm dependability. Request/Response and Communication are the two basic sublayers of the CoAP framework. Whereas the request/ response sublayer is in charge of connectivity, the messaging sublayer is in charge of message dependability and redundancy. CoAP supports four communications configurations: confirmable, non-confirmable, piggyback, and separate, as shown in Figure 2.8. Piggyback is a direct communication technique between a client and a server that involves the server sending its answer to the message immediately after receiving it. In contrast, the separate configuration is utilized when the server answer is delivered in a message distinct from the ACK. The delivery of this message by the server might take a while. In the same way, as HTTP uses GET, PUT, and DELETE signal requests, so does CoAP (Campos et al., 2018). These requests are used to receive, create, amend, and delete messages accordingly (Figure 2.8).

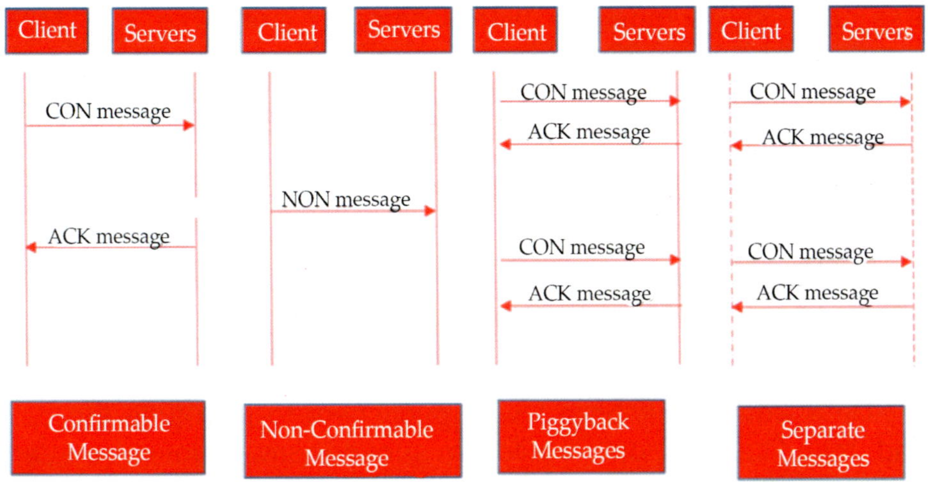

Figure 2.8. Diagram of CoAP messages.

Source: Tara Salman, Creative Commons License.

2.6.5. XMPP

It is a communications protocol initially conceived for instant messaging and data transmission programs. IETF defined it more than 10 years ago. Therefore, it is widely known and has demonstrated internet-wide effectiveness. It has subsequently been repurposed for Computer network applications and as an SDN protocol. This reuse of the same protocol is possible because of its XML-based extensibility. XMPP provides both publish/subscribe and request/response architectures, and it depends upon the application builder to decide which paradigm to utilize. It is intended for near-real-time scenarios and enables low-latency short messages effectively. It does not offer any service quality assurances and is impractical for M2M connectivity. In addition, XML communications create extra overhead because of the large number of headers and tagging formats, which increases the vital energy usage for Computer networks. Consequently, XMPP is utilized infrequently in Computer networks, but there is growing interested in upgrading its framework to enable Computer network uses (Shukla & Tripathi, 2018).

KEYWORD

Service quality is a measure of how an organization understands its users' needs and fulfills their expectations.

2.6.6. DDS

It's another publish/subscribe standard for M2M connectivity by the OMG (Object Management Group). The primary advantage of this standard is that it provides good service quality levels and consistency assurances because it is based on a broker-less topology compatible with Computer networks and M2M connectivity. It gives 23 high-quality service levels, providing a wide range of criteria such as security, immediacy, priority, endurance, dependability, and so on. It distinguishes between 2 sublayers:

- data-centric publish-subscribe
- data-local reconstruction (Sheng et al., 2013).

Remember

The publisher layer is in charge of the sensory dissemination of the data.

The 1st is in charge of information transmission to subscribers, whereas the 2nd is customizable and provides for simple DDS incorporation at the application level.

Data writers collaborate with publishers to negotiate the data and modifications distributed to subscribers. Subscribers are the recipients of sensory information sent to Computer network applications. Data readers receive published information and transmit it to subscribers, and topics are released. Conversely, in broker-based systems, data producers and readers assume the broker's role (Mowery & Simcoe, 2002).

This part provided a high-level overview of some of the numerous established session layer standards used by Computer networks. These session layer standards rely heavily on the application, and selecting one over another depends on the application's requirements. It is important to remember that MQTT is utilized most frequently in Computer networks because of its low complexity and energy consumption. Deciding on these standards requires taking into account both organizational and application-specific factors. The key differences and similarities between these various session layer standards are outlined in Table 2.1 (Meingast et al., 2006).

Table 2.1. Tabular Data about Computer Networks Transport Layer Protocols Contrast

Protocols	UDP/TCP	Security and Quality of Service	Topology	Max Length (Bytes)	Header Size (Bytes)
MQTT	TCP	Both	Pub/Sub	5	2
CoAP	UDP	Both	Req/Res	20	4
AMQP	TCP	Both	Pub/Sub	–	8
DDS	TCP/UDP	Quality of service	Pub/Sub	–	–
XMPP	TCP	Security	Both	–	–

Source: Tara Salman, Creative Commons License.

2.7. MANAGEMENT PROTOCOLS

The two major management protocols for Computer networks that support heterogeneous communication—connectivity amongst various data links—are covered in this part. Because of the variability of guidelines and standards at different networking layers, management standards play a significant role in Computer network. For systems using Computer networks, there is a fundamental need for diverse and straightforward communication between many standards at the same or separate tiers. In Computer networks, it remains challenging to ease communication at various layers; prevailing standards primarily enable communication across the same layer (Leiner et al., 1997).

KEYWORD

A data link is the means of connecting one location to another for the purpose of transmitting and receiving digital information (data communication).

2.7.1. Interconnection of Heterogeneous Datalinks

As Computer network environments depend on numerous MAC standards, compatibility between these technologies presents a difficulty that must be addressed. IEEE 1905.1 guidelines provide this compatibility by incorporating an abstraction layer on top of these diverse MAC protocols. This generalization conceals the variability of the many standards without necessitating any changes to the architecture of every MAC. This system is based on the abstraction layer utilized to send and receive packets, known as CMDU (control message data units), across all standards-compliant devices, as depicted in Figure 2.9 (Cirani et al., 2018).

All IEEE 1905.1-compliant machines comprehend a prevalent ALME (abstraction layer management entity) protocol that provides various services such as (Figure 2.9):

- Neighbor finding;
- Configuration exchange;
- Configuration change confirmation;
- Measured traffic statics transfer;
- Flow routing rules;
- Safety affiliations (Wigand et al., 2005).

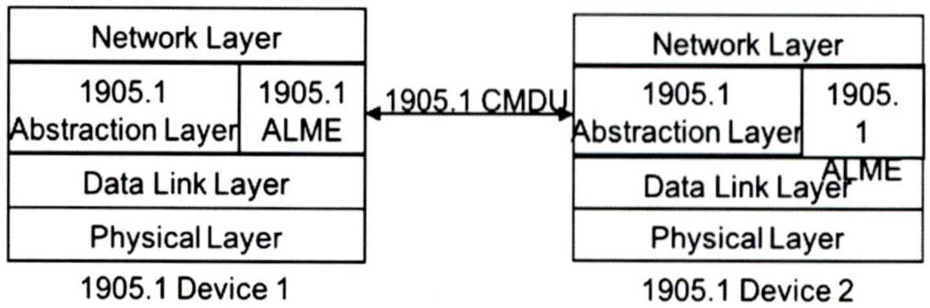

Figure 2.9. Schematic of IEEE 1905.1 protocol configuration.

Source: Tara Salman, Creative Commons License.

2.7.2. Smart Transducer Interface

IEEE 1451 is a series of protocols designed to manage various analog transducers and devices. The primary concept behind this protocol is to employ plug-and-play recognition using standardized TEDSs (Transducer electronic data sheets). In addition to the data from the devices, every transducer carries a TEDS that provides all of the data requested by the measuring system, like device ID, features, and interface. Data sheets are integrated memory stored inside the transducer or device and feature a standardized encoding scheme to comprehend a wide range of sensor kinds and uses. Memory use is reduced by using tiny XML-based communications that are accepted by various manufacturers and programs (Triantafyllou et al., 2018).

2.8. SECURITY IN COMPUTER NETWORKS PROTOCOLS

Another essential component of the applications that use Computer networks is privacy, which can be seen embedded in virtually every layer of the standards that underpin Computer networks. Dangers are lurking in every tier, from the data link to the network to the session to the application layer. This part provides a quick overview of the safety protocols built into the computer networks and standards covered in the preceding sections of this review.

2.8.1. MAC

It can provide various security options by exploiting the Security Enabled Bit located in the Frame Control field of the header (Gazis et al., 2015). The following are examples of required security measures: secrecy, authentication, stability, access control methods, and encrypted time-synchronized connections.

2.8.2. 6LoWPAN

It does not provide any security features by itself. Conversely, pertinent documents cover security risks, needs, and strategies to take into account at the network layer of Computer network. For instance, the potential for redundant EUI-64 interface addresses—which are meant to be unique—is covered in RFC 4944. The security concerns brought up by the problems in RFC 4944 are covered in RFC 6282. RFC 6568 discusses potential safety implementation methods for restricted wireless sensing devices (Zhu et al., 2010).

ACTIVITY 2.1.

Enlist some networking protocols and standards of internet technologies Also discuss why these protocols and standards are necessary for smooth functioning of internet technologies.

2.8.3. RPL

It provides varying levels of security by including a Security field following the four-byte ICMPv6 packet headers. This field contains information about the status of safety and the encryption algorithm used to secure the message. RPL assists in data validity, semantic security, recovery, secrecy, and key distribution. Unprotected, preinstalled, and verified are the protection levels in RPL (Houimli et al., 2017).

2.8.4. Application Layer

TLS or SSL can be used as a transport layer standard in applications, allowing for extra protection. Furthermore, multiple identifications and encryption techniques can be employed to manage the various degrees of security that are necessary depending on the situation (Stallings, 2004).

It is essential to highlight that various novel security techniques are also being explored, and these methods are designed to work well on resource-limited Computer network devices.

2.9. SUMMARY

A thorough overview of standards for Computer networks is given in this chapter. The IETF, IEEE, the ITU, and numerous other organizations have all participated in the creation of similar protocols, and countless additional are now under. Because there are so many of them, the explanation of each procedure will only be a few sentences long. Links to more material have been supplied. This chapter aims to offer developers and network operators an understanding of the various protocols used in Computer networks and guidance on picking amongst them.

REVIEW QUESTIONS

1. What is the purpose of Computer networks?
2. What are the most common Data Link Standards?
3. What is the role of MAC Standards in networking?
4. What are the different types of Routing Standards?
5. What are the most widely used Network Standards?
6. How do Transport Layer Standards facilitate communication between two computers?
7. What are the different types of Management Standards used in networking?

MULTIPLE CHOICE QUESTIONS

1. Which of the following data link standards is used in most Ethernet networks?

a. IEEE 802.3
b. IEEE 802.11
c. IEEE 802.15
d. IEEE 802.2

2. Which of the following is a computer network used for exchanging data over a network?

a. RIP
b. DHCP
c. FTP
d. OSPF

3. Which of the following MAC standards defines the protocol for exchanging packets between nodes in a network?

a. IEEE 802.3
b. IEEE 802.15

c. IEEE 802.2

d. IEEE 802.11

4. Which routing standards are used to find the most efficient route between two nodes in a network?

a. OSPF

b. BGP

c. RIP

d. All of the above

5. Which network standards define how data can be transmitted over a network?

a. Ethernet

b. IP

c. Token ring

d. All of the above

Answers to Multiple Choice Questions

1. (a); 2. (c); 3. (a); 4. (d); 5. (d)

REFERENCES

1. Aijaz, A., & Aghvami, A. H., (2015). Cognitive machine-to-machine communications for Internet-of-Things: A protocol stack perspective. *IEEE Internet of Things Journal, 2*(2), 103–112.
2. Akbar, M. S., Hussain, Z., Sheng, M., & Shankaran, R., (2022). Wireless body area sensor networks: Survey of MAC and routing protocols for patient monitoring under IEEE 802.15. 4 and IEEE 802.15. 6. *Sensors, 22*(21), 8279.
3. Al-Fuqaha, A., Guizani, M., Mohammadi, M., Aledhari, M., & Ayyash, M., (2015). Internet of things: A survey on enabling technologies, protocols, and applications. *IEEE Communications Surveys & Tutorials, 17*(4), 2347–2376.
4. Ashok, S., & Krishnaiah, R. V., (2013). Overview and evaluation of Bluetooth low energy: An emerging low-power wireless technology. *International Journal, 3*(9), 11734–11753.
5. Ayoub, W., Samhat, A. E., Nouvel, F., Mroue, M., & Prévotet, J. C., (2018). Internet of mobile things: Overview of LoRaWAN, DASH7, and Nb-IoT in LPWANs standards and support mobility. *IEEE Communications Surveys & Tutorials, 21*(2), 1561–1581.
6. Beck, K., (1999). Embracing change with extreme programming. *Computer, 32*(10), 70–77.
7. Campos, J., Colteryahn, S., & Gagneja, K., (2018). Ipv6 transmission over BLE using raspberry pi 3. In: *2018 International Conference on Computing, Networking*

and Communications (ICNC) (Vol. 1, pp. 200–204). IEEE.

8. Cao, J., Guo, C., Lu, G., Xiong, Y., Zheng, Y., Zhang, Y., & Chen, C., (2012). Datacast: A scalable and efficient reliable group data delivery service for data centers. In: *Proceedings of the 8th International Conference on Emerging Networking Experiments and Technologies* (Vol. 1, pp. 37–48).
9. Cetinkaya, O., & Akan, O. B., (2015). A DASH7-based power metering system. In: *2015 12th Annual IEEE Consumer Communications and Networking Conference (CCNC)* (Vol. 1, pp. 406–411). IEEE.
10. Choi, Y., Choi, Y., Kim, D., & Park, J., (2017). Scheme to guarantee IP continuity for NFC-based IoT networking. In: *2017 19th International Conference on Advanced Communication Technology (ICACT)* (Vol. 1, pp. 695–698). IEEE.
11. Cirani, S., Ferrari, G., Picone, M., & Veltri, L., (2018). *Internet of Things: Architectures, Protocols, and Standards* (Vol. 1, pp. 3–9). John Wiley & Sons.
12. Dong, X., Yu, J., Luo, Y., Chen, Y., Xue, G., & Li, M., (2014). Achieving a practical, scalable, and privacy-preserving data-sharing service in cloud computing. *Computers & Security, 42*, 151–164.
13. Dujovne, D., Watteyne, T., Vilajosana, X., & Thubert, P., (2014). 6TiSCH: Deterministic IP-enabled industrial internet (of things). *IEEE Communications Magazine, 52*(12), 36–41.
14. Gartner, J., (2014). *Gartner's 2014 Hype Cycle for Emerging Technologies Maps the Journey to Digital Business* (Vol. 11, No. 1, pp. 1–6). GARTNER, Inc.[online].
15. Gazis, V., Görtz, M., Huber, M., Leonardi, A., Mathioudakis, K., Wiesmaier, A., & Vasilomanolakis, E., (2015). A survey of technologies for the internet of things. In: *2015 International Wireless Communications and Mobile Computing Conference (IWCMC)* (Vol. 1, pp. 1090–1095). IEEE.
16. Gomez, C., Oller, J., & Paradells, J., (2012). Overview and evaluation of Bluetooth low energy: An emerging low-power wireless technology. *Sensors, 12*(9), 11734–11753.
17. Görmüş, S., Aydın, H., & Ulutaş, G., (2018). Security for the internet of things: A survey of existing mechanisms, protocols, and open research issues. *Journal of the Faculty of Engineering and Architecture of Gazi University, 33*(4), 1247–1272.
18. Grabia, M., Markowski, T., Mruczkiewicz, J., & Plec, K., (2017). Design of a DASH7 low-power wireless sensor network for industry 4.0 applications. In: *2017 IEEE International Conference on RFID Technology & Application (RFID-TA)* (Vol. 1, pp. 254–259). IEEE.
19. Hansen, P. B., (1975). The programming language is the concurrent pascal. *IEEE Transactions on Software Engineering,* (2), 199–207.
20. Hasan, M., Hossain, E., & Niyato, D., (2013). Random access for machine-to-machine communication in LTE-advanced networks: Issues and approaches. *IEEE Communications Magazine, 51*(6), 86–93.

21. Houimli, M., Kahloul, L., & Benaoun, S., (2017). Formal specification, verification, and evaluation of the MQTT protocol in the internet of things. In: *2017 International Conference on Mathematics and Information Technology (ICMIT)* (Vol. 1, pp. 214–221). IEEE.
22. Hui, J., & Thubert, P., (2011). *Compression Format for IPv6 Datagrams Over IEEE 802.15. 4-Based Networks (No. rfc6282)* (2nd edn., pp. 6–9).
23. Isomaki, M., Nieminen, J., Gomez, C., Shelby, Z., Savolainen, T., & Patil, B. (2015). IPv6 over BLUETOOTH (R) Low Energy. *Internet Engineering Task Force (IETF) 4*(1), 6–9.
24. Karagiannis, V., Chatzimisios, P., Vazquez-Gallego, F., & Alonso-Zarate, J., (2015). A survey on application layer protocols for the internet of things. *Transaction on IoT and Cloud Computing, 3*(1), 11–17.
25. Kim, A. N., Hekland, F., Petersen, S., & Doyle, P., (2008). When HART goes wireless: Understanding and implementing the WirelessHART standard. In: *2008 IEEE International Conference on Emerging Technologies and Factory Automation* (Vol. 1, pp. 899–907). IEEE.
26. Kim, E., Kaspar, D., & Vasseur, J. P., (2012). *Design and Application Spaces for IPv6 Over Low-Power Wireless Personal Area Networks (6LoWPANs) (No. rfc6568),* (Vol. 1, pp. 3–9).
27. Lee, Y. U., & Kavehrad, M., (2012). Two hybrid positioning system design techniques with lighting LEDs and ad-hoc wireless network. *IEEE Transactions on Consumer Electronics, 58*(4), 1176–1184.
28. Leiner, B. M., Cerf, V. G., Clark, D. D., Kahn, R. E., Kleinrock, L., Lynch, D. C., & Wolff, S. S., (1997). The past and future history of the Internet. *Communications of the ACM, 40*(2), 102–108.
29. Locke, D., (2010). MQ telemetry transport (MQTT) v3. 1 protocol specification. *IBM Developer Works Technical Library, 15*(1), 5–9.
30. Madhyastha, H. V., Isdal, T., Piatek, M., Dixon, C., Anderson, T., Krishnamurthy, A., & Venkataramani, A., (2006). iPlane: An information plane for distributed services. In: *Proceedings of the 7th Symposium on Operating Systems Design and Implementation* (Vol. 1, pp. 367–380).
31. Meingast, M., Roosta, T., & Sastry, S., (2006). Security and privacy issues with health care information technology. In: *2006 International Conference of the IEEE Engineering in Medicine and Biology Society* (Vol. 1, pp. 5453–5458). IEEE.
32. Mohammadi, M., Al-Fuqaha, A., Guizani, M., & Oh, J. S., (2017). Semisupervised deep reinforcement learning in support of IoT and smart city services. *IEEE Internet of Things Journal, 5*(2), 624–635.
33. Montenegro, G., Kushalnagar, N., Hui, J., & Culler, D., (2007). *Transmission of IPv6 Packets Over IEEE 802.15. 4 Networks (No. rfc4944),* (Vol. 1, pp. 2–9).
34. Mowery, D. C., & Simcoe, T., (2002). Is the Internet a US invention?— Economic and

technological history of computer networking? *Research Policy, 31*(8, 9), 1369–1387.

35. Nieminen, J., Savolainen, T., Isomaki, M., Patil, B., Shelby, Z., & Gomez, C., (2015). *Ipv6 Over Bluetooth (r) Low Energy (No. rfc7668*), (Vol. 1, pp. 2–9).
36. Oliveira, L., Rodrigues, J. J., Kozlov, S. A., Rabêlo, R. A., & Albuquerque, V. H. C. D., (2019). MAC layer protocols for the internet of things: A survey. *Future Internet, 11*(1), 16.
37. Pardo-Castellote, G., (2003). Omg, data-distribution service: Architectural overview. In: *23rd International Conference on Distributed Computing Systems Workshops, 2003; Proceedings.* (Vol. 1, pp. 200–206). IEEE.
38. Park, M., (2015). IEEE 802.11 ah: Sub-1-GHz license-exempt operation for the internet of things. *IEEE Communications Magazine, 53*(9), 145–151.
39. Pongle, P., & Chavan, G., (2015). A survey: Attacks on RPL and 6LoWPAN in IoT. In: *2015 International Conference on Pervasive Computing (ICPC)* (Vol. 1, pp. 1–6). IEEE.
40. Poole, I., (2014). *Weightless Wireless—M2M White Space Communications-Tutorial, 1*, 3–9.
41. Raza, S., & Voigt, T., (2010). Interconnecting WirelessHART and legacy HART networks. In: *2010 6th IEEE International Conference on Distributed Computing in Sensor Systems Workshops* (DCOSSW) (Vol. 1, pp. 1–8). IEEE.
42. Rivera, J., & Van, D. M. R., (2014). *Gartner's 2014 Hype Cycle for Emerging Technologies Maps the Journey to Digital Business* (Vol. 1, No. 2, pp. 3–8). Connecticut, EEUU: Gartner Group.
43. Saint-Andre, P., (2011). *Extensible Messaging and Presence Protocol (XMPP): Core (No. rfc6120), 3*(1), 4–8.
44. Salman, T., & Jain, R., (2017). Networking protocols and standards for the internet of things. *Internet of Things and Data Analytics Handbook, 1*, 215–238.
45. Salman, T., & Jain, R., (2019). *A Survey of Protocols and Standards for the Internet of Things* (Vol. 1, pp. 5–8). arXiv preprint arXiv:1903.11549.
46. Shelby, Z., Hartke, K., & Bormann, C., (2014). *The Constrained Application Protocol (CoAP) (No. rfc7252),* (Vol. 1, pp. 4–6).
47. Sheng, Z., Yang, S., Yu, Y., Vasilakos, A. V., McCann, J. A., & Leung, K. K., (2013). A survey on the IETF protocol suite for the internet of things: Standards, challenges, and opportunities. *IEEE Wireless Communications, 20*(6), 91–98.
48. Shukla, A., & Tripathi, S., (2018). Security challenges and issues of internet of things: Possible Solutions. In: *Proceedings of 3rd International Conference on Internet of Things and Connected Technologies (ICIoTCT)* (Vol. 1, pp. 26, 27).
49. Stallings, W., (2004). *Computer Networking with Internet Protocols and Technology* (Vol. 1, pp. 4–8). Upper Saddle River, NJ, USA: Pearson/Prentice Hall.
50. Standard, O. A. S. I. S., (2012). Oasis advanced message queuing protocol (AMQP) version 1.0. *International Journal of Aerospace Engineering Hindawi* (Vol. 2, No. 1,

pp. 2–7). www.Hindawi.com (accessed on 10 April 2023).

51. Tilkov, S., & Vinoski, S., (2010). Node.js: Using JavaScript to build high-performance network programs. *IEEE Internet Computing, 14*(6), 80–83.
52. Triantafyllou, A., Sarigiannidis, P., & Lagkas, T. D., (2018). Network protocols, schemes, and mechanisms for the internet of things (IoT): Features, open challenges, and trends. *Wireless Communications and Mobile Computing, 2018*, (Vol. 1, pp. 1–5).
53. Wigand, R. T., Steinfield, C. W., & Markus, M. L., (2005). Information technology standards choices and industry structure outcomes: The case of the US home mortgage industry. *Journal of Management Information Systems, 22*(2), 165–191.
54. Winter, T., Thubert, P., Brandt, A., Hui, J., Kelsey, R., Levis, P., & Alexander, R., (2012). *RPL: IPv6 Routing Protocol for Low-Power and Lossy Networks (No. rfc6550)* (Vol. 1, pp. 2–6).
55. Wong, A. C. W., Dawkins, M., Devita, G., Kasparidis, N., Katsiamis, A., King, O., & Burdett, A. J., (2012). A 1 V 5 mA multimode IEEE 802.15. 6/Bluetooth low-energy WBAN transceiver for biotelemetry applications. *IEEE Journal of Solid-State Circuits, 48*(1), 186–198.
56. Zhu, Q., Wang, R., Chen, Q., Liu, Y., & Qin, W., (2010). IoT gateway: Bridging wireless sensor networks into the internet of things. In: *2010 IEEE/IFIP International Conference on Embedded and Ubiquitous Computing* (Vol. 1, pp. 347–352). IEEE.

CHAPTER 3

HARDWARE AND SOFTWARE USED IN COMPUTER NETWORKS

UNIT INTRODUCTION

The practical application of technology in today's world is meant to produce tangible commercial benefits, as seen by Turboinstitut. The use of information technology and the provision of extra processing power can boost worker productivity, open up new company prospects, and enable greater flexibility. Beginning with a definition of hardware, this chapter describes the software and hardware parts of a computer network (Yakubailik et al., 2018).

Hardware describes the actual parts of a computer system that carry out its input, processing, storing, and output functions. In what way hardware can serve the aims of the company and the computer network should be the primary factor taken into account by a corporation when making hardware decisions.

People should choose and arrange components while understanding the trade-offs between total system performance and cost, control, and complexity to create an effective and efficient system. Manufacturers, for instance, make an effort to match the components of an automobile to the application for which it is intended. For instance, racing automobiles need particular tires, transmissions, and engine types. When choosing a drivetrain for a racing car, it's crucial to weigh the amount of engine power that can be sent to the wheels against the transmission's cost, control, and number of gears (complexity). In a similar way, businesses set together computers that are useful, efficient, and well-suited to the jobs that need to be done (Thrall, 1999).

The IS solutions that different firms opt for can be fairly different because the business requires, and their significance varies at each organization. To make wise purchase selections, those choosing the computer hardware for their firm must thoroughly understand both current and future business requirements. Take a look at the examples below of how to use business knowledge to make significant hardware decisions:

1. The NOAA is a scientific organization whose goals are to conserve and manage coastal and marine resources as well as comprehend and forecast changes in the Earth's ecosystem. To fulfill its mandate, the NOAA creates severe storm warnings and daily weather predictions. The NOAA realized it needed greater computational power and backup storage. In order to handle more precise information and sharpen the resolution of meteorological conditions, it recently updated from a single machine to two more potent computer systems. The two brand-new devices, stratus and cirrus, have four times as much computing power as the old one. The Cirrus computer, which is kept in a different location, also serves as a backup for the Stratus computer. The Cirrus can take over in minutes if the Stratus fails.
2. With 1.5 million followers and 223 branch locations, the North Carolina State Workers' Credit Union is the 4th-largest credit union in the nation. The credit union constantly seeks ways to cut costs while enhancing client service. Consequently, it made a large investment in computer hardware to upgrade more than 3k desktop computers to modern, affordable, flexible systems.
3. On Boston's picturesque waterfront sits the 426-room, four-diamond-rated Seaport Hotel. The guest house installed tablets in each room based on the findings of focus group discussions and guest feedback. These computers enable guests to access current hotel and neighborhood attraction information, obtain traffic updates and weather forecast, have unrestricted Internet, and make free local and long-distance calls online (Ganesh, 2021).

These illustrations show that selecting the appropriate computer hardware necessitates grasping how it relates to the data system and the company's requirements. Moreover, hardware goals complement the data system and the organization's present-day and upcoming demands but are subordinate to them.

Learning Objectives

At the end of this chapter, readers will be able to learn:

- Components of hardware used in computer networks;
- Processing and memory devices in computer networks;
- Various secondary storage, input, and output devices;
- Overview of the Software used in the computer networks;
- Operating systems of the software;
- Utility programs and applications of the software in computer networks.

Key Terms

- Computing
- Data
- Device
- Hardware
- Memory
- Network
- Operating systems
- Software
- Storage

3.1. HARDWARE COMPONENTS

Hardware components consist of the roles of input, processing, data storage, and output (*see* Figure 3.1).

Figure 3.1. The input-process-output concept.

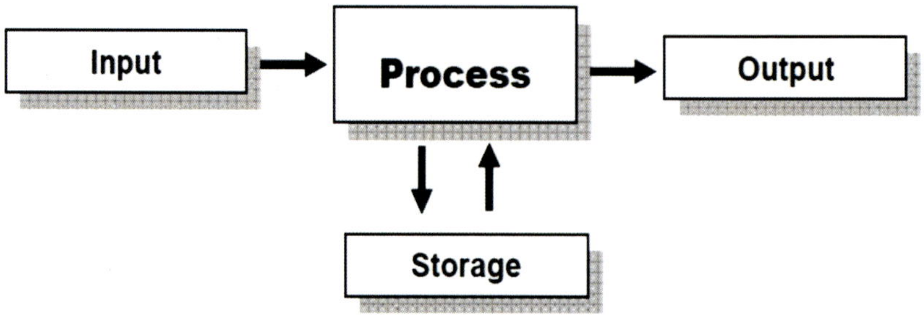

Source: General Note, Creative Commons License.

These elements consist of the CPU, peripheral devices, telecommunications equipment, secondary and primary storage devices, and devices for exchanging data (CPU). The CPU comprises the CU, the ALU(arithmetic/logic unit), and the register storage sections (Herbst et al., 1999).

A crucial component of a computer system is its capacity to process (order and manipulate) data. Processing is carried out through the interaction of one or more central processing units (CPU) with primary storage. The arithmetic/logic unit and the control unit (CU) are the two main components of each CPU. Mathematical calculations and logical comparisons are carried out by the ALU. The CU coordinates data flow into and out of the ALU, primary storage, secondary storage, and different output devices while progressively accessing and decoding program instructions. The CPU and primary memory, which stores data and program instructions, are closely related.

After learning about the fundamental hardware components and how they work, readers are now prepared to look at processing capacity. These three characteristics determine a hardware device's capabilities (Saputra, 2022).

3.2. PROCESSING AND MEMORY DEVICES: POWER, SPEED, AND CAPACITY

The system unit, also known as the box or cabinet housing the CPU and memory, is where the processing-related parts are kept.

All additional computer hardware, including the keyboard and display, is either linked indirectly or directly to the system unit casing. As mentioned, organizational goals and IS objectives should come first when choosing memory and processing devices. This section looks into the traits of these significant devices (Wright et al., 2013) (Figure 3.2).

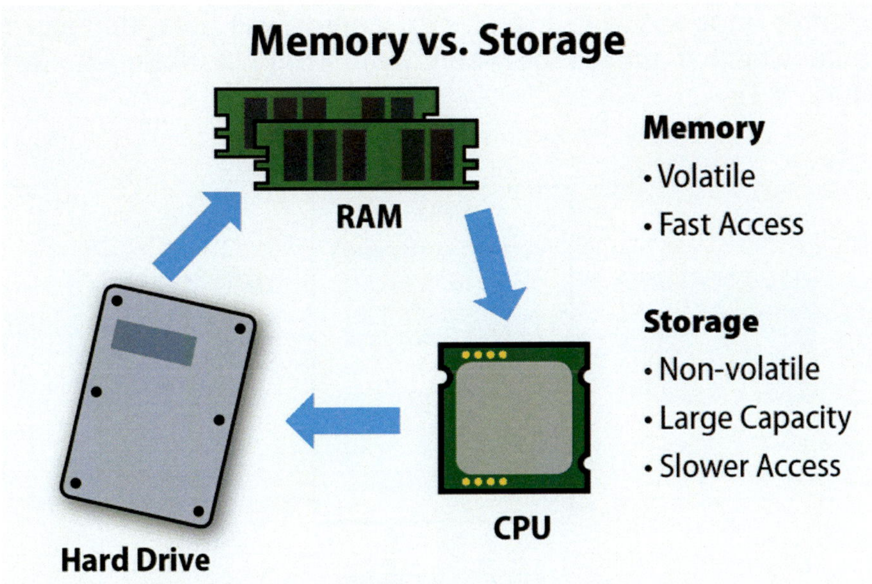

Figure 3.2. Illustration of the memory vs. storage.

Source: Christine Taylor, Creative Commons License.

3.2.1. Processing Characteristics and Functions

Organizations measure processing speed using a range of metrics because timely output and effective processing are crucial. These metrics include clock speed and the length of a machine cycle.

3.2.1.1 Clock Speed

The duty cycle, which determines how quickly each CPU generates a sequence of electronic pulses that influences machine cycle time, is produced by each CPU. The electronic cycle, or pulses, of the CPU "clock," determine how the CU will instruct. The duration of each instruction is at least equal to the time elapsed between pulses. Each command can be carried out more quickly the more often the pulses are sent. Personal computers have clock speeds in the several GHz range or trillions of cycles per second (Raj et al., 2019).

3.2.1.2 Physical Characteristics of the CPU

Physical limitations also affect Processor speed. Most CPUs are made up of groups of digital circuits that are printed on silicon chips, or chips, each of which is no larger than the tip of an eraser. The electrical current must move from point A to point B through a material (often silicon) to switch on or off a logic gate within the CPU. Lowering the distances between the spots or the medium's impedance to the electric charge will both increase the rate at which it moves between them (Belo & Marques, 2012) (Figure 3.3).

Figure 3.3. Schematic of the central processing unit (CPU).

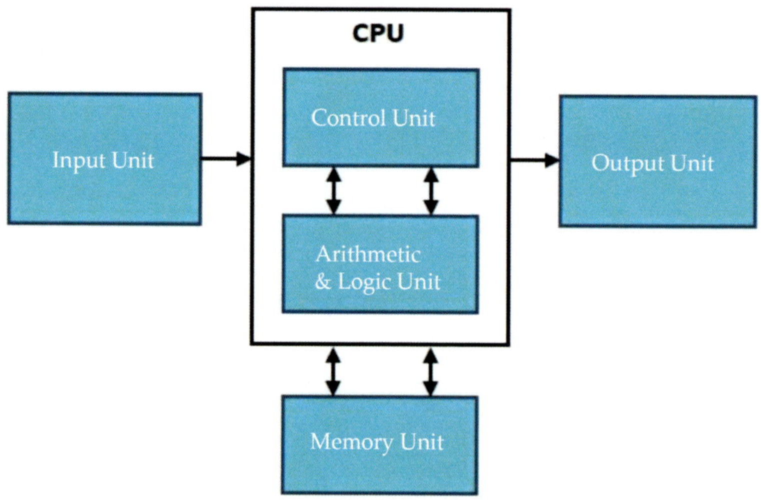

Source: Tutorials Point, Creative Commons License.

3.2.2. Memory Characteristics and Functions

Memory offers the Processor a functioning storage area for program instructions and data by being physically close by (to reduce access time). The main benefit of memory is that it gives the Processor access to data and instructions quickly.

3.2.2.1. Storage Capacity

Memory devices have thousands of transistors engraved on a silicon chip, similar to the CPU. Every circuit conducts electrical current (turned on) or does not (off). Circuit states that are both on and off are used to store data in memory. A character, such as a letter A, is typically represented by 8 bits. A byte is formed by eight bits (B). The most common unit of measurement for storage space is the byte, with one byte standing in for one bit of data. With much more than 126 million objects and 530 kilometers of bookcases, the Library of Congress' collection would need nearly 20 terabytes of digital storage data. Units for assessing computer storage capacity are listed in Table 3.1.

3.2.2.2. Types of Memory

There are numerous types of memory. Random access memory can temporarily store instructions or data (RAM). RAM is transient and brittle; if the current is interrupted or switched off, RAM transistors lose their contents. RAM modules are directly located on the computer's main circuit board or in peripheral cards connecting to the main circuit board. Millions of switches sensitive to electric current shifts make up these RAM chips (Mello et al., 2005). The simultaneous use of many processors to carry out the same activity to quickly get results.

Table 3.1. Comparison for Various Forms of Data Storage

Name	Abbreviation	Number of Bytes
Byte	B	1
Kilobyte	KB	2^{10} or approximately 1,024 bytes
Megabyte	MB	2^{20} or 1,024 kilobytes (about 1 million)
Gigabyte	GB	2^{30} or 1,024 megabytes (about 1 billion)
Terabyte	TB	2^{40} or 1,024 gigabytes (about 1 trillion)
Petabyte	PB	2^{50} or 1,024 terabytes (about 1 quadrillion)
Exabyte	EB	2^{60} or 1,024 petabytes (about 1 quintillion)

Source: Office Depot, Creative Commons License.

Another type of memory is read-only memory (ROM), which is typically nonvolatile. Because the circuit states in ROM are fixed, its information is not discarded if the power is turned off. For information and instructions that don't change over time, such as programs and data from the computer's maker and the commands that tell the computer how to start up when the power is switched on, ROM offers eternal storage.

3.2.3. Multiprocessing

Multiprocessing is the correlation method of two or more instructions, and it takes many different forms.

3.2.3.1. Multicore Microprocessor

A multicore microprocessor integrates two or more independent engines into a single computer to share the workload and increase processing capacity. When compared to its two-lane predecessor, a dual-core processor can accommodate up to twice as many vehicles without requiring each car to travel at twice the speed. A dual-core CPU also makes it possible to do two things simultaneously: play a game and burn a CD. In the market for multicore processors, Intel, AMD, and IBM are vying for first place (Hayashi et al., 2020) (Figure 3.4).

Figure 3.4. Architecture of the multiprocessor microprocessor.

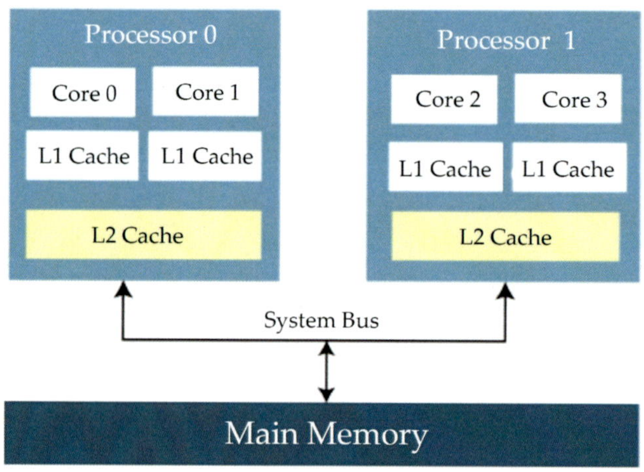

Source: Java Point, Creative Commons License.

By releasing new quad-core chips, Intel and AMD have enhanced dual processors. Four CPUs are combined onto a single chip for the Intel Core i7, allowing them to share an L3 cache. The AMD's quad-core, 3.4 GHz Phenom II X4 Black Edition CPU was just released. Even though the AMD clock speed is somewhat quicker than the Intel Core i7, there is little point in comparing the clock speeds of two CPUs with distinct designs. The CPU must be integrated with the main memory and the other computer components for the system to function. Based on the outcomes of numerous computer benchmarks, the Intel Core i7 processor beats out the AMD Phenom processor. Eight processor cores were featured in the Power7 CPU from IBM. The chip offers a

32-core processor because each core can do four jobs or threads. Electric utilities can process more than 85 million reads per day in a smart grid thanks to this potent processor, up from less than 1 million reads per day in a traditional [power] system. (Arvanitis & Krystalli, 2021)"

Did you Know?

The global parallel computing market size was valued at USD 9.79 billion in 2020 and is expected to grow at a CAGR of 14.6% from 2021 to 2028, driven by the increasing demand for efficient computing systems in data-intensive applications such as AI, machine learning, and big data analytics.

3.2.3.2. Parallel Computing

Through links that enable many processors to run concurrently or in parallel processing, another type of multiprocessing, speeds up processing.

The most common parallel computing applications are modeling, simulation, and data analysis. In medicine, parallel computing is utilized to create new imaging systems that can do ultrasound scans more quickly and accurately, allowing clinicians to diagnose patients more accurately. Engineers can build virtual models of new items instead of physical ones, test how they function using parallel computing and then adjust design and material choices as necessary. By simulating the appearance and motion of new designs on digital models, clothes designers can cut the production time for a seasonal apparel collection from six months to just over one month (Udhayakumar & Murugaboopathi, 2020) (Figure 3.5).

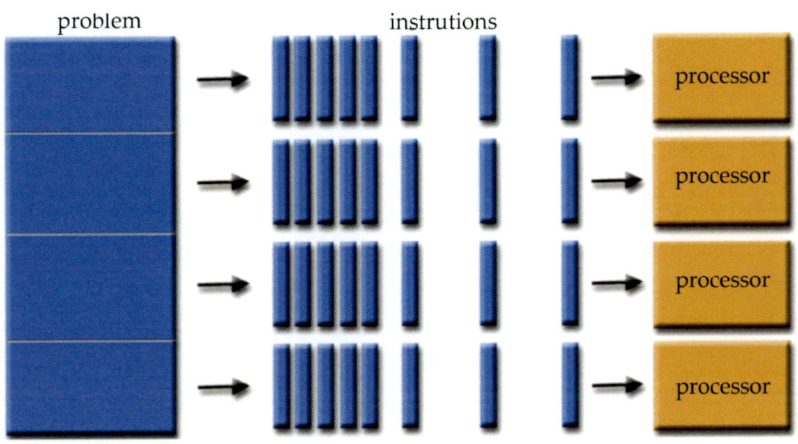

Figure 3.5. Illustration of the parallel computing.

Source: Mobile CSP, Creative Commons License.

3.2.3.3. Grid Computing

Network virtualization entails using several computers, frequently owned by numerous people or organizations, to collaborate to address a common issue. One inexpensive method for parallel processing is called grid computing. The grid comprises several computers—possibly thousands—working together to tackle massive similar processing issues. A central server that serves as the grid leader and network monitor is essential to the success of distributed systems. The computing effort is broken down into smaller tasks by the managing server, which then distributes the work to computers on the grid that (at least momentarily) have the extra processing power. The central server also keeps track of the processing, and if one of the grid members fails to finish a subtask, it will restart or redistribute the task. Once each subtask is completed, the controlling server combines the results, then moves on to the next task until the entire job is finished (Kotenko et al., 2015) (Figure 3.6).

Figure 3.6. Schematic of the grid computing.

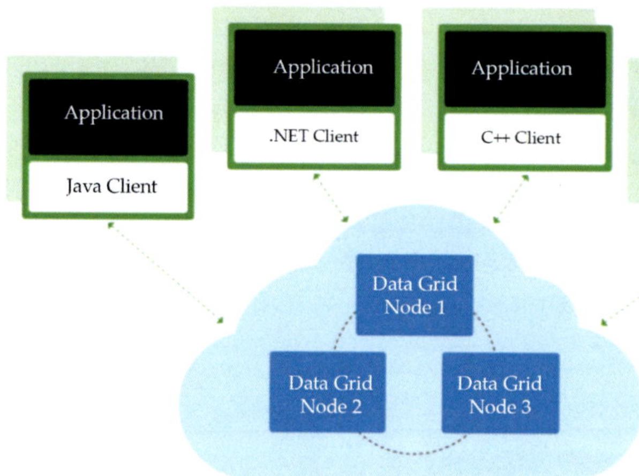

Source: Hazel Cast, Creative Commons License.

To tap into the underutilized computing capacity of home and office computers and create a massive public computing grid, IBM started the Global Community Grid initiative in 2004. To evaluate potential treatments for novel and drug-resistant flu viruses like H1N1, researchers at the University of Texas Medical Branch took advantage of the computing capacity of more than 1 million connected devices. According to Stan Watowich, the principal investigator at UTMB, "we anticipate identifying novel influenza medication candidates in less than a month. We can focus more intently and swiftly transition from computer calculations to lab testing (Kim & Chung, 2003).

3.3. SECONDARY STORAGE, INPUT, AND OUTPUT DEVICES

As they can see, memory plays a significant role in determining the total power of a computer system. The data and commands the CPU needs to process can only be stored in a small amount of memory. Moreover, more permanent storage of data, commands, and information is required by computers than is possible with main memory. This is accomplished by secondary storage, often known as persistent storage (Lindstrom & Vitter, 1985).

Secondary storage has more capacity, is more cost-effective, and is nonvolatile compared to memory. Most secondary storage options are significantly cheaper than memory. However, secondary storage is much slower than memory due to the electromechanical operations needed. Understanding the essential characteristics of secondary storage media and devices—access method, capacity, and portability—is necessary for making the right choice (Lian et al., 2022).

3.3.1. Secondary Storage Devices

Magnetic tapes, magnetic discs, and optical discs are the most widely used secondary storage media. While some of these media, like magnetic tape, only permit sequential accesst, others, like optical and magnetic discs, allow direct and consecutive access.

3.3.1.1. Magnetic Tapes

Magnetic tape is a common secondary storage medium. Magnetic portions of the tape represent bits. A linked list storage media is magnetic tape. Magnetic tape is typically less expensive than disc storage, despite slower access. it is frequently used to back up hard drives and store data off-site for disaster recovery. As technology advances, tape storage systems will have more extensive storage and faster transfer rates. Since dozens of tape cartridges may now be housed in a compact space, large, massive tape drives have indeed been replaced by much smaller tape cartridge devices that are just a few millimeters in diameter. These newer devices require significantly less floor space (Coffman & Hofri, 1986).

TIPS

Magnetic tapes can be cost-effective for infrequently accessed data, but it's crucial to consider tape durability, longevity, and environmental conditions. Regular testing and maintenance are also recommended to prevent data loss.

3.3.1.2. Magnetic Disks

Iron oxide also coats magnetic discs, which can be Mylar film or thin metal platters. Magnetic discs use tiny, magnetized patches to represent bits, similar to magnetic tape. Companies that must respond promptly to client demands employ magnetic discs and direct access storage technologies that enable swift data retrieval. If the data is saved on a direct access storage device, a manager can quickly determine a customer's credit history or the number of seats left on a specific aircraft (Chen et al., 1994) (Figure 3.7).

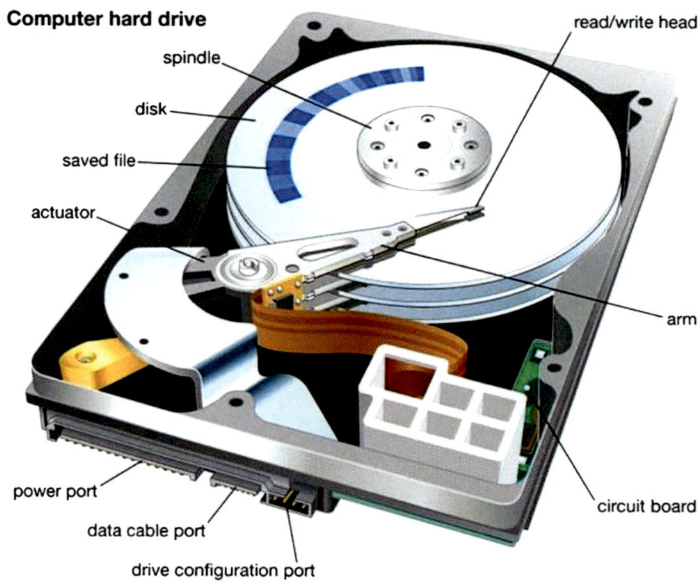

Figure 3.7. Schematic of the hard disk and its components.

Source: Britannica, Creative Commons License.

3.3.1.3. RAID

Data storage requirements for businesses are growing quickly. Several hundreds of gigabytes are frequently used in modern storage setups. The loss of vital business data can force a company out of business; hence posting the company's data online entails a significant business risk. A disc storage device's most important mechanical parts—the disc drives, the fans, and other input/output devices—can break, which is a source of concern (Coffman & Hofri, 1986).

Nowadays, businesses need their data storage systems to be robust, which means they can keep working even if one or more crucial parts fail with little to no performance loss. RAID is a technique for storing data so that the lost data on that drive can be restored during a hard drive failure. In this method, data is distributed uniformly over multiple physical disc drives utilizing the redundant storage method of stripping. For its film production clients and TV, Point360, a post-production firm with headquarters in Burbank, California, edits, masters, reformats, and archives video data. The company adopted a RAID storage solution to increase security and manage the growing storage needs of high-definition video and complex visual effect rendering (McKusick, 1996).

3.3.1.4. Virtual Tape

A storage method known as virtual tape makes less often used data appear to be saved on tape cartridges, even though some portions may be kept on faster hard discs. Virtual tape server is another name for software with a data backup system. A comprehensive storage-management system that shifts data to slower but less expensive forms of storage media when individuals utilize the data less frequently can be used with virtual tape. Data access times, the total cost of ownership, and the floor area required by tape operations can all be decreased thanks to virtual tape technology. More than 400 TB of data related to running this 581-bed academic health hospital are maintained by the IS department at Boston Medical Center. The firm implemented a virtual tape management system to meet stringent regulatory standards, keep data storage expenses in check, and handle a 50% annual data growth rate (Wibawa, 2015).

Remember

Virtual tape controllers provide replication, transparent tracking, and synchronization of the logical tape volumes.

3.3.1.5. SAN

As seen in Figure 3.8, a SAN (storage area network) connects everything through networks, computer servers, and distributed storage devices. High-speed communications channels are frequently utilized to speed up the storage and retrieval of data. Even though SAN technology is still relatively new, many businesses successfully and effectively store crucial data on it. Almost 713,000 Australians subscribe to Austar, a significant pay-TV company that offers digital satellite services. To keep track of every transaction and client interaction, the organization uses a 60-terabyte SAN. According to CIO Dean Walters, all of the information is valuable. "We gather much intelligence about our customers' attitudes, openness, and moods through those touch points. We discover crucial information about customers' inclination to stop using the service (Grossman & Silverman, 1973) (Figure 3.8).

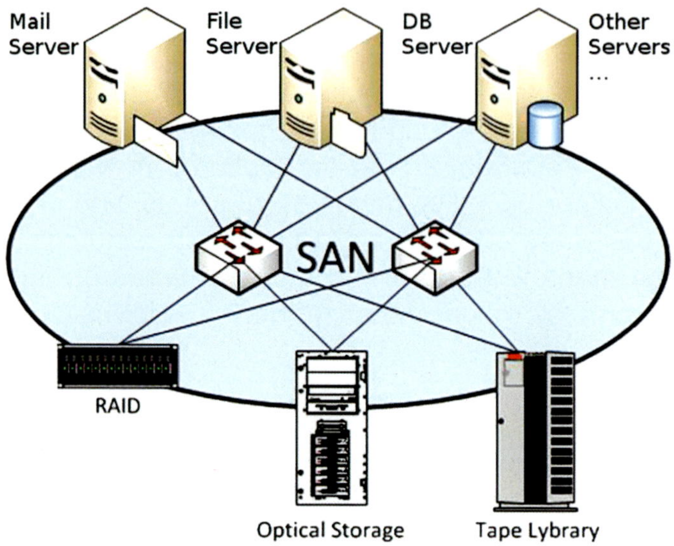

Figure 3.8. Illustration of the storage area network (SAN).

Source: Fiktoria, Creative Commons License.

3.3.1.6. Optical Discs

CD-ROM (compact disc read-only memory) has a 740 MB data storage capacity and is a standard optical disc. A CD-ROM disc is "read-only," meaning it cannot be changed once information is recorded. A tool that can collect data on a disk drive is a CD burner, sometimes a CD recorder. The two most popular types of systems that can print CDs, either once or frequently (CD-RW), are CD-recordable (CD-R) and CD-rewritable (CD-RW) (in the case of CD-RW). CD-RW technology makes data backup on CDs possible for PC users (Grossman & Silverman, 1973).

3.3.1.7. Digital Video Disc (DVD)

A DVD (digital video disc) is a five-inch-diameter disc that resembles a CD-ROM and can hold up to several gigabytes of data or around 135 minutes of digital video (*see* Figure 3.9). This storage medium is frequently used for movies, video games, and software packages (Christodoulakis, 1984) (Figure 3.9).

DVDs have replaced digital audio and rewritable CDs as the popular format for exchanging movies and photographs. A single-sided DVD has a capacity of 4.7 GB, and double-sided DVDs have a total of 9.4 GB, whereas a CD can contain roughly 740 MB of data. Recons can be created on record-only discs or rewritable discs. Rewritable DVD formats are not all interchangeable with one another.

Figure 3.9. Image of an optical disk drive.

Source: Tikhomirov Sergey, Creative Commons License.

At least three times as much data can be stored on a Blu-ray high-definition video disc than on a DVD. Although this new format may also store computer data, it is mainly used in home entertainment systems to store high-definition video (Arato & Benczur, 1981).

3.3.1.8. Solid-State Secondary Storage Devices

As opposed to optical media, memory chips are where data is kept in solid-state storage (SSD) devices. These memory chips use less power than magnetic data storage devices and offer faster data access. Moreover, SSDs are less brittle than hard disc drives since they contain fewer moving parts. The SSD is recommended for portable laptops because of all these features. The high cost per gigabyte of data storage and the limited capacity of SSDs currently are two drawbacks. As a constantly evolving technology, SSDs will become more affordable and capable (McKellar & Wong, 1978).

One illustration of a frequently used SSD is a USB flash drive (Figure 3.10). External USB flash drives that may be removed and written to are called flash drives. Most are less than an ounce in weight and have storage capacities ranging from 1 GB to 64 GB. Based on a technology known as X4, which stores 4 bits of data in each of the millions of small storage components on a chip called cells, SanDisk creates flash drives with storage capacities of up to 64 GB (Figure 3.10).

Figure 3.10. Image of a USB flash drive.

Source: SANDISK, Creative Commons License.

With roughly 100 people, Marketing Architects offers its clients radio, television, and telephone marketing programs. The company uses SSD technology to store data to deliver faster response times at lower storage costs than other alternatives (Yue & Wong, 1973).

Secondary storage generally requires more capacity, increased portability, and direct access techniques. While choosing a particular form of storage, the demands of both the business and the individual users should be considered. In general, organizational performance and efficiency can be improved by quickly accessing vast amounts of data and information (Omiecinski et al., 1994).

3.3.2. Input Devices

Input and output devices are typically how people interact with computers for the first time. These gadgets are the system's entry points, allowing them to give the computer information and commands and request output. The computer's UI comprises hardware and software that let them communicate with a computer system, including input and output devices (Jacob, 1996).

While choosing input and output devices, an organization should consider its business objectives, much like determining other computer system components. For instance, several restaurant chains employ computerized terminals or handheld input devices that enable servers to enter orders quickly and correctly. The ability to track stock and promote it to customers has also reduced costs (Jacob et al., 1994).

Hundreds of devices can be used for data input, from more general-purpose user input to those with unique purposes for capturing detailed data.

3.3.2.1. Personal Computer Input Devices

A keypad and a computer pointing device are the most popular input devices to enter data, including characters, text, and simple commands. Modern keyboards that are faster, more customizable, and more pleasant are being created by several companies. These keyboards, like the split keyboard, made famous by Microsoft and others, are intended to prevent wrist and hand problems brought on by prolonged keyboard use. They may type text with the keys and draw on the touchpad with the same keyboard (Card et al., 1991) (Figure 3.11).

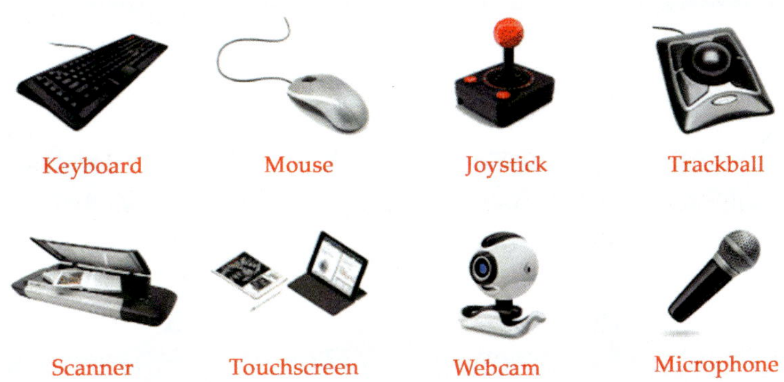

Figure 3.11. Schematic of the personal computer input devices.

Source: Tutorials Mate, Creative Commons License.

Icons, menus, and instructions on the screen are selected using the pointing device to point at and click them. In response, the computer performs various tasks, like data entry into the computer system.

3.3.2.2. Speech-Recognition Technology

With voice-recognition technology, a computer with a microphone or other speech-input device may understand human speech as a substitute for typing in data or receiving directions. Most basic systems have a minimal word vocabulary or need to train to identify their speech patterns. Modern systems don't require users to break their voices into distinct words to recognize continuous speech. The military and the government use highly sophisticated methods to decipher voices they have never heard before and comprehend various languages (MacKenzie et al., 1991).

Businesses that must deal with consumers regularly are eager to lower their support expenses when enhancing the quality of their services. For instance, SBI Funds Management is an Indian investment management company serving over 5.8 million clients. The company implemented a speech-recognition technology to replace all the operations that live agents formerly offered. Customers will not need to wait for live agents to become accessible, saving money in addition to that gained from lowering the number of employees. Users communicate with the system using their voice rather than touching the phone's keypad (Mackinlay et al., 1990).

3.3.2.3. Digital Cameras

Digital cameras capture and store pictures or videos. Images are electronically saved in the camera when they snap pictures. The photos can be downloaded to a computer or stored on a flash card. The photographs can be edited, sent to another place, copied into another program, or printed after being saved to the computer's hard drive. They could, for instance, use a digital camera to take a picture of their project team, save it, and then post it online or include it in a report on the project's progress. Regarding photo quality and features like zoom, flash, exposure adjustments, special effects, and even video capture, digital cameras have surpassed film cameras used by photographers. They can enhance the image with sound and calligraphy using the appropriate software (Kessler et al., 1995) (Figure 3.12).

Figure 3.12. Illustration of the various types of digital cameras.

Source: Ashley Maas, Creative Commons License.

Full-featured, high-resolution digital camera models are available from Nikon, Canon, Pentax, Casio, Olympus, Sony, Panasonic, and other camera manufacturers for less than $250. For less than $150, some manufacturers offer compact camcorders (Ballagas et al., 2006).

3.3.2.4. Touch-Sensitive Screens

Modern screen technology enables the displays to serve as input and output devices. The software can be run, or a computer activity triggered by touching specific areas of a sensitive screen. Gesture screens are regularly used at gas stations so that clients can choose the grade of gas they want and request an invoice, at fast-food restaurants so that order takers can enter customers' needs, and at hotel information desks so that visitors can ask questions about nearby restaurants and bars, and at theme parks so that visitors can get directions. Also, they are utilized in airport and department store kiosks (Zhai, 1998).

3.3.2.5. Optical Data Readers

Users can scan papers using a specialized scanner called an optical signal reader. OMR (visual mark recognition) and OCR (optical character recognition) are the two types of OCR (optical data readers). When standardized tests use pens to fill in the boxes on OMR paper, commonly known as a "mark sense form," they employ OMR scanners for test marking and other uses. OMR systems, which are used in standardized exams like the GMAT and SAT, are being taken into consideration as a way to record electors' decisions on election day. In contrast, most OCR readers scan and identify characters using reflected light. OCR readers use specialized software to turn typewritten or handwritten documents into electronic data. This information can be shared, altered, and sent to hundreds of people over computer networks after being entered (Wanderley & Orio, 2002).

TIPS

The technology offers secure, encrypted data transmission as an alternative to paper processes, resulting in improved supply chain tracking, reduced errors, and less time spent on data entry. The transportation industry developed EDI in the 1960s to simplify transaction information management.

According to Missouri law, police officers must record information about each traffic stop and report it to the State Attorney General. Using OMR technology, the St. Peters Police Department decided to abide by this. The department created a traffic stop data card, which the officer fills out during each traffic stop, to record the necessary information. The cards are returned and scanned at the end of each shift. The findings are condensed into two formats: an overview report to give the state attorney general the information they need and a more in-depth examination using graphs and charts to ensure the agency is serving the requirements of the people (Kim et al., 2005).

3.3.2.6. Magnetic Ink Character Recognition (MICR) Devices

Cheques, credit applications, financial records, and other documents in the 1950s overran the banking industry. The industry created magnetic ink character recognition (MICR), a technique for quickly reading this data, to address this overflow and process documents more quickly. A unique magnetic ink is used to write MICR data on the bottom of a check or other form to aid special and routine inspections. This ink has a special character set that people and computers can read when printing data (Wood et al., 2005).

3.3.2.7. Pen Input Devices

KEYWORD

Screenwriting or scriptwriting is the art and craft of writing scripts for mass media such as feature films, television productions or video games. It is often a freelance profession.

Users can execute a command or have the computer perform a task by touching a touch screen with a pen input device. Users can also enter handwritten notes and draw pictures of items and figures. Pen input necessitates specialized hardware and software. Text can be generated from screenwriting using handwriting recognition software. With the help of its hardware partners, Microsoft, with its Tablet PC, can convert handwriting into textual content and store the "digital ink" exactly how it is written. E-mails may be written and delivered using a pen, and users can also annotate Word documents, PowerPoint, and even manual charts on paper. Then, such information can be moved, underlined, searched for, and turned into text. This interface has the potential to be widely used once it is developed. If using a keyboard makes them uncomfortable, pen input may be appealing. The success of pen input hinges on how well and inexpensively handwriting can be read and converted into digital form (Lapointe et al., 2011).

3.3.2.8. Radio Frequency Identification

Using a mobile device called a tag, an RFID (radio frequency identification) system transmits data that an RFID reader reads and processes following the requirements of a computer network program. One common use for RFID is adding a microchip to retail products and installing readers inside stores that track the stock on the shelves to identify when frames need replenishment. Remember that the RFID tag chip's EPROM (erasable programmable read-only memory) component stores information about the object to which the tag is connected. Its memory can be updated by a radio-frequency signal as the item's status changes. The information provided by the tag may include identity, geographic data, or specifics about the tagged item, such as the item's date of manufacture, retail price, color, or purchase date (Taveira & Choi, 2009).

RFID technology is used at the Newmount Leeville Gold Mine in Nevada to monitor workers, machinery, and vehicles. For the corporation to track where miners are operating and promptly locate them in the event of an accident, RFID tags are installed in the miners' cap lamps and fastened to trucks and equipment. These tags broadcast real-time position data (Tsukada & Yasumura, 2001).

3.3.3. Output Devices

Computer systems deliver information to decision-makers at all organizational levels so they may address a business issue or seize a business opportunity. Moreover, the output of one computer system might serve as the input for another. This output's chosen format could be digital, audio, or visually appealing. Output devices deliver the appropriate information to the appropriate person in the suitable design at the proper time, regardless of the content or form of the output (Jacob et al., 1993).

KEYWORD

Audio is sound that is within the acoustic range of human hearing.

3.3.3.1. Display Monitors

The outputs from the computer are displayed on a display monitor. Early monitors were called CRTs since they displayed images using a cathode-ray tube. One or more beam of electrons is produced by the cathode ray tubes. A marker on the screen, known as a pixel, illuminates when the beams hit a phosphorescent substance (phosphor) deposited on the inner surface of the screen. A pixel is a small area of color or light that appears on a touchscreen display. There are just two states it can be in: on or off. As the phosphor begins to dim, the beam of electrons sweeps across the screen to strike it, relighting it (Eisenberg, 2002) (Figure 3.13).

Many competent cells (pixels) made of electrodes and neon and xenon gases that are electrically converted into plasma (electrically charged atoms and negatively charged particles) in a plasma display are used to produce the display's light. Using the data in the video feed, the plasma display illuminates the pixels to create an image. Red, green, and blue light make up each pixel in a display. The intensity of the lights is adjusted on the plasma display to provide a broad spectrum of colors. Plasma displays can create high-quality images with great resolution and accurate color representation (Burdea et al., 1996).

Figure 3.13. Image of display monitor.

Source: Tony Hoffman, Creative Commons License.

Liquid crystals, an organic substance that resembles oil and is sandwiched between two polarizers, are used in LCDs to create characters and graphic pictures on a backlit screen. Because they are brighter and flicker-free and don't release the kind of radiation that some CRT users are concerned about, these displays are friendlier on their eyes than CRTs. Also, compared to CRT monitors of the same size, LCD monitors are smaller and consume less than half the energy (Dicarlo & Banajee, 2000).

A layer of organic material is sandwiched between two conductors in an organic light-emitting diode (OLED), which is then layered between a crystal top plate and a glass bottom plate. Bright, electro-luminescent light is created directly from the organic substance when an electric charge is introduced to the 2 conductors. OLEDs can produce more precise and vibrant colors than CRTs and LCDs, and because they do not need a backlight, their displays can be flexible and only half as thick as LCDs. The fact that OLEDs do not crack when dropped is another significant benefit. By layering transparent OLED films over a conventional LCD panel, OLED technology may also produce 3D video displays that give the illusion of depth without using 3D glasses or laser optics. Both 2D and 3D content can be displayed on the iZ3D monitor. To coincide with the release of James Cameron's film

Avatar, the manufacturer sold a 22-inch version of the monitor for $300 (Eisenberg et al., 2003).

Power consumption is crucial when choosing which type of monitor to buy because most users leave their laptops on for hours. LCD monitors typically use between 35% and 50% less electricity than plasma screens, though this varies from model to model. Even less power is used by 18 OLED monitors than by LCD monitors (Ware, 1996).

3.3.3.2. Printers and Plotters

Physical copies are printed on paper using a printer. For forms like blank check forms, invoicing forms, and so forth, printers with different Laser printers are usually faster than inkjet printers and can handle the larger volume. Modern printers enable companies to provide customized printed output for each customer utilizing standard paper and full-color data input (Balasubramanian & Dalal, 1997).

The quantity of sheets printed per minute is often used to gauge a printer's speed (ppm). The quality or resolution of a printer's output, like that of a display screen, is determined by the amount of dots produced per inch (dpi). The print quality of a 600-dpi printer is superior to a 300-dpi printer. Each time a page is printed, the inkjet or laser cartridge consumed is a recurring expense associated with operating a printer. Some can be configured to work with various paper inkjet printers. Laser printers can print in color at 6 to 25 ppm and in black and white at 25 to 60 ppm. For less than $200, one may get an inkjet printer with a black-and-white print speed of 12 to 40 ppm and a color print speed of 5 to 20 ppm (Waal et al., 2007).

KEYWORD

A **display** screen is a visual output device that presents information in a visible form. It can be an image, text, or graphics.

Hard-copy output devices called plotters are commonly utilized for general design work. Businesses often use these devices to produce blueprints, schematics, and drawings of new buildings or items on paper or acetate. Typical plot widths are 24 and 36 inches, while the length might range from a few inches to several feet, depending on the situation (Bornman et al., 2001).

3.3.3.3. Digital Audio Player

A gadget that can store, manage, and play online music files is known as an audio player. A standard format for compressing sound sequences into tiny files without sacrificing sound quality when played is MP3 (MPEG-1 Audio Layer-3). When a sound file is compressed, it takes fewer seconds to download and uses fewer resources on a hard drive.

Remember

Digital Audio Players revolutionized on-the-go music listening and continue to offer advanced features such as gapless playback and customizable sound settings.

Downloading music via the World Wide Web (WWW) and other sources can be done using a variety of music players that are approximately the size of a pack of cigarettes. These gadgets can store music for hours and have no moving parts. The iPod MP3 device and the iTunes Online Store make it easy to search for music online, listen to a sample, and download it safely and legally. Affordably, Apple entered the digital music business. With a 2.5-inch screen and the ability to play video, the Apple iPod can play some TV shows they may download from the iTunes Music Store. Other MP3 producers include Motorola, whose Rokr device is the first iPhone that works with Dell, Sony, Samsung, iTunes, and Iomega (Hudson, 2004).

The Apple iPod Touch is a music player with a 3.5-inch-wide screen that can also play movies and TV shows, show photos, and access the Internet. As a result, they can use it to access their e-mail, view YouTube videos, and buy music online. The view is automatically adjusted when the display is rotated from portrait to landscape. To fit the lighting conditions, an ambient light sensor modifies brightness (Bawden, 1985).

ACTIVITY 3.1.

How does the choice of hardware components affect the overall performance and capabilities of an information system, and what factors should be considered when selecting hardware components for a specific application?

3.3.3.4. eBooks

An eBook is a traditional printed book's digital media equivalent. More than 30k free eBooks and more than 100k other eBooks are available, according to the Project Gutenberg Online Book Catalog. eBooks can be downloaded to personal computers or specialized hardware units called eBook readers from Project Gutenberg (www.gutenberg.org) and many other places. The gadgets cost between $250 and $350 and download files of recent releases and best-sellers are less than $10.00 each. 19 eBooks have screens that range in size from 5 to 8 inches, weigh less than three-quarters of a pound, and are an about one-half inch thick. eBooks can be readily grasped in one hand because they are more compact than most paperbacks. For readers with impaired vision, the text size can often be enlarged on e-readers (Dixit, 1991).

3.4. OVERVIEW OF SOFTWARE

Computer programs make up the software that manages how computer hardware functions. Programs for computers are collections of instructions. The documentation describes the program functionalities to assist the user in using the computer system. The application displays some documentation on screen, while other forms are found in other sources, like printed manuals. End-User License Agreements are often read and accepted before commercial software is used (EULAs). Before using the program, which can fall under one of two categories: systems or application software, they often need to read the EULA and click an "I agree" button (El-Gayar & Fritz, 2006).

Systems software is a group of applications created to coordinate the operations and features of the devices and different software applications running on the computer system. Each sort of systems software is designed for a specific CPU architecture and hardware category. Applications that assist users in resolving specific computing issues are called application software. Application software often resides on the computer's hard drive before being loaded into memory and executed. Application software may also be kept on CDs, DVDs, USB-powered flash drives, or keychain storage devices (Cox & Gifford, 1997). There is a growing selection of application software available online. A web-delivered software application, often known as an RIA (rich Internet application), combines the hardware resources of the PC and Web server to provide beneficial software services via a Web browser interface. When choosing the optimal strategy for procuring application software, an individual, group, or company should carefully assess their needs and goals (Mellado & Rosado, 2012).

3.5. SYSTEMS SOFTWARE

One of the most important tasks of systems software is managing how computer hardware operates. Application programs also support the ability of systems software to solve issues. Operating systems and utility programs are examples of several systems software (Gifford et al., 1985).

3.5.1. Operating Systems

A group of software applications known as an operating system (OS) manages a computer's hardware and serves as an interface for application programs.

Operating systems can control a single computer, a network of computers, or a single computer used by several users. The following are some examples of the many OS, computer, and user combinations (Garmpis, 2011):

i. A single user and one computer. One user at a time is permitted under this arrangement, frequently found in personal.
ii. A single computer shares several users. This setup is characteristic of more giant mainframe computers that support simultaneous use by hundreds of users or even thousands of users.
iii. Numerous people are using many computers. This system is typical of a computer network, such as a local network with several connected computers or an extensive network with tens of connected computers worldwide.
iv. Specialized computers Many computers with specific purposes, like those that operate high-tech military aircraft, spacecraft, image sensors, or home appliances, typically use this type of technology.

The operating system (OS), which is essential to the overall operation of the computer system, is often stored on a disc. A computer system's operating system (OS) is loaded into memory as needed once it has "booted up" or started. Moreover, a USB-connected thumb drive, CD, or DVD can start a computer. Because it can be used to create the computer if the primary hard disc has issues, a storage device with some or all of the OS is frequently called a "rescue disc. (Hasselbring, 2000)"

The group of software applications that make up the operating system carry out several tasks, such as the following (Figure 3.14):

- Providing networking capability;
- Managing system memory;
- Performing standard computer hardware functions;
- Managing processing tasks;
- Managing files;
- Controlling access to system resources.

Did you Know?

According to a report by Statcounter, as of January 2022, the most commonly used operating system worldwide on desktop and laptop computers was Windows, with a market share of 76.24%, followed by macOS at 16.35% and Linux at 1.92%.

Figure 3.14. Illustration of system software.

Source: Bestweb, Creative Commons License.

3.5.1.1. Common Hardware Functions

Certain hardware-related operations that any application must carry out include (Choi et al., 2003):

- Get input from the keypad or another input devices;
- Fetch information from disks;
- Store information on the storage device;
- Display output on a monitor or printer.

A complete set of instructions is necessary for each of these jobs. The operating system (OS) transforms a simple request into a specific collection of instructions the hardware needs. The OS is a middleman between the software and the hardware. A typical OS carries out hundreds of these activities, converting each one into one or more hardware instructions. When peripheral devices require attention, a mistake, or something unusual occurs in the system, the OS tells the user (Helps & Renshaw, 2004).

3.5.1.2. User Interface and Input/Output Management

So long as a UI, which enables users to access and engage with the computer system, is one of the most crucial tasks performed by any OS. The early mainframe and laptop user interfaces were command-based (Phani et al., 2007).

With a command-based UI, the computer must be given written commands to perform simple tasks. For instance, the computer would wipe or delete the file 00TAXRTN if the instruction ERASE 00TAXRTN was entered. Some instructions for modifying files and copying data from one directory to another include RENAME and COPY (Olsen et al., 1985).

While using a GUI (graphical user interface), humans can communicate commands to the computer system by selecting items from menus and images known as icons. Many believe that GUIs are more straightforward since users intuitively understand the functionality. The most popular GUI available today is Windows from Microsoft. As its name implies, Windows is based on using a window or a section of the display screen set aside for a particular application. Several windows may be visible at once on the screen. Windows 7 offers strong support for interacting with its GUI through touch, building on the iPhone's success, primarily made possible by its distinctive and sophisticated multitouch user interface (Myers et al., 1997).

KEYWORD

The user interface (UI) is the point of human-computer interaction and communication in a device.

3.5.1.3. Hardware Independence

Programs must request services from the OS through a predetermined application program interface (API). With APIs, programmers can build application software without being familiar with the operating system's inner workings (Layton et al., 2017).

3.5.1.4. Memory Management

The OS also manages memory access and makes the most available memory and storage. Most modern OSs handle the memory more effectively than legacy OSs do. The computer can efficiently execute program instructions and speed up processing thanks to the memory-management feature found in many operating systems. Upgrading to a newer OS and adding more memory are two ways to improve the performance of an old computer (Weiss et al., 1986).

Most operating systems support VR memory, which allows space on the hard disc to complement RAM's immediate, usable memory range. Paging is a technique used in virtual memory that allows programs or portions of programs to be switched between memory and one or more storage drives. As a result, more jobs can run simultaneously, and the CPU's idle time is decreased (Xiao & Wang, 2019).

3.5.1.5. Processing Tasks

The task-management capabilities of modern OSs control all processing activities. Task management distributes computer resources to maximize the effectiveness of each system's resources. With task management software, multiple users can use the same computer simultaneously, and one user can run numerous programs or tasks simultaneously (multitasking) (time-sharing) (Rayner et al., 2007).

Users can utilize multiple applications simultaneously when using an OS with multitasking features. Most computer users don't realize how creative multitasking OSs are since they exploit them to their advantage. Users can work in one application, quickly switch to another, and then promptly return to the original program to continue where they left off without having to exit it. Better yet, while they are working in one program's foreground, one or more other programs may be working silently in the background, sorting databases, printing documents, or carrying out other time-consuming tasks that would otherwise take up all of their computer's resources and prevent them from doing other work. Users can save a significant amount of time and effort by multitasking (Chandrasekaran, 1987).

More than one person can utilize a computer system at once thanks to time sharing. For instance, 15 customer care agents may simultaneously input sales information into a computer system for a mail-order business. In a different scenario, thousands of individuals may be using an online computer service at once to access stock prices and other business news.

Scalability is the capacity of a computer to manage a growing number of concurrent users efficiently. This functionality is essential for systems like mainframe computers or web servers supporting many users. Personal computer operating systems (OSs) rarely need to manage tasks involving numerous users because they are typically designed for a single user (Brysbaert et al., 2000).

KEYWORD

Scalability is the property of a system to handle a growing amount of work.

3.5.1.6. Networking Capability

Most operating systems provide networking features that allow machines to connect in a network to exchange information and use computing resources. Users can set up home or office networking for exchanging Web access, printers, storage, and data on Computers running the Mac, Linux operating systems, or Windows. The HomeGroup feature in Windows 7 makes sharing files, printers, music, and images with others on a local network simple. Larger server operating systems are explicitly created for computer networking environments (Lambourne et al., 2010) (Figure 3.15).

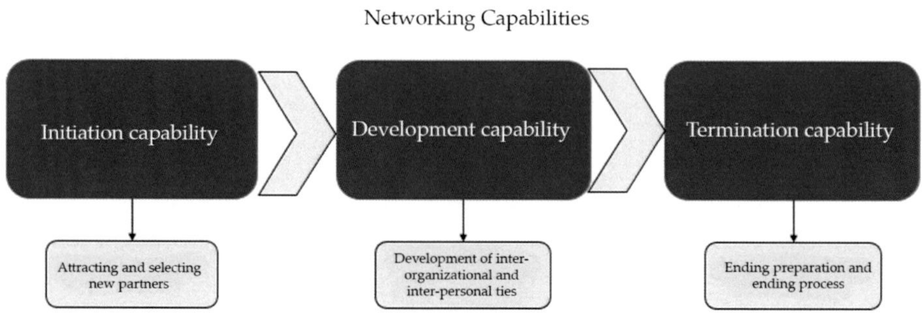

Figure 3.15. Schematic of networking capabilities.

Source: Cristian R. Foguesatto, Creative Commons License.

3.5.1.7. Access to System Resources and Security

Computers regularly handle sensitive data that can be accessible across networks, thus the operating system (OS) must provide a high level of safeguarding against unwanted access to the data and applications of the users. A login process that requires users to enter an identifying code, such as a username and a match passcode, is often created by the operating system (OS). If the passcode does not reflect the identity number or the identifying code is wrong, the users are able to access the computer. Many operating systems require users to update their passwords frequently, such as every 20 to 40 days. If a user successfully signs on to the system, the OS restricts access to only those components of the system for which the client has been given permission. Who uses the system, for how long, and by whom is tracked by the OS (Hidayatullah & Ma'Arif, 2017).

3.5.1.8. File Management

The OS controls files to ensure that secondary storage files are accessible when needed and are secured against access by unwanted users. On centrally positioned discs or tape drives, many systems can accommodate numerous users who store their files. The OS keeps track of each file's storage location and authorized users. If multiple users simultaneously seek access to the same file, the System must decide what to do. File management is required even on standalone personal computers with just one user to track where files are, their sizes, when they were generated, and who authored them (Agarwal & Nenkova, 2022).

3.5.2. Current Operating Systems

OSs from the past were quite simple. However, more sophisticated operating systems have been created, combining sophisticated functions and stunning graphical effects (Peters, 1973).

3.5.2.1. Microsoft PC Operating Systems

Personal computer operating systems (OSs) have continuously advanced since a little firm called Microsoft created PC-DOS and MS-DOS to serve the IBM desktop computer released in the 1980s. The command-driven user interfaces of PC-DOS and MS-DOS were challenging to learn and operate. The usability, processing power, dependability, and capacity to support new computer hardware components have increased with each OS version (McKinney et al., 1999). In the fall of 2001, Microsoft debuted Windows XP, which is said to stand for the fantastic computing experience they will have. Windows' first consumer editions were notoriously unreliable and frequently crashed, necessitating annoying and time-consuming reboots. Microsoft aimed to increase consumer reliability with XP (Novac et al., 2017). With the intention of delivering an operating system that was more stable and secure, Microsoft developed Windows Vista in 2007. Several new features are part of the new operating system. Vista's most recent iterations come with a 3D GUI dubbed Aero. Therefore, many users must buy more powerful Computers to meet Windows Vista with Aero's system requirements. One other problem was that some devices and applications made for Windows XP would not function on Vista (Figure 3.16).

In 2009, Windows 7, the following version, was introduced with updates and new features. According to most analysts, Windows 7 is "Vista done well." After fixing a few Windows Vista problems, Windows 7 added new windows manipulation features that make it simpler for users to search, access, and operate with data in files. Moreover, it has enhanced apps and home networking capabilities. Netbooks and touch displays are well supported by Windows 7, ushering in a new era of mobile computing devices (Baseman et al., 1995).

KEYWORD

Data is information that has been translated into a form that is efficient for movement or processing.

Figure 3.16. Picture of window vista.

Source: Office of Information, Creative Commons License.

TIPS

Keep your Microsoft PC operating system updated with the latest security patches and perform regular antivirus scans. Optimizing system settings and minimizing unnecessary applications can also improve performance. Finally, create regular backups of important data.

3.5.2.2. Apple Computer Operating Systems

Apple devices have utilized non-Intel microprocessors created by Apple, Motorola, and IBM and a proprietary Apple OS dubbed the Mac OS. In contrast, IBM system platforms have historically used one of the Windows OSs with Intel CPUs (often referred to as Wintel for this reason). Yet, Intel CPUs are used in newer Apple computers. Apple computers are also prevalent, particularly in publishing, academia, visual design, music, movies, and media, even though Wintel machines still account for most of the commercial PC market (Hagedoorn et al., 2001).

The Apple OSs also have developed throughout the years and frequently offer functionality that Microsoft does not. But, as they battle for consumers, Windows and Mac platforms have been created to share many of the same features. Mac OS X, a brand-new operating system for the Mac based on the UNIX platform, was introduced in July 2001. It contained a new user interface that gave users a fresh visual experience. Elements like windows, scroll bars, buttons, and fluid animation were illuminated and partially translucent to improve the user's experience (Harris, 1983).

Apple has repeatedly updated OS X since its first release. The most recent OS X update, Snow Leopard (version 10.6), was made available in 2009 to compete with Windows 7. Snow Leopard comes with Time Machine, a potent backup tool that enables users to restore deleted items and observe how their system appeared in the past. Multiple desktops that let users pose in front of imagined scenery, a robust system search tool, and other new apps are also included with Snow Leopard. Due to the lack of widespread virus or spyware attacks to date, Macs are likewise regarded as being relatively secure (Lorch & Smith, 1998).

Mac users can set up their computer to run both Mac OS X and Windows Vista and then choose which platform to use when they boot their computer because Mac OS X operates on Intel CPUs. Dual booting is a term used to describe such a setup. Macs can dually boot into Windows, but the reverse is not possible. OS X can only be used on Apple devices, according to Apple. However, Linux and other operating systems can use dual boot on Windows PCs (Bala et al., 2015).

3.5.2.3. Linux

Linus Torvalds created the Linux operating system while he was a student in Finland in 1991. The OS's source code is accessible to everyone and distributed under the GNU General Public License. As a result, it is referred to as an open-source operating system. However, this does not imply that Linux and its many variants must be free; businesses and creators are free to charge for a version as long as the programming language is still accessible. Linux is merely an operating system's kernel, which controls hardware, maintains files, splits processes, and does other things. Numerous Linux configurations can be used, each with a unique mix of features and programs to create an entire operating system. A distribution of Linux is the term used to describe each of these mixtures. Several distributions can be downloaded for free (Wang et al., 2016).

Linux is accessible via various sources, including the Internet. Caldera OpenLinux and Red Hat Linux are two common variations. Several major computer manufacturers, including IBM, Hewlett-Packard, and Intel, support Linux. For instance, IBM employs hundreds of programmers who use Linux. For workstations, distributed systems, and even supercomputers, Linux is a popular operating system. There is no lack of developers and engineers for Linux-based systems because most computer science and engineering graduates are conversant with Linux. Open architecture's flexibility makes it simple to adapt Linux to various demands (Appavoo et al., 2005).

Google has created its own OS called Chrome OS, which is based on Linux. Chrome is designed for mobile; PCs and its primary focus is on Web-based data and services. These services include web surfing, e-mail, social networking sites, and Google online applications (Xiao et al., 2019).

3.6. UTILITY PROGRAMS

Utility software aids in doing maintenance on a computer system or fixing issues. For instance, specific utility programs combine and organize data collections, monitor the progress of computer operations, compress data files before storing or sending them over a network (saving time and space), and carry out other crucial functions. Specific utility software can improve and extend the trouble-free operation of computer systems (Alderighi et al., 1999).

Utility software can also aid in protecting and securing data. Digital rights management (DRM) systems, for instance, are used by the publishing and film industries to stop unauthorized duplication of copyright-protected publications and motion pictures. The intellectual property is stored in files that are encoded so that only versions that have been obtained legitimately can be recognized and played by eBook readers and media players. DRM has drawn criticism for limiting consumers' freedom and rights. Record labels have already abandoned DRM methods to gain the support of their patrons.

Users can buy utility programs individually even though many PC utility apps are pre-installed on computers (Ong et al., 2008) (Figure 3.17).

Figure 3.17. Illustration of components of utility programs.

Source: TeachingCS, Creative Commons License.

3.7. APPLICATION SOFTWARE

Application software harnesses the power of a computer to enable people, workgroups, and the entire organization to carry out specified tasks and solve problems. Application programs communicate with the operating system, and the operating system instructs the computer hardware to carry out the required operations.

Although some programs are more specialized, they all assist them in carrying out common operations like writing and formatting text documents, doing computations, or organizing information. The medical industry uses application software to prolong and save lives. For instance, Swedish Medical Center in Seattle, Washington, employs Oracle content management software to access patient records whenever and wherever required (Dehlinger & Dixon, 2011).

Application software is used for various tasks, from business analysis to enhancing personal efficiency. Application software, for instance, can assist sales managers in tracking sales of a new product in a test market. IntelliVid software watches video feeds from store security cameras and alerts security when a customer acts suspiciously. This book uses application software in most computerized business duties and activities. We start by looking into the many kinds and uses of application software (Aerts et al., 2004).

3.7.1. Types and Functions of Application Software

Application software is the secret to maximizing the capabilities of any computer system. A business can create a unique program for a particular purpose (proprietary software) or buy and employ an already-existing software package. Moreover, specific commercial software can be changed, resulting in a hybrid of commercial and customized methods.

Remember

Application software is created to execute a certain set of tasks.

A lot of businesses employ commercial software to support business operations. According to Forrester Research, Microsoft Office is used by 80% of businesses. 37 Important considerations for choosing commercial software also include the following: (1) Can they use the software with the hardware and operating system they have chosen? (2) Would the software satisfy the specified vital business requirements? (3) Is the developer a trustworthy and financially stable business? and (4) Are the overall costs of buying, setting up, and sustaining the software positively contrasting with the anticipated business benefits? (Alkhatib, 1992)

Several commercial software packages can be changed, effectively combining commercial and customized methods. To track patients with the H1N1 flu and others who may have been exposed to it, El Camino Hospital in Mountain View, California, modified Microsoft's Amalga e-health management system.

Using an application service provider (ASP) is another way to get a software package specifically designed for them. A business known as an ASP can offer users the software, network access, and computer hardware necessary to execute the software from their premises. An ASP can make a sophisticated business software package simpler so that users can set it up and maintain it more easily. ASPs offer contract modification of commercial software, speed up the rollout of new applications, assist IS managers in avoiding implementation challenges, lessen the requirement for numerous highly qualified IS staff people, and lower project start-up costs. Such a strategy enables businesses to focus more time and resources on more crucial tasks. For instance, to handle its business intelligence, Rapid Advance, a well-known cash advance service for small to medium-sized businesses (SMBs), employs Business Objects and Crystal Reports, software provided by SAP (BI). Real-time access to sales data, partner data, and crucial corporate reporting is provided via the system (Dutke & Reimer, 2000).

The use of an ASP exposes an organization to certain dangers, including the possibility that sensitive data will be compromised due to unauthorized access by employees or by computer hackers; the possibility that the ASP will be unable to keep its computers and network operational as reliably as is required; and the possibility that a natural disaster will render the ASP's data center inoperable, thus temporarily preventing the organization from conducting business. These are all legitimate concerns that need to be addressed by an ASP (Wilkie & Kitchenham, 2000).

KEYWORD

Software as a service is a software licensing and delivery model in which software is licensed on a subscription basis and is centrally hosted.

Software as a service (SaaS) is a new way of distributing software made possible by the substantial overhead associated with an ASP building, operating, managing, and supporting numerous specialized programs for numerous enterprises. Software as a Service (SaaS) enables companies to pay a monthly service fee or a per-use price to subscribe to Web-delivered business application software. Like ASP, SaaS vendors host software on their own servers and offer online access. SaaS typically uses a Web browser-based user interface. By distributing its active applications among numerous firms, SaaS can save costs. For instance, an ordinary SaaS supplier may offer customer relationship management software to Sears, JCPenney, and Walmart. It is significantly less expensive to offer one excellent SaaS solution to thousands of organizations than to create the software from scratch for each one individually (Kapoor & Agarwal, 2017) (Figure 3.18).

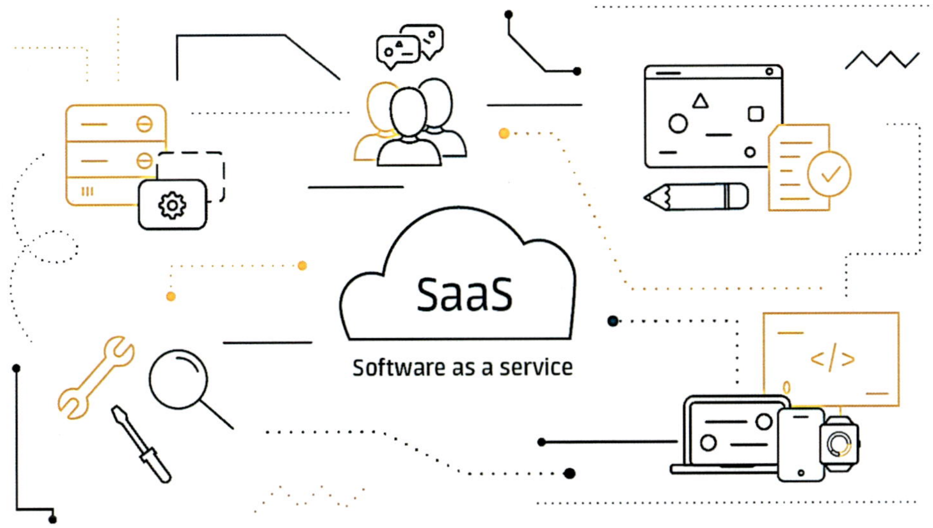

Figure 3.18. Schematic of software as a service (SaaS).

Source: Avsystem, Creative Commons License.

SaaS and new web development tools have given rise to the cloud computing paradigm, a new way of thinking about computing. Using computing resources, such as data storage and software, through the Internet instead of local PCs is called cloud computing. Powerful Web programming languages and methodologies have enabled developers to produce Web-based software that is competitive with installation software. With cloud computing, they use a Web browser to access software downloaded and delivered from a Web server rather than installing, saving, and running it on their machine. Usually, the Web server also houses the data that the software produces. For instance, the Tableau program enables users to import data from databases or spreadsheets to create effective representations that deliver insightful insights. The advantage of cloud computing is that it makes it simple to collaborate with others by sharing papers online (Boehm, 1981).

3.7.2. Personal Application Software

Many computer programs exist that can be used to benefit people at work, home, and school. The features of personalized application software are enumerated. There are probably millions of other private computer programs available besides these general-purpose ones that are designed to carry out more specific tasks, such as helping them with their taxes, getting in shape, losing weight, getting medical advice, writing wills, as well as other official papers, fixing their computer, fixing their car, writing music, and editing their photos and videos. This category of software, often known as user software or personal productivity software, consists of all-purpose tools and applications that cater to user requirements (Van Gorp & Comuzzi, 2013).

3.7.2.1. Word Processing

Word processing software can be essential for creating reports, memos, or term papers. Today's personal computers almost all come with word processing software preinstalled. Documents can be created, edited, and printed using these programs. Most provide a wide range of capabilities, including ones for verifying spelling, making tables, inputting formulas, producing pictures, and much more. Like other similar books, this book was written using a word processing program on a home computer (Bergin, 2006).

A group of individuals can use a word-processing tool to work together on a project. For instance, this book's writers and editors tracked and modified the chapter files using Microsoft Word's Transition Words and Reviewing capabilities. With these tools, they can add remarks or edit a document, which a colleague can review and accept or reject (Figure 3.19).

Figure 3.19. Floe diagram of word processing.

Source: Sunybroome, Creative Commons License.

3.7.2.2. Spreadsheet Analysis

People use spreadsheets to create budgets, predict earnings, examine insurance policies, compile income tax information, and evaluate assets. Spreadsheets should be taken into consideration if there are computations and numbers involved. Spreadsheet features include visuals, a constrained database, data analysis, built-in business features, and many others. Current value, internal return rate, and monthly loan payments are only business tasks. Another full function of many spreadsheet systems is optimization. Under certain restrictions, optimization enables the spreadsheet to maximize or minimize a quantity. For instance, a modest furniture producer who creates tables and chairs would desire to increase sales. The limitations might include a finite amount of timber, a certain number of people who can put the chairs and tables together, or a finite number of hardware fasteners that might be needed. The spreadsheet may decide how many chairs and tables to make with labor and material limits to optimize revenues using an optimization capability (Chakravarty et al., 2006).

3.7.2.3. Database Applications

Data storage, manipulation, and retrieval are all made possible by the database software. These applications come in handy when they need to edit a lot of data and create documents and reports. Data combining, editing, and sorting are examples of database manipulations. A database application has many different applications. They can maintain a list of their CD collection, the possessions in their residence, tax information, and expenditures. A student club can utilize a database to keep track of members' names, contact information, and dues payments. A database application in the company can assist with processing sales orders, inventory control, ordering new supplies, sending letters to clients, and paying personnel. Database management systems can be used to keep track of purchases, goods, and clients, evaluate meteorological data to produce forecasts for the coming days and compile the findings of medical research. A database may serve as the user interface for another application. For instance, they can enter and store income tax data in a database application, then export the results to other programs like a spreadsheet or one used for tax preparation (Dehlinger & Dixon, 2011).

KEYWORD

A **database management system (or DBMS)** is essentially nothing more than a computerized data-keeping system.

3.7.2.4. Graphics Programs

Creating eye-catching graphs, pictures, and drawings using today's graphics software is simple. Develop advertising brochures, promotions, and full-color presentations with graphics software. If they are required to lecture at school or business, they can create and show their slides using a graphics application. They can use a graphics program to assist in creating a PowerPoint, a painting, or an animation. Many types of clip art, including pictures of people meeting, medical devices, telecommunications devices, entertainment, and much more, are included in most (Buchanan, 1993).

3.7.2.5. Personal Information Managers

Individuals, organizations, and groups can use personal information managers (PIMs) to store relevant information, such as a task checklist or a list of names and addresses. These typically offer a spot to write notes and an appointment calendar. Moreover, a PIM's data can be linked. For instance, they can connect a calendar meeting with a sales manager to the manager's contact information in the address book. The address book's entry for the sales manager is accessed and published on the computer monitor when users click the meeting in the calendar. A PIM software program is an example, such as Microsoft Outlook. By enabling users to view calendars, to-do lists, e-mail, social networking sites, contacts, and other data from a single page, Web portals like iGoogle and others facilitate PIM.

ACTIVITY 3.1.

How do different types of software used in information systems (such as system software, application software, and utility programs) differ in terms of their purpose and functionality, and what are some examples of each type?

They can schedule and organize group meetings using some PIMs. They can upload PIM data and sync it with other network users' calendars and schedules with the same PIM application if a desktop or mobile device is linked to one. Several PIMs also let them organize e-mails to invite people to meetings. Users click a link or button when they receive invitations to be added to the guest list instantly (Aerts et al., 2004).

3.7.3. Mobile Application Software

Recall that OS X iOS, Android, and WebOS are operating systems created specifically for cellphones. Software developers now have the chance to create programs tailored for mobile use on a small display thanks to the APIs and software developer kits designed for these operating systems. And they have. Tens of thousands of programs have been created by outside developers specifically for the iPhone and the mobile user apps that come with the OS. Numerous Apple apps are free; others cost 99 cents and hundreds of dollars. For $999.99, users may prepare for the California bar test with the BarMax iPhone App. Users of Android smartphones can also find 43,000,000 mobile apps in the Android Market. Although the Palm WebOS software development kit was only recently made available, many more applications may soon be available than the present dozens (Offutt, 2002).

3.8. SUMMARY

- The chapter "Hardware and Software in Computer networks" is about the components and software that make up modern computer networks. A computer network is a collection of hardware, software, data, people, and processes that work together to provide useful information for decision making and problem-solving.
- The chapter starts by discussing the various hardware components used in computer networks, such as the CPU, memory devices, motherboard, power supply, and cooling systems. It then covers processing and memory devices in more detail, including their speed and performance, types of memory, and the role of cache memory in performance enhancement. The chapter also explores various secondary storage, input, and output devices, such as hard disk drives, solid-state drives, optical storage devices, keyboard, mouse, scanners, printers, monitors, and speakers.
- After discussing the hardware components of computer networks, the chapter moves on to an overview of software used in computer networks. It explains the difference between system software and application software, with examples of each. The chapter then delves into operating systems, including their definition, function, types, and user interfaces. Finally, the chapter explores utility programs and applications of software in computer networks, such as system utilities, application programs, and software as a service (SaaS) and cloud-based applications.

REVIEW QUESTIONS

1. What are the different components of hardware used in computer networks, and how do they work together to process and store data?
2. What are the processing and memory devices used in computer networks, and how do they affect the performance of the system?
3. What are some examples of secondary storage, input, and output devices used in computer networks, and how do they work?
4. What is the difference between system software and application software used in computer networks, and what are some examples of each?
5. What is an operating system, and why is it important in computer networks? What are some common types of operating systems used today?
6. What are some examples of utility programs used in computer networks, and how do they help optimize the system's performance?
7. What is software as a service (SaaS), and how does it differ from traditional software applications installed on a computer?
8. What are the key features and benefits of cloud-based applications used in computer networks?

9. How can you assess the performance of the hardware components in a computer network, and what steps can you take to optimize its performance?
10. What are some potential security risks associated with using software in computer networks, and how can you protect against them?

MULTIPLE CHOICE QUESTIONS

1. What is a common input device used in computer networks?

a. Monitor
b. Printer
c. Keyboard
d. Speakers

2. Which of the following is a primary storage device used in computer networks?

a. Hard disk drive
b. Solid-state drive
c. USB flash drive
d. RAM

3. Which of the following is an example of a secondary storage device used in computer networks?

a. RAM
b. CPU
c. Hard disk drive
d. Optical drive

4. What is an operating system?

a. A type of software application used in computer networks
b. A set of hardware components used in computer networks
c. The user interface used in computer networks
d. The system software that manages hardware and software resources

5. Which of the following is not an example of an operating system?

a. Windows
b. Mac OS
c. Linux
d. Microsoft Office

6. Which of the following is a type of utility program used in computer networks?

a. Word processor
b. Spreadsheet software

c. Antivirus software
d. Presentation software

7. **What is software as a service (SaaS)?**
   a. A type of system software used in computer networks
   b. A type of cloud-based application used in computer networks
   c. A type of application software installed on a computer
   d. A type of programming language used in computer networks
8. **What is the function of a device driver in computer networks?**
   a. To manage the operating system
   b. To manage input and output devices
   c. To manage storage devices
   d. To manage application software
9. **Which of the following is a benefit of cloud-based applications in computer networks?**
   a. Improved system security
   b. Reduced hardware costs
   c. Increased system speed
   d. Improved user interface
10. **Which of the following is a potential security risk associated with using software in computer networks?**
    a. Malware infections
    b. Hardware failure
    c. Network congestion
    d. System crashes

Answers to the Multiple-Choice Questions

1. (c); 2. (d); 3. (c); 4. (d); 5. (d); 6. (c); 7. (b); 8. (b); 9. (b); 10. (a)

REFERENCES

1. Adler, R. M., (1995). Emerging standards for component software. *Computer, 28*(3), 68–77.
2. Aerts, A. T. M., Goossenaerts, J. B., Hammer, D. K., & Wortmann, J. C., (2004). Architectures in context: On the evolution of business, application software, and ICT platform architectures. *Information & Management, 41*(6), 781–794.

3. Agarwal, O., & Nenkova, A., (2022). Temporal effects on pre-trained models for language processing tasks. *Transactions of the Association for Computational Linguistics, 10*, 904–921.
4. Alderighi, L., Gans, P., Ienco, A., Peters, D., Sabatini, A., & Vacca, A., (1999). Hyperquad simulation and speciation (HySS): A utility program for the investigation of equilibria involving soluble and partially soluble species. *Coordination Chemistry Reviews, 184*(1), 311–318.
5. Alkhatib, G., (1992). The maintenance problem of application software: An empirical analysis. *Journal of Software Maintenance: Research and Practice, 4*(2), 83–104.
6. Appavoo, J., Auslander, M., Butrico, M., Da Silva, D. M., Krieger, O., Mergen, M. F., & Xenidis, J., (2005). Experience with K42, an open-source, Linux-compatible, scalable operating-system kernel. *IBM Systems Journal, 44*(2), 427–440.
7. Arato, M., & Benczur, A., (1981). Dynamic placement of records and the classical occupancy problem. *Computers & Mathematics with Applications, 7*(2), 173–185.
8. Arvanitis, P., & Krystalli, P., (2021). Mobile assisted language learning (MALL): Trends from 2010 to 2020 using text analysis techniques. *European Journal of Education, 4*(1), 13–22.
9. Bala, K., Sharma, S., & Kaur, G., (2015). A study on smartphone based operating system. *International Journal of Computer Applications, 121*(1), 2–10.
10. Balasubramanian, R., & Dalal, E., (1997). Method for quantifying the color gamut of an output device. In: *Color Imaging: Device-Independent Color, Color Hard Copy, and Graphic Arts II* (Vol. 3018, pp. 110–116).
11. Ballagas, R., Borchers, J., Rohs, M., & Sheridan, J. G., (2006). The smart phone: A ubiquitous input device. *IEEE Pervasive Computing, 5*(1), 70–77.
12. Baseman, K. C., Warren-Boulton, F. R., & Woroch, G. A., (1995). Microsoft plays hardball: The use of exclusionary pricing and technical incompatibility to maintain monopoly power in markets for operating system software. *The Antitrust Bulletin, 40*(2), 265–315.
13. Bawden, D., (1985). Computer output devices: A tutorial review. *Journal of Information Science, 11*(1), 1–8.
14. Belo, O., & Marques, A., (2012). Archiving business operational data heritage. *Procedia Technology, 1*, 107–111.
15. Benlian, A., & Hess, T., (2011). Comparing the relative importance of evaluation criteria in proprietary and open-source enterprise application software selection–a conjoint study of ERP and office systems. *Computer Networks Journal, 21*(6), 503–525.
16. Bergin, T. J., (2006). The origins of word processing software for personal computers: 1976–1985. *IEEE Annals of the History of Computing, 28*(4), 32–47.
17. Boehm, B. W., (1981). An experiment in small-scale application software engineering. *IEEE Transactions on Software Engineering*, (5), 482–493.

18. Bornman, E., Alant, E., & Meiring, J., (2001). The use of a digital voice output device to facilitate language development in a child with developmental apraxia of speech: A case study. *Disability and Rehabilitation, 23*(14), 623–634.
19. Brysbaert, M., Van, W. I., & De Deyne, S., (2000). Age-of-acquisition effects in semantic processing tasks. *Acta Psychologica, 104*(2), 215–226.
20. Buchanan, R. L., (1990). Using spreadsheet software for predictive microbiology applications. *Journal of Food Safety, 11*(2), 123–134.
21. Buchanan, R. L., (1993). Developing and distributing user-friendly application software. *Journal of Industrial Microbiology and Biotechnology, 12*(3–5), 251–255.
22. Buncic, P., Sanchez, C. A., Blomer, J., Franco, L., Harutyunian, A., Mato, P., & Yao, Y., (2010). CernVM–a virtual software appliance for LHC applications. In: *Journal of Physics: Conference Series, 219*(4), 042003.
23. Burdea, G., Richard, P., & Coiffet, P., (1996). Multimodal virtual reality: Input-output devices, system integration, and human factors. *International Journal of Human-Computer Interaction, 8*(1), 5–24.
24. Capra, E., Francalanci, C., & Slaughter, S. A., (2012). Is software "green"? Application development environments and energy efficiency in open source applications. *Information and Software Technology, 54*(1), 60–71.
25. Card, S. K., Mackinlay, J. D., & Robertson, G. G., (1991). A morphological analysis of the design space of input devices. *ACM Transactions on Computer Networks (TOIS)*, *9*(2), 99–122.
26. Chakravarty, S., Dogan, K., & Tomlinson, N., (2006). A hedonic study of network effects in the market for word processing software. *Decision Support Systems, 41*(4), 747–763.
27. Chandrasekaran, B., (1987). Towards a functional architecture for intelligence based on generic information processing tasks. In: *IJCAI* (Vol. 87, pp. 1183–1192).
28. Chen, P. M., Lee, E. K., Gibson, G. A., Katz, R. H., & Patterson, D. A., (1994). RAID: High-performance, reliable secondary storage. *ACM Computing Surveys (CSUR), 26*(2), 145–185.
29. Choi, H. R., Kim, H. S., Park, B. J., Park, N. K., & Lee, S. W., (2003). An ERP approach for container terminal operating systems. *Maritime Policy & Management, 30*(3), 197–210.
30. Christodoulakis, S., (1984). Estimating block selectivities. *Computer Networks, 9*(1), 69–79.
31. Coffman, E. G., & Hofri, M., (1986). Queueing models of secondary storage devices. *Queueing Systems, 1*, 129–168.
32. Corral, L., Sillitti, A., & Succi, G., (2015). Software assurance practices for mobile applications: A survey of the state of the art. *Computing, 97*, 1001–1022.
33. Cox, A. B., & Gifford, F., (1997). An overview to geographic computer networks. *The Journal of Academic Librarianship, 23*(6), 449–461.

34. De Waal, E. E., Kalkman, C. J., Rex, S., & Buhre, W. F., (2007). Validation of a new arterial pulse contour-based cardiac output device. *Critical Care Medicine, 35*(8), 1904–1909.
35. Dehlinger, J., & Dixon, J., (2011). Mobile application software engineering: Challenges and research directions. In: *Workshop on Mobile Software Engineering* (Vol. 2, pp. 29–32).
36. Denaro, G., Polini, A., & Emmerich, W., (2004). Early performance testing of distributed software applications. In: *Proceedings of the 4th International Workshop on Software and Performance, 1*, 94–103.
37. Dicarlo, C. F., & Banajee, M., (2000). Using voice output devices to increase initiations of young children with disabilities. *Journal of Early Intervention, 23*(3), 191–199.
38. Dixit, S. S., (1991). Quantization of color images for display/printing on limited color output devices. *Computers & Graphics, 15*(4), 561–567.
39. Dutke, S., & Reimer, T., (2000). Evaluation of two types of online help for application software. *Journal of Computer Assisted Learning, 16*(4), 307–315.
40. Ebert, C., & Jones, C., (2009). Embedded software: Facts, figures, and future. *Computer, 42*(4), 42–52.
41. Eisenberg, M., (2002). Output devices, computation, and the future of mathematical crafts. *International Journal of Computers for Mathematical Learning, 7*, 1–44.
42. Eisenberg, M., Eisenberg, A., Hendrix, S., Blauvelt, G., Butter, D., Garcia, J., & Nielsen, T., (2003). As we may print: New directions in output devices and computational crafts for children. In: *Proceedings of the 2003 Conference on Interaction Design and Children, 1*, 31–39.
43. El-Gayar, O., & Fritz, B. D., (2006). Environmental management computer networks (EMIS) for sustainable development: A conceptual overview. *Communications of the Association for Computer Networks, 17*(1), 34.
44. Ganesh, E. N., (2021). Study of self-organizing wireless hardware and software parts of the network sensor networks. *Current Trends in Information Technology; Programmed Efficiently; The Execution of the Data, 11*(3), 12–16.
45. Garmpis, A., (2011). Design and development of a web-based interactive software tool for teaching operating systems. *Journal of Information Technology Education: Research, 10*(1), 1–17.
46. Gifford, D. K., Baldwin, R. W., Berlin, S. T., & Lucassen, J. M., (1985). An architecture for large scale computer networks. *ACM SIGOPS Operating Systems Review, 19*(5), 161–170.
47. Grossman, D. D., & Silverman, H. F., (1973). Placement of records on a secondary storage device to minimize access time. *Journal of the ACM (JACM), 20*(3), 429–438.
48. Hagedoorn, J., Carayannis, E., & Alexander, J., (2001). Strange bedfellows in the personal computer industry: Technology alliances between IBM and Apple. *Research Policy, 30*(5), 837–849.

49. Harris, J. R., (1983). Apple computer, Inc. v. franklin computer corp.-does a ROM a computer program make. *Jurimetrics J., 24*, 248.
50. Hasselbring, W., (2000). Computer network integration. *Communications of the ACM, 43*(6), 32–38.
51. Hayashi, V. T., Arakaki, R., & Ruggiero, W. V., (2020). OKIoT: Trade off analysis of smart speaker architecture on open knowledge IoT project. *Internet of Things, 12*, 100310.
52. Helps, C. R. G., & Renshaw, S. A., (2004). Design of a flexible case-study instructional module for operating systems for information technology. In: *Proceedings of the 5th Conference on Information Technology Education, 1*, 56–59.
53. Herbst, K., Littlejohns, P., Rawlinson, J., Collinson, M., & Wyatt, J. C., (1999). Evaluating computerized health computer networks: Hardware, software and human ware: Experiences from the Northern Province, South Africa. *Journal of Public Health, 21*(3), 305–310.
54. Hidayatullah, A. F., & Ma'Arif, M. R., (2017). Pre-processing tasks in Indonesian Twitter messages. In: *Journal of Physics: Conference Series* (Vol. 801, No. 1, p. 012072). IOP Publishing.
55. Hudson, S. E., (2004). Using light emitting diode arrays as touch-sensitive input and output devices. In: *Proceedings of the 17th Annual ACM Symposium on User Interface Software and Technology, 1*, 287–290.
56. Jacob, R. J., (1996). Human-computer interaction: Input devices. *ACM Computing Surveys (CSUR), 28*(1), 177–179.
57. Jacob, R. J., Leggett, J. J., Myers, B. A., & Pausch, R., (1993). Interaction styles and input/output devices. *Behavior & Information Technology, 12*(2), 69–79.
58. Jacob, R. J., Sibert, L. E., McFarlane, D. C., & Mullen, Jr. M. P., (1994). Integrality and separability of input devices. *ACM Transactions on Computer-Human Interaction (TOCHI), 1*(1), 3–26.
59. Kapoor, R., & Agarwal, S., (2017). Sustaining superior performance in business ecosystems: Evidence from application software developers in the iOS and Android smartphone ecosystems. *Organization Science, 28*(3), 531–551.
60. Keller, A., & Hüsig, S., (2009). Ex ante identification of disruptive innovations in the software industry applied to web applications: The case of Microsoft's vs. Google's office applications. *Technological Forecasting and Social Change, 76*(8), 1044–1054.
61. Kelly, D. F., (2007). A software chasm: Software engineering and scientific computing. *IEEE Software, 24*(6), 120–119.
62. Kessler, G. D., Hodges, L. F., & Walker, N., (1995). Evaluation of the CyberGlove as a whole-hand input device. *ACM Transactions on Computer-Human Interaction (TOCHI), 2*(4), 263–283.
63. Kim, M. S., & Chung, S. C., (2003). Identification of nonlinear characteristics for precision servomechanisms. In: *Proceedings of the ASPE 2003 Annual Meeting, 1*, 167–170.

64. Kim, Y. S., Soh, B. S., & Lee, S. G., (2005). A new wearable input device: SCURRY. *IEEE Transactions on Industrial Electronics, 52*(6), 1490–1499.

65. Kotenko, I., Saenko, I., & Ageev, S., (2015). Countermeasure security risks management in the internet of things based on fuzzy logic inference. In: *2015 IEEE Trustcom/BigDataSE/ISPA, 1*, 654–659.

66. Lambourne, K., Audiffren, M., & Tomporowski, P. D., (2010). Effects of acute exercise on sensory and executive processing tasks. *Med. Sci. Sports Exerc., 42*(7), 1396–402.

67. Lapointe, J. F., Savard, P., & Vinson, N. G., (2011). A comparative study of four input devices for desktop virtual walkthroughs. *Computers in Human Behavior, 27*(6), 2186–2191.

68. Layton, K. J., Kroboth, S., Jia, F., Littin, S., Yu, H., Leupold, J., & Zaitsev, M., (2017). Pulseq: A rapid and hardware-independent pulse sequence prototyping framework. *Magnetic Resonance in Medicine, 77*(4), 1544–1552.

69. Lian, X., Liu, C., Fu, J., Liu, X., Ren, Q., Wan, X., & Wang, L., (2022). Design of plasmonic enhanced all-optical phase-change memory for secondary storage applications. *Nanotechnology, 33*(49), 495204.

70. Lim, S. L., Bentley, P. J., Kanakam, N., Ishikawa, F., & Honiden, S., (2014). Investigating country differences in mobile app user behavior and challenges for software engineering. *IEEE Transactions on Software Engineering, 41*(1), 40–64.

71. Lindstrom, E. E., & Vitter, J. S., (1985). The design and analysis of bucketsort for bubble memory secondary storage. *IEEE Transactions on Computers, 34*(03), 218–233.

72. Lorch, J. R., & Smith, A. J., (1998). Apple Macintosh's energy consumption. *IEEE Micro, 18*(6), 54–63.

73. MacKenzie, I. S., Sellen, A., & Buxton, W. A., (1991). A comparison of input devices in element pointing and dragging tasks. In: *Proceedings of the SIGCHI Conference on Human Factors in Computing Systems, 1*, 161–166.

74. Mackinlay, J., Card, S. K., & Robertson, G. G., (1990). A semantic analysis of the design space of input devices. *Human–Computer Interaction, 5*(2, 3), 145–190.

75. Maggio, M., Hoffmann, H., Santambrogio, M. D., Agarwal, A., & Leva, A., (2010). Controlling software applications via resource allocation within the heartbeats framework. In: *49th IEEE Conference on Decision and Control, 1,* 3736–3741.

76. McKellar, A. C., & Wong, C. K., (1978). Dynamic placement of records in linear storage. *Journal of the ACM (JACM), 25*(3), 421–434.

77. McKINNEY, C. J., MacCormac, E. R., & Welsh-Bohmer, K. A., (1999). Hardware and software for tachistoscopy: How to make accurate measurements on any PC utilizing the Microsoft Windows operating system. *Behavior Research Methods Instruments and Computers, 31*, 129–136.

78. McKusick, M. K., (1996). Secondary storage and filesystems. *ACM Computing Surveys (CSUR), 28*(1), 217–219.

79. Mellado, D., & Rosado, D. G., (2012). An overview of current computer networks security challenges and innovations J. UCS special issue. *Journal of Universal Computer Science, 18*(12), 1598–1607.
80. Mello, D., Cordiano, F., Gerosa, A., Padalino, M., Gagliano, C., Renna, G., & Franco, G., (2005). In-line monitor introduction to prevent metallic contamination in wet bench. In: *Solid State Phenomena, 108*, 637–642.
81. Mohanty, A., Alam, A., Sarkar, R., & Chaudhury, S., (2021). Design and development of digital game-based learning software for incorporation into school syllabus and curriculum transaction. *Design Engineering, 8*, 4864–4900.
82. Myers, B. A., McDaniel, R. G., Miller, R. C., Ferrency, A. S., Faulring, A., Kyle, B. D., & Doane, P., (1997). The amulet environment: New models for effective user interface software development. *IEEE Transactions on Software Engineering, 23*(6), 347–365.
83. Nagappan, M., & Shihab, E., (2016). Future trends in software engineering research for mobile apps. In: *2016 IEEE 23rd International Conference on Software Analysis, Evolution, and Reengineering, 5*, 21–32.
84. Novac, O. C., Novac, M., Gordan, C., Berczes, T., & Bujdosó, G., (2017). Comparative study of Google Android, Apple iOS and Microsoft Windows phone mobile operating systems. In: *2017 14th International Conference on Engineering of Modern Electric Systems (EMES)* (pp. 154–159). IEEE.
85. Offutt, J., (2002). Quality attributes of web software applications. *IEEE Software, 19*(2), 25–32.
86. Olsen, Jr. D. R., Dempsey, E. P., & Rogge, R., (1985). Input/output linkage in a user interface management system. *ACM SIGGRAPH Computer Graphics, 19*(3), 191–197.
87. Omiecinski, E., Lee, L., & Scheuermann, P., (1994). Performance analysis of a concurrent file reorganization algorithm for record clustering. *IEEE Transactions on Knowledge and Data Engineering, 6*(2), 248–257.
88. Ong, M. E. H., Tan, E. H., Yan, X., Anushia, P., Lim, S. H., Leong, B. S. H., & Anantharaman, V., (2008). An observational study describing the geographic-time distribution of cardiac arrests in Singapore: What is the utility of geographic computer networks for planning public access defibrillation? (PADS Phase I). *Resuscitation, 76*(3), 388–396.
89. Peters, P. A., (1973). Advanced logging system-II: Balloon logging: A look at current operating systems. *Journal of Forestry, 71*(9), 577–579.
90. Phani, A. M. R. V. A., Kumar, D. J., & Kumar, G. A., (2007). *Operating Systems for Wireless Sensor Networks: A Survey Technical Report, 3*, 1–30.
91. Raj, J. R. F., Vijayalakshmi, K., & Priya, S. K., (2019). Medical image denoising using multi-resolution transforms. *Measurement, 145*, 769–778.
92. Rayner, K., Li, X., Williams, C. C., Cave, K. R., & Well, A. D., (2007). Eye movements during information processing tasks: Individual differences and cultural effects. *Vision Research, 47*(21), 2714–2726.

93. Saputra, F., (2022). The role of human resources, hardware, and databases in mass media companies. *International Journal of Advanced Multidisciplinary, 1*(1), 47–55.
94. Shin, I., (2006). Adoption of enterprise application software and firm performance. *Small Business Economics, 26*, 241–256.
95. Stytz, M. R., (2004). Considering defense in depth for software applications. *IEEE Security & Privacy, 2*(1), 72–75.
96. Taveira, A. D., & Choi, S. D., (2009). Review study of computer input devices and older users. *Intl. Journal of Human–Computer Interaction, 25*(5), 455–474.
97. Thrall, S. E., (1999). Geographic computer network (GIS) hardware and software. *Journal of Public Health Management and Practice, 5*(2), 82–90.
98. Tsukada, K., & Yasumura, M., (2001). Ubi-finger: Gesture input device for mobile use. In: *Ubicomp 2001 Informal Companion Proceedings, 11*, 4–10.
99. Udhayakumar, U., & Murugaboopathi, G., (2020). Enhanced security using hybrid parallel integrity key data service access control method in virtual cloud. *Journal of Green Engineering, 10*(2), 342–359.
100. Van, G. P., & Comuzzi, M., (2013). Lifelong personal health data and application software via virtual machines in the cloud. *IEEE Journal of Biomedical and Health Informatics, 18*(1), 36–45.
101. Wanderley, M. M., & Orio, N., (2002). Evaluation of input devices for musical expression: Borrowing tools from HCI. *Computer Music Journal, 26*(3), 62–76.
102. Wang, H., Chen, Z., Xiao, G., & Zheng, Z., (2016). Network of networks in Linux operating system. *Physica A: Statistical Mechanics and its Applications, 447*, 520–526.
103. Ware, C., (1996). Multimedia output devices and techniques. *ACM Computing Surveys (CSUR), 28*(1), 181–183.
104. Weiss, B., Weisz, J. R., & Bromfield, R., (1986). Performance of retarded and nonretarded persons on information-processing tasks: Further tests of the similar structure hypothesis. *Psychological Bulletin, 100*(2), 157.
105. Wibawa, I. N. G. S., (2015). Hierarchy and characteristic of storage devices. *International Research Journal of Management, IT and Social Sciences, 2*(3), 1–4.
106. Wilkie, F. G., & Kitchenham, B. A., (2000). Coupling measures and change ripples in C++ application software. *Journal of Systems and Software, 52*(2, 3), 157–164.
107. Wood, E., Willoughby, T., Rushing, A., Bechtel, L., & Gilbert, J., (2005). Use of computer input devices by older adults. *Journal of Applied Gerontology, 24*(5), 419–438.
108. Wright, C. D., Hosseini, P., & Diosdado, J. A. V., (2013). Beyond von-Neumann computing with nanoscale phase-change memory devices. *Advanced Functional Materials, 23*(18), 2248–2254.
109. Xiao, G., Zheng, Z., Yin, B., Trivedi, K. S., Du, X., & Cai, K. Y., (2019). An empirical study of fault triggers in the Linux operating system: An evolutionary perspective. *IEEE Transactions on Reliability, 68*(4), 1356–1383.

110. Xiao, Y., & Wang, W. Y., (2019). Quantifying uncertainties in natural language processing tasks. In: *Proceedings of the AAAI Conference on Artificial Intelligence* (Vol. 33, No. 1, pp. 7322–7329).

111. Yakubailik, O. E., Kadochnikov, A. A., & Tokarev, A. V., (2018). Web geographic computer network and the hardware and software ensuring rapid assessment of air pollution. *Optoelectronics, Instrumentation and Data Processing, 54*, 243–249v.

112. Yamada, S., & Osaki, S., (1985). Software reliability growth modeling: Models and applications. *IEEE Transactions on Software Engineering*, (12), 1431–1437.

113. Yue, P. C., & Wong, C. K., (1973). On the optimality of the probability ranking scheme in storage applications. *Journal of the ACM (JACM), 20*(4), 624–633.

114. Zhai, S., (1998). User performance in relation to 3D input device design. *ACM SIGGRAPH Computer Graphics, 32*(4), 50–54.

CHAPTER 4

UNDERSTANDING COMPUTER NETWORK SECURITY

UNIT INTRODUCTION

Security is defined in basic terms as:

"Continuously shielding a thing from illegal access is called security."

It is the condition of remaining or feeling safe from harm. This item in that condition may be an individual, an entity like a corporation, or a tangible asset like a personal computer or a folder. An item can attain a physical or conceptual condition of security. Physically, a certain facility is secure when an enclosure-like fence surrounds it, contains secure zones inside and outside, and can withstand intrusion. This level of security may be ensured if the four protective mechanisms, deterrent factor, prevention measures, detection systems, and reaction are in effect (Onwubiko, 2009).

Deterrence is typically the initial defensive line for potential invaders. It operates by generating an environment designed to terrify invaders (Roy et al., 2010). Occasionally, this may include cautions of serious repercussions for security breaches.

Prevention is the strategy for preventing attackers from entering the system's features (Ciampa, 2012). Proxy servers, demilitarized zones (DMZs), and access devices such as passwords, access cards, and fingerprinting are examples of barriers that enable only permitted people to use and enter a facility.

Detection happens whenever the intruder has gained the system's access or is currently doing so. Signals generated by the detecting procedure include intrusion alarm warnings (Bejtlich, 2013). Occasionally, these signals might be in real-time or kept for later study by the security staff.

The reaction is an aftereffect process that attempts to compensate for the failure of the preceding three mechanisms. It attempts to block and prevent future facility damage or access.

The regions beyond the perimeter of the protected systems can be guarded via cable and wall fencing, motion sensors, security lights, closed circuit television (CCTV), concealed seismic sensing devices, or other optoelectronic and electromagnetic systems (White et al., 1995). Electronic boundaries such as firewalls and user passwords might strengthen the system's internal security.

Learning Objectives

After this chapter, readers will comprehend the following:

- The fundamentals of security for computer networks;
- The distinction between data protection and network security;
- Attacks using IPV4 and security problems with IPV6;
- Protection of computer networks;
- Types of network protection;
- Potential implications for network security.

Key Terms

- Attacks
- Authentication
- Firewall
- Integrity
- Internet
- Network
- Protection
- Security
- Software
- Technologies
- Viruses

4.1. UNDERSTANDING COMPUTER NETWORK SECURITY

Digital barriers – often known as firewalls – are either software or hardware employed to protect the sensitive areas of any information system unit against the outside environment and reduce the possible damage caused by an invader (Lincke & Holland, 2007).

A condition of hypothetical security, often known as pseudo security. Many feel that an asset may be secure so long as no one beyond the primary functional group has information about its presence.

This represents virtual security in that it is not practically implemented by constructing walls, providing user credentials, or constructing a router firewall; rather, it is built on a mindset. The idea rests on the requirement to know the foundation, which means that an individual is not hazardous if he or she does not possess information that may compromise the security of a system, such as a network (Brooks, 2013).

KEYWORD

A **router firewall** is a physical device that controls the incoming and outgoing traffic through an Internet connection.

In actual systems employing this security concept, security is ensured by the notion that only people with accountability and trustworthiness can access the system and that no one else must be made aware of this (Zhuang et al., 2013). In essence, the ideology is founded on the assumption that individuals participating will never depart. If they do so, the system's security will be compromised. There are several instances wherein STO has already been utilized successfully. Examples include Pepsi, McDonalds, and other corporations that have, for years, relied on a handful of trustworthy staff to keep their proprietary formulas protected. Nonetheless, the STO as a whole has been exploited by several software developers to conceal their programs.

In 1994, Matt Blaze discovered a weakness in the Escrowed Encryption Standard (Clipper) that could have been utilized to circumvent law enforcement agencies' surveillance. Laze's finding made encrypted communication with Clipper technologies simpler to access without passwords than was earlier feasible (Strebe, 2006).

4.1.1. Computer Security

This subject, a subfield of Computer Science, focuses on creating a secure ecosystem for computer usage. It emphasizes "user conduct" and the procedures necessary to maintain a safe environment for everyone who uses computers (Lehtinen & Gangemi, 2006). Hence, this topic includes four areas of significance: the research of computer morality, the creation of hardware and software standards, and the creation of guiding principles. It is a complicated research subject, including mathematically precise cryptographic technique constructions. This is not the emphasis of this book.

Remember

Lock down your network like Fort Knox with strong encryption, access controls, and security protocols.

4.1.2. Network Security

As is common knowledge, computer networks are dispersed clusters of computers that are either strongly connected, indicating they exchange many services from a computer system, or loosely linked, indicating they exchange only the resources necessary for the network to function.

Currently, the focused object has shifted whenever computer network security is discussed. It is now a network rather than a single machine (Ohta & Chikaraishi, 1993). Hence, computer network security constitutes a subfield of computer security. It is still a discipline of computer science, although it is far more expansive than computer security.

It entails establishing a safe environment for a computer network, encompassing all of its numerous resources, all of its stored and in-transit information, and all of its regular users. It is an increasingly sophisticated study area than computer security because it has a broader scope and requires more intricate mathematical formulations of cryptography, transmission, communications, and exchange protocols, including practice guidelines.

4.2. NETWORK SECURITY

System and network technologies are crucial for several different uses. Security is necessary for applications and networks. Given that network security is crucial, there is a severe dearth of simply implementable security measures. There is a "miscommunication" between those designing security technologies and those constructing networks (Roy et al., 2010). The Open Systems Interface (OSI) concept is the foundation for network design, a well-established procedure. Several protocol layers may be coupled to construct stacking that facilitates modular development. Each layer implementation can be altered later without impacting other levels, providing for developmental adaptability.

In comparison to network design, secure network design is not a well-established procedure. There is no system for coping with the intricacies of security needs. Network design offers more advantages than secure network architecture (Marin, 2005).

Network security also does not necessitate the protection of both endpoints. When sending data, the communication channel should not be susceptible to assault. A prospective intruder may attack the communication route, steal the encrypted information, decode it, and reinsert false messages. As crucial as it is to protect the devices and secure the communication, it is as vital to secure the intermediary network.

While constructing a secure network, these key considerations must be taken into account:

1. Authorized users are granted the capacity to send messages via or from a particular network.
2. Confidentiality – Information on the network is treated with confidentiality.
3. Verify that network consumers are those whom they proclaim to be through authentication.
4. Integrity – Verify that the message was not changed during transmission.
5. Nonrepudiation guarantees that the user will not deny utilizing the network (Lye & Wing, 2005).

KEYWORD

Authentication is the act of proving an assertion, such as the identity of a computer system user.

A successful network security strategy takes into account security challenges, prospective attackers, the desired level of protection, and the variables that render a network at risk of attack. Many devices are designed to reduce the computer's susceptibility to network assaults. These technologies include encrypting, intrusion detection, firewalls, security management, and authentication systems. Companies throughout the globe utilize a mix of these tools. "Intranets" are linked to the internet and sufficiently shielded from it (Pawar & Anuradha, 2015).

Due to network defects, the network structure itself is in charge. Addressing internet security challenges substantially facilitates the creation of safe network protection solutions (Daya, 2013). In order to identify and protect against Internet assaults, it is necessary to study their many forms. Most intrusion detection devices are intended to identify the most prevalent assaults.

Packets are injected to cause issues during network incursions for the reasons listed:

1. Inappropriate utilization of resources;
2. Meddling with the desired operation of a system resource;
3. Acquiring system knowledge, including usernames and logins, for use in future attacks (Liang & Xiao, 2012).

4.3. DIFFERENCE BETWEEN DATA SECURITY AND NETWORK SECURITY

Data security is the component of security that enables the conversion of a customer's data into unintelligible information for transmission (Baker & Wallace, 2007). Regardless of whether this nonsensical data is stolen, the communication cannot be decoded without a passcode. This security approach is partly successful. Strong encryption was once readily cracked, but this is no longer true. In order to remain one point ahead of hackers, cryptographic techniques must continually change.

Using a secure network for sending ciphertext across a network is helpful. This will safeguard the ciphertext, reducing the likelihood that many individuals will seek to decipher it. A secure network would also prohibit unapproved communications into the network (Ben-Asher & Gonzalez, 2015). Thus, strong ciphers and attack-resistant networks are necessary.

Figure 4.1. Network and data link in OSI model.

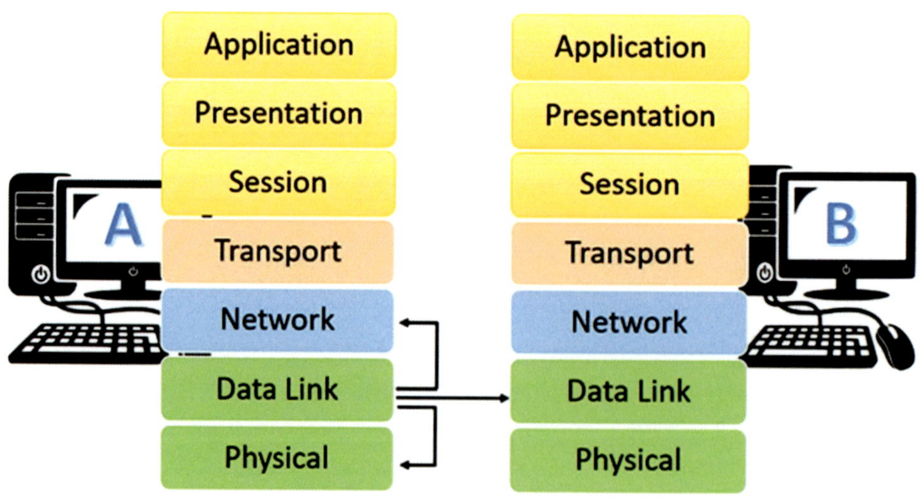

Source: Guru99, Creative Commons License.

Figure 4.1 demonstrates the link between network and data in the OSI model (Posey et al., 2014). Since that cryptography occurs at the application level, application developers are conscious of its existence. The user may choose from a range of data security techniques. Network security is essentially the responsibility of the physical layer. In addition to the physical layer, other layers are utilized to ensure the requisite network security. Authentication takes happen on such a layer that lies above the physical one. Physical network-layer security requires failure monitoring, intrusion detection techniques, and smart prevention and mitigation tactics.

4.4. VULNERABLE SECURITY ASPECTS IN INTERNET ARCHITECTURE

Businesses' use of protected private networking or intranets is a response to Internet security concerns. The Internet Engineering Task Force (IETF) recently implemented security features to many levels of the Internet Protocol Suite (Fraiji et al., 2018). These security measures provide for the practical protection of data components as they traverse a network. Both present and future implementations of the Internet Protocol are evaluated for their security implications. While protocol security applies, not all assaults are protected. Examining these assaults to see whether extra security measures are necessary.

The Internet Protocol Security architecture is standardized of internet security. IP security refers to both IPv6 and the present version (IPv4) (Landwehr & Goldschlag, 1997). Although new approaches, like IP sec, have been created to solve a few of the internet's major infamous flaws, they appear insufficient.

Figure 4.2 of IPsec implementation to provide secure communications IPsec provides a point-to-point system wherein one party encrypts while the other decrypts with identical keys or credentials. IPsec operates in two modes: transport and tunnel mode (Wählisch et al., 2013).

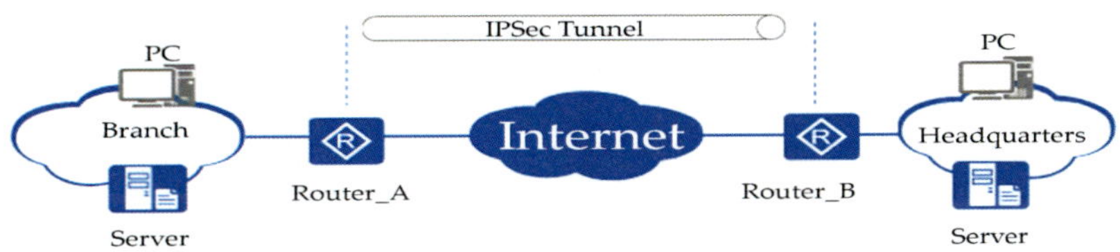

Figure 4.2. Visual representation of IPsec implementation.

Source: Huawei, Creative Commons License.

4.5. ATTACKS THROUGH IPV4 AND SECURITY ISSUES IN IPV6

4.5.1. Common Internet Attack Methods

The most prevalent Internet assault techniques are categorized. Cyberattacks, including eavesdropping and phishing, are designed to acquire system understanding or personal data (Durdağı & Buldu, 2010). Assaults are conceivable.

Viruses, trojans, and worms can potentially disrupt the planned operation of a system. A denial of service (DoS) attempted attack is another assault that occurs when system resources are spent inadequately. Land assaults, surf assaults, and teardrop attacks are further forms of network infiltration.

These assaults are not as common as DoS attacks. However, they are nevertheless utilized, despite not being named.

4.5.1.1. Viruses

Viruses are malicious, self-replicating programs that infect and propagate via files (Caicedo et al., 2009). The virus penetrates the system and then becomes activated upon file opening (Figure 4.3).

Figure 4.3. Illustration of the viruses attack on computers.

Source: Investor Media, Creative Commons License.

4.5.1.2. Trojans

Trojans may seem to the users as innocent programs, yet they have harmful intentions. Generally, Trojan horses transmit a payload, typically a virus (Radhakrishnan et al., 2007).

TIPS

Be wary of opening e-mail attachments or downloading files from untrusted sources to avoid unwittingly installing Trojan malware.

4.5.1.3. Eavesdropping

Eavesdropping is when an unauthorized person intercept conversation. Passive eavesdropping happens when an individual secretly listens to networked communications. Active eavesdropping happens whenever the attacker listens and puts information into the communications channel (Žagar et al., 2007). Thus, the signals may become garbled. This technique can be employed to steal critical data.

4.5.1.4. Phishing

Phishing is gaining sensitive information from a person, group, or organization (Ullrich et al., 2014). Phishers deceive consumers into divulging private data like credit card numbers, login passwords for internet banking, and other private details.

4.5.1.5. Denial of Service

Denial of Service is an attack when a system receives too many queries and cannot interact with the clients (Choudhary, 2009). When the system waits for the interaction to conclude, it consumes resources. Ultimately, the system will no longer be able to react to queries, leaving it unusable.

4.5.1.6. IP Spoofing

In order to obtain access to certain other desktop computers, spoofing involves a computer's address mimicking that of a trustworthy computer. The intruder's identity is masked in several ways, challenging identification and prevention. Existing IP protocol tech is incapable of eliminating IP spoofing (Bi et al., 2007).

4.5.2. Internet Security Technologies

As long as data is accessible and exchanged through the Internet, Internet risks will remain a serious worry for worldwide society.

Several defensive and detection techniques were created to counteract these threats (Ahmed et al., 2014).

4.5.2.1. Firewall

The firewall is a popular device for border protection or boundary defense. The goal of a firewall is to prevent external traffic, but it may also block internal traffic. The primary line of security against invaders is a firewall (Szigeti & Risztics, 2004). It prohibits illegal access to and from a private connection. Firewalls can be built into the hardware, software, or a combination (Figure 4.4).

Figure 4.4. Schematic of the firewall internet security.

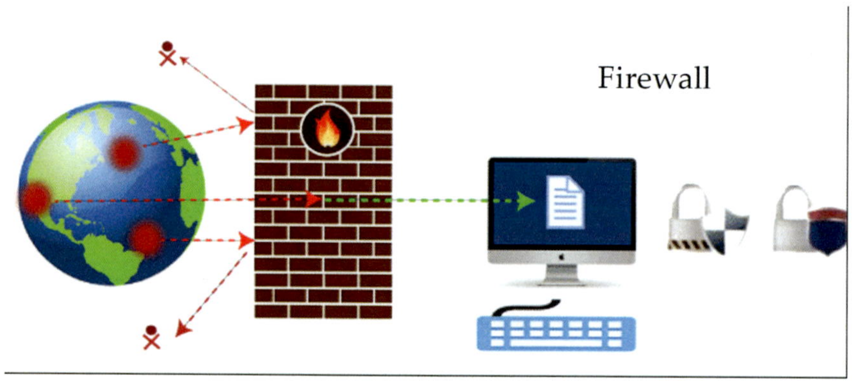

Source: Java Point, Creative Commons License.

4.5.2.2. Cryptographic Systems

Currently, cryptography is a vital and commonly employed technique in the field of security engineering (Shanmugaraja & Chandrasekar, 2012). Using codes and ciphers to transform information into unintelligible data was required. Hence, this garbled data is transported securely over the network.

4.5.2.3. Secure Socket Layer

SSL is a standard protocol for establishing high privacy between an internet browser and an internet site. SSL is designed to provide secure communication, or channel, between a browser on a computer and a web server to ensure that all data sent within the tunnel is safeguarded. SSL enables users to identify servers utilizing certificates (Yang et al., 2007). To establish their identity, clients provide the server with a certificate.

4.5.2.4. Intrusion Detection System

IDS is an extra security mechanism that assists in the deterrence of computer intrusions. IDS systems may detect threats using both hardware as well as software (Shiranzaei & Khan, 2018). IDS solutions monitor connections to ascertain whether or not an attack has been performed. Even though various intrusion detection systems (IDS) monitor and alarm when an attack happens, others seek to avert the assault.

4.6. SECURITY IN COMPUTER NETWORK

The network security industry is following in its predecessors' footsteps. The same approaches are employed with the inclusion of biometric identification. Biometric authentication is much more secure than password protection. This might greatly decrease illegal system access. The software component of network security continues to evolve (Pawar & Anuradha, 2015). Regularly, newer firewalls and encryption strategies are deployed. The ongoing study contributes to comprehending present advances and predicting future advancements in the discipline. In network security, Software and Hardware Deployments are the two primary deployments.

Incorporating computer and network security, information security is an even broader area of research. This research may be found in several disciplines, including computer engineering, business administration, information studies, and science and engineering. It entails establishing a secure environment for information and data. In this paradigm, data or information can be transported via communication routes or stored in server databases. This necessitates the study of increasingly intricate mathematical designs of encryption, communication, transportation, exchange protocols, and practice guidelines, but also the status of both information and data in transit. They are not being discussed here.

KEYWORD

Network security consists of the policies, processes and practices adopted to prevent, detect and monitor unauthorized access, misuse, modification, or denial of a computer network and network-accessible resources.

4.6.1. Securing the Computer Network

Developing security in a computer network paradigm necessitates the development of secure areas for several resources (Rutledge & Hoffman, 1986). According to the above description, a resource is safe in this paradigm if it is secured from interior and exterior illegal access. These are items, whether tangible or not. Protecting a thing involves preventing unwanted access from inside and outside the entity. Simply put, it aims to safeguard items. System items either exist or do not exist. Inside a computer network paradigm, the actual objects are the system's physical resources, and the non-real objects are the system's data and information, both in transit and in memory.

4.6.2. Hardware

Safeguarding hardware resources entails safeguarding and includes:

i. End-user objects comprising interface hardware components like a keypad, mice, touchpad, and other input devices (Aydın et al., 2009).
ii. Hacker-vulnerable network objects such as firewalls, ports, routers, switches, and gateways.
iii. Network communication routes to avoid snooping on network communications.

4.6.3. Software

KEYWORD

A **database** is an organized collection of structured information, or data, typically stored electronically in a computer system.

Safeguarding software resources include safeguarding hardware-based applications, server protocols, operating systems, web browsers, software applications, and copyrighted material stored on networked storage drives and databases (Davies & Price, 1984). It also entails securing client software, such as stock holdings, financial information, property investment records, photos or images, and other frequently kept personal information on home and office computers.

4.7. FORMS OF PROTECTION

Now, it is understood which model items are protected or require protection. The next section examines quickly, reserving specifics for later, the means and methods of preserving these items. Many services, including access control, confidentiality, authentication, and integrity, are employed to prevent unwanted utilization of system resources.

4.7.1. Access Control

The system utilizes this feature in conjunction with user-supplied identification information like a passcode to identify who uses which of its services (Menell, 1986). The next section looks at several software and hardware-based access control methods (Figure 4.5).

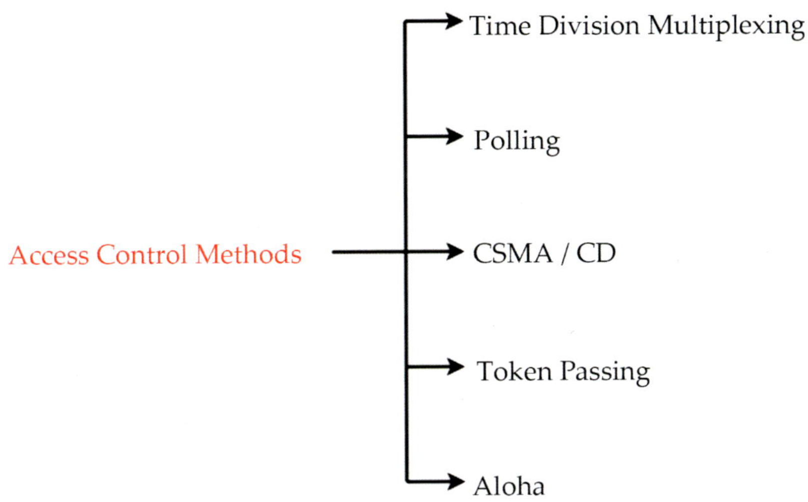

Figure 4.5. Illustration of the access control methods.

Source: Gate Vidyalay, Creative Commons License.

4.7.1.1. Hardware Access Control Systems

Fast technological advancements have produced effective access control technologies that are both open and adaptable while maintaining appropriate protection against hazards. The following basic access control tools come into this category:

4.7.1.2. Access Terminal

Terminal access points (APs) are now so advanced that in addition to identifying users, they effectively validate access privileges, regulate APs, and interact with host systems (Wolf & Pfitzmann, 2000). This can be accomplished through various biometric authentication methods and real-time anti-intrusion sensors. Network technology has enabled these devices to be linked to a monitoring program or operate offline.

4.7.1.3. Visual Event Monitoring

This valuable and quickly expanding kind of access control that combines several real-time tools, such as audio and video data, aerial pictures, and global positioning system (GPS) technology, to detect places (Mullender & Tanenbaum, 1984).

4.7.1.4. Identification Cards

As a form of access control throughout structures, banking establishments, and other prohibited locations, these cards, often referred to as proximity cards, have become quite prevalent in recent years. Cards can be bar-coded, magnetic, contact chip, or a mix.

4.7.1.5. Biometric Identification

This is likely the most rapidly expanding control access technology in use nowadays. Biometrics, eye, and speech recognition are a few of the most prevalent types (Harahap & Khairina, 2021). However, fingerprint identification provides enhanced security.

4.7.1.6. Video Surveillance

This replaces traditional CCTV and is getting more favor as an access control instrument. With rapid networking technology and electronic cameras, pictures may be captured, processed, and acted upon within moments.

4.7.1.7. Software Access Control Systems

KEYWORD

Point of Access means Provider's border router which is used to establish connectivity from Provider's systems to its Internet service provider and the public Internet.

There are two forms of software access control: point-of-access monitoring and distant monitoring. Personal actions can be tracked via a PC-based program at the point of access (POA). The program can also be linked to a network, machine, or machine of individual choosing (Nguyen et al., 2020). The program gathers and maintains access occurrences and other system-related events and downloads access privileges to access terminals.

In remote status, the terminals may be connected through modems, telephone service, and all wireless links. These terminals may, on occasion, if necessary, be equipped with automatic phoning at predetermined periods or a periodic reporting attendant.

4.7.2. Authentication

The purpose of authentication is to determine the user's identity. User identity, particularly of distant users, is challenging since many users, particularly those with malicious intent, may pose as real users when they are not. This service offers a system that can confirm that a user is whom he or she purports to be depending on the user's attributes (Figure 4.6).

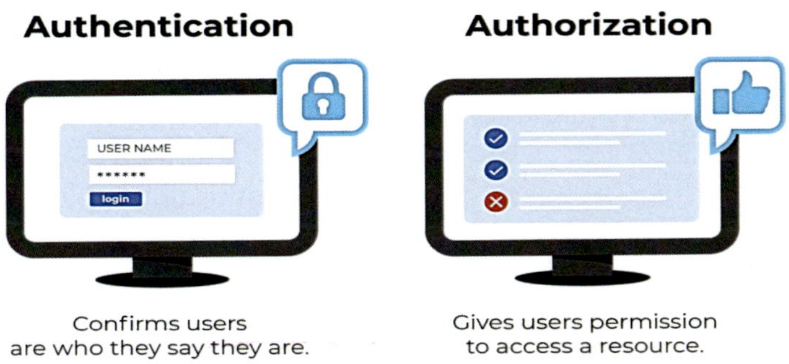

Figure 4.6. Authentication as a form of protection.

Source: Okta, Creative Commons License.

Physically, any or all of the below user elements may be used to authenticate a user or user surrogates:

1. **Username:** A username is a unique identifier used by a person to access a computer system or online service. It typically consists of a combination of letters, numbers, and/or symbols chosen by the user. Usernames are used to distinguish one user from another and are often required in conjunction with a password for authentication purposes. Usernames may also be used to create a public identity or handle for a user within a particular online community or social network. It is important for users to choose a strong, unique username that is not easily guessable or associated with personal information to ensure the security of their accounts.
2. **Passcode or Password:** Both passwords and passcodes are authentication mechanisms used to verify a user's identity and grant access to a secure system or device. Passwords are typically associated with an account and are longer and more complex than passcodes, which are used to unlock a device and are usually shorter. Both should be strong, unique, and not shared to prevent unauthorized access.
3. **Retinal Images:** The individual stares at an electrical gadget that records the image of his or her eye's retina; the program then matches this mapping with a comparable map recorded on the system.
4. **Fingerprints:** The user pushes on or occasionally places a certain finger on a gadget that generates a replica of the user's fingerprints and afterward matches it with a comparable picture on the computer user files (Sergent, 1995).

5. **Physical Location:** The exact position of the system making an entrance attempt is verified to confirm that the request originates from a recognized and approved place. In networks, the client computer's Internet protocol (IP) addresses are matched to that in the system user record to verify the client's location. This strategy is typically employed with other security precautions as it cannot ensure security on its own. It grants access to the specified system to anyone who can access the client's computer if used individually.
6. **Identification Cards:** These are progressively being used as authentication papers (Cohen, 1987). Anyone who possesses the card is granted access to the desired system. Similar to the case with specific geographical authentication, card identification is often a second-level authentication method because anybody possessing the card can acquire access to the intended system.

Did you Know?

Confidentiality is a form of protection in networks that ensures that data is kept private and only accessible to authorized users, typically through encryption and access controls.

4.7.3. Confidentiality

The confidentiality service prevents unwanted exposure of system information and data. When information leaves one end of a network, for instance, a client's computer on a network, it enters an environment that cannot be trusted. So, the data recipient may not have complete faith that no third party, such as a cryptanalysis or a man-in-the-middle, has intercepted the data. The current service employs encryption techniques to guarantee that no such incidents occur when the data is public.

Encryption safeguards the communication network against eavesdroppers (Stytz & Whittaker, 2003). Sniffers are applications created for and put on communication channels to spy on network activity, analyzing all network activity on certain network segments. Sniffers are simple to create and deploy but challenging to detect. The encryption procedure employs an encryption technique and codes to change plaintext at the origin into ciphertext, which is often incomprehensible, before recovering it at the sink. The algorithm for encryption might be either symmetrical or asymmetrical.

Symmetric encryption, also known as secret key encryption, scrambles and decrypts the message using the same cryptographic method and a shared key. Asymmetric encryption, often called encryption with a public key, employs two keys: a shared key accessible to everyone and a secret key accessible only to the recipient and the sender (Menell, 2017). The sender and recipient both own a set of these credentials, a public, and a secret. A communication is encrypted using the disclosed public key of the recipient. The recipient decrypts the communication using his or her secret key upon reception.

4.7.4. Integrity

The integrity service safeguards data from active threats, including those that may modify it (François et al., 2012). Similarly, to data privacy, data in transit between communicating and receiving entities are vulnerable to several risks from cybercriminals, spies, and cryptologists who aim to intercept and manipulate the data for their purposes. With the use of encryption and hash methods, this solution maintains the integrity of temporary data.

A hash function generates a code from the input message M. Often, the code is referenced as a hashing or a message signal. A unidirectional hash function generates the message's signature, similar to fingerprints. Hence, the hash algorithm ensures the message's integrity and validity. The sender attaches the signature to the communication before sending it to the receiver.

4.8. FUTURE SCOPE OF NETWORK SECURITY

The collection of apps will have the greatest impact on Internet security. Future security might mimic the immune response. The immune system guards against assaults and develops for more formidable adversaries. Likewise, network security will function as an immune system (Figure 4.7).

Figure 4.7. Illustration of the scope of future computer networks security.

Source: Skill Monk, Creative Commons License.

ACTIVITY 4.1.

Can you provide an example of a common network security threat and explain how you would address it?

Although the biometric initiative may have started long ago, it is not followed extensively. Numerous security advancements occur inside the same information security currently used, with few modifications. Following numerous years of development, security flaws, such as circumventing or modifying the security mechanisms, required modification and must be closed. Several layers of protection can prohibit their access.

4.9. SUMMARY

- Understanding Computer Network Security introduces computer network security, including an explanation of its fundamentals, the distinction between data security and network security, and susceptible security features in internet design. The chapter also discusses IPV4 assaults and IPV6 security challenges, computer network security, network defense methods, and the future of network security. The reader should be able to comprehend the core ideas of network security and the accompanying difficulties by the conclusion of the chapter.

REVIEW QUESTIONS

1. What is computer network security? Explain its importance.
2. How is data security different from network security?
3. What are some of the vulnerable security aspects of Internet architecture? Explain their significance.
4. What are the common attacks through IPV4? How can they be prevented?
5. What are the security issues in IPV6? How can they be addressed?
6. What are the forms of protection of computer networks? Explain their functions.
7. What is the future scope of network security? How can it be leveraged to improve network security?

MULTIPLE CHOICE QUESTIONS

1. What is the difference between data security and network security?

a. They are the same thing
b. Data security refers to the protection of the data, while network security refers to the protection of the network
c. Network security refers to the protection of the data, while data security refers to the protection of the network
d. None of the above

2. Which of the following is not a vulnerable security aspect in internet architecture?

a. Routers
b. Firewalls
c. DNS
d. Web servers

3. Which IPV version has more security issues?

a. IPV4

b. IPV6
c. Both have equal security issues
d. Neither has any security issues

4. What is the most common attack through IPV4?

a. Spoofing
b. Denial of Service (DoS)
c. Man-in-the-Middle (MitM)
d. None of the above

5. What is a form of protection for computer networks?

a. Firewalls
b. Intrusion Detection Systems (IDS)
c. Virtual Private Networks (VPN)
d. All of the above

6. Which of the following is not a future scope of network security?

a. Artificial Intelligence (AI)
b. Internet of Things (IoT)
c. Blockchain
d. None of the above

7. What is the main objective of computer network security?

a. Protecting hardware
b. Protecting data
c. Preventing network outages
d. All of the above

Answers to Multiple Choice Questions

1. (b); 2. (b); 3. (b); 4. (a); 5. (d); 6. (d); 7. (b)

REFERENCES

1. Ahmed, A. S., Hassan, R., & Othman, N. E., (2014). Security threats for IPv6 transition strategies: A review. In: *2014 4th International Conference on Engineering Technology and Technopreneuship (ICE2T)* (Vol. 1, pp. 83–88). IEEE.
2. Aydın, M. A., Zaim, A. H., & Ceylan, K. G., (2009). A hybrid intrusion detection system design for computer network security. *Computers & Electrical Engineering, 35*(3), 517–526.

3. Baker, W. H., & Wallace, L., (2007). Is information security under control?: Investigating quality in information security management. *IEEE Security & Privacy, 5*(1), 36–44.
4. Bejtlich, R., (2013). *The Practice of Network Security Monitoring: Understanding Incident Detection and Response* (Vol. 2, No. 1, pp. 5–10). No Starch Press.
5. Ben-Asher, N., & Gonzalez, C., (2015). Effects of cyber security knowledge on attack detection. *Computers in Human Behavior, 48*, 51–61.
6. Bi, J., Wu, J., & Leng, X., (2007). IPv4/IPv6 transition technologies and univer6 architecture. *International Journal of Computer Science and Network Security, 7*(1), 232–243.
7. Brooks, R. R., (2013). *Introduction to Computer and Network Security: Navigating Shades of Gray* (Vol. 1, pp. 2–6). CRC Press.
8. Caicedo, C. E., Joshi, J. B., & Tuladhar, S. R., (2009). IPv6 security challenges. *Computer, 42*(2), 36–42.
9. Choudhary, A. R., (2009). In-depth analysis of IPv6 security posture. In: *2009 5th International Conference on Collaborative Computing: Networking, Applications and Worksharing* (Vol. 1, pp. 1–7). IEEE.
10. Ciampa, M., (2012). Security+ guide to network security fundamentals. *Cengage Learning, 2*(1), 5–7.
11. Cohen, F., (1987). Computer viruses: Theory and experiments. *Computers & Security, 6*(1), 22–35.
12. Davies, D. W., & Price, W. L., (1984). *Security for Computer Networks: An Introduction to Data Security in Teleprocessing and Electronic Funds Transfer* (Vol. 1, pp. 2–4). John Wiley & Sons, Inc.
13. Daya, B., (2013). *Network Security: History, Importance, and Future* (Vol. 4, No. 2, pp. 5–8). University of Florida Department of Electrical and Computer Engineering.
14. Durdağı, E., & Buldu, A., (2010). IPV4/IPV6 security and threat comparisons. *Procedia-Social and Behavioral Sciences, 2*(2), 5285–5291.
15. Fraiji, Y., Azzouz, L. B., Trojet, W., & Saidane, L. A., (2018). Cyber security issues of Internet of electric vehicles. In: *2018 IEEE Wireless Communications and Networking Conference (WCNC)* (Vol. 1, pp. 1–6). IEEE.
16. François, J., Aib, I., & Boutaba, R., (2012). FireCol: A collaborative protection network for the detection of flooding DDoS attacks. *IEEE/ACM Transactions on Networking, 20*(6), 1828–1841.
17. Harahap, M. K., & Khairina, N., (2021). Copyright protection of scientific works using digital watermarking by embedding DOI QR code. *Journal of Computer Networks, Architecture and High Performance Computing, 3*(2), 234–240.
18. Landwehr, C. E., & Goldschlag, D. M., (1997). Security issues in networks with Internet access. *Proceedings of the IEEE, 85*(12), 2034–2051.
19. Lehtinen, R., & Gangemi, Sr. G. T., (2006). *Computer Security Basics: Computer Security* (Vol. 3, No. 1, pp. 7–9). "O'Reilly Media, Inc."

20. Liang, X., & Xiao, Y., (2012). Game theory for network security. *IEEE Communications Surveys & Tutorials, 15*(1), 472–486.
21. Lincke, S. J., & Holland, A., (2007). Network security: Focus on security, skills, and stability. In: *2007 37th Annual Frontiers in Education Conference-Global Engineering: Knowledge Without Borders, Opportunities Without Passports* (Vol. 1, p. F1D-10). IEEE.
22. Lye, K. W., & Wing, J. M., (2005). Game strategies in network security. *International Journal of Information Security, 4*, 71–86.
23. Marin, G. A., (2005). Network security basics. *IEEE Security & Privacy, 3*(6), 68–72.
24. Menell, P. S., (1986). Tailoring legal protection for computer software. *Stan. L. Rev., 39*(1), 1329.
25. Menell, P. S., (2017). Rise of the API copyright dead: An updated epitaph for copyright protection of network and functional features of computer software. *Harv. JL & Tech., 31*(1), 305.
26. Mullender, S. J., & Tanenbaum, A. S., (1984). Protection and resource control in distributed operating systems. *Computer Networks (1976), 8*(5, 6), 421–432.
27. Nguyen, G., Dlugolinsky, S., Tran, V., & García, Á. L., (2020). Deep learning for proactive network monitoring and security protection. *IEEE Access, 8*, 19696–19716.
28. Ohta, T., & Chikaraishi, T., (1993). Network security model. In: *Proceedings of IEEE Singapore International Conference on Networks/International Conference on Information Engineering'93* (Vol. 2, pp. 507–511). IEEE.
29. Onwubiko, C., (2009). Functional requirements of situational awareness in computer network security. In: *2009 IEEE International Conference on Intelligence and Security Informatics* (Vol. 1, pp. 209–213). IEEE.
30. Pawar, M. V., & Anuradha, J., (2015). Network security and types of attacks in network. *Procedia Computer Science, 48*, 503–506.
31. Posey, C., Roberts, T. L., Lowry, P. B., & Hightower, R. T., (2014). Bridging the divide: A qualitative comparison of information security thought patterns between information security professionals and ordinary organizational insiders. *Information & Management, 51*(5), 551–567.
32. Radhakrishnan, R., Jamil, M., Mehfuz, S., & Moinuddin, M., (2007). Security issues in IPv6. In: *International Conference on Networking and Services (ICNS'07)* (Vol. 1, p. 110). IEEE.
33. Roy, S., Ellis, C., Shiva, S., Dasgupta, D., Shandilya, V., & Wu, Q., (2010). A survey of game theory as applied to network security. In: *2010 43rd Hawaii International Conference on System Sciences* (Vol. 1, pp. 1–10). IEEE.
34. Rutledge, L. S., & Hoffman, L. J., (1986). A survey of issues in computer network security. *Computers & Security, 5*(4), 296–308.
35. Sergent, R. S., (1995). A fourth amendment model for computer networks and data privacy. *Va. L. Rev., 81*, 1181.

36. Shanmugaraja, P., & Chandrasekar, S., (2012). Accessible methods to mitigate security attacks on ipv4 to ipv6 transitions. *European Journal of Scientific Research, 77*(2), 165–173.

37. Shiranzaei, A., & Khan, R. Z., (2018). IPv6 security issues—A systematic review. *Next-Generation Networks: Proceedings of CSI-2015,* 41–49.

38. Strebe, M., (2006). *Network Security Foundations: Technology Fundamentals for IT Success* (Vol. 4, No. 1, pp. 7–10). John Wiley & Sons.

39. Stytz, M. R., & Whittaker, J. A., (2003). Software protection: Security's last stand? *IEEE Security & Privacy, 1*(1), 95–98.

40. Szigeti, S., & Risztics, P., (2004). Will IPv6 bring better security? In: *Proceedings 30th Euromicro Conference, 2004* (Vol. 1, pp. 532–537). IEEE.

41. Ullrich, J., Krombholz, K., Hobel, H., Dabrowski, A., & Weippl, E., (2014). IPv6 security: Attacks and countermeasures in a nutshell. In: *8th {USENIX} Workshop on Offensive Technologies {WOOT}, 14*(1), 7–11.

42. Wählisch, M., Schmidt, T. C., & Vahlenkamp, M., (2013). Backscatter from the data plane–threats to stability and security in information-centric network infrastructure. *Computer Networks, 57*(16), 3192–3206.

43. White, G. B., Fisch, E. A., & Pooch, U. W., (1995). *Computer System and Network Security* (Vol. 7, pp. 2–8). CRC press.

44. Wolf, G., & Pfitzmann, A., (2000). Properties of protection goals and their integration into a user interface. *Computer Networks, 32*(6), 685–700.

45. Yang, X., Ma, T., & Shi, Y., (2007). Typical DoS/DDoS threats under ipv6. In: *2007 International Multi-Conference on Computing in the Global Information Technology (ICCGI'07)* (Vol. 1, p. 55). IEEE.

46. Žagar, D., Grgić, K., & Rimac-Drlje, S., (2007). Security aspects in IPv6 networks–implementation and testing. *Computers & Electrical Engineering, 33*(5, 6), 425–437.

47. Zhuang, R., Zhang, S., Bardas, A., DeLoach, S. A., Ou, X., & Singhal, A., (2013). Investigating the application of moving target defenses to network security. In: *2013 6th International Symposium on Resilient Control Systems (ISRCS)* (Vol. 1, pp. 162–169). IEEE.

CHAPTER 5

WIRELESS NETWORKING

UNIT INTRODUCTION

Equipment that enables multiple computers to interact using common network protocols but without network cables is known as wireless networking (Zhang et al., 2019). Any technique that accomplishes this might technically be referred to as wireless networking. The first analog cellphone introduced the idea of wireless technology into the world.

The aforementioned technologies are collectively known as 11.5G, omitting analog, and are viewed as rival technologies because each is anticipated to release fiercely competitive products, according to industry analysts (Bernardos et al., 2014). However, the present lingo typically refers to LANs that are wireless. This technology, driven by the rise of cross-vendor industry norms like "IEEE 802.11," has shaped several accessible wireless solutions that are gaining popularity in businesses and educational institutions and in complex applications where web wiring is impossible, like in warehouse operations or point-of-sale handheld devices.

Learning Objectives

At the end of this chapter, readers will be able to learn the following:

- Various types of wireless links;
- Different types of wireless networks;
- Various standards of WLAN;
- Different elements of the wireless networks;
- Electromagnetic interference in wireless networks.

Key Terms

- Communication
- Connection
- Electromagnetic interference
- Radio
- Reflection
- Safety
- Security
- Space network
- Technologies
- Wireless

5.1. WIRELESS LINKS

The wireless connections are listed in subsections.

5.1.1. Terrestrial Microwave

In order to carry out terrestrial microwave communication, earth-based transmitters and receivers resembling satellites are utilized. The low gigahertz frequency of terrestrial microwaves makes it so that communication can only take place in a direct line with the source. The distance between each relay station is around 48 kilometers (30 miles) (Zamalloa & Krishnamachari, 2007) (Figure 5.1).

Figure 5.1. Illustration of the terrestrial microwave technology.

Source: Teachoo, Creative Commons License.

Remember

Cellular and PCS systems work together to provide wireless communication for mobile devices.

5.1.2. Cellular and PCS systems

They use a variety of different methods for radio transmission. The systems divide the territory that is covered into a number of distinct geographical areas (Davis et al., 2003). Each region is equipped with a radio relay antenna and a low-powered transceiver so that calls can be transmitted from one area to the next.

5.1.3. Radio and Spread Spectrum Technologies

Wireless local area networks utilize both low-frequency radio communication and high-frequency radio technologies, very similar to digital cellular networks. Wireless local area networks make use of spread spectrum technology to make it easier for a large number of devices to communicate with one another inside a confined location (Xylomenos et al., 2001). IEEE 802.11 is the standard that defines Wi-Fi, which is a widely used radio communication technology that uses open standards.

5.1.4. Free-Space Optical Communication

This makes use of either visible or invisible light for the purpose of communication (Balakrishnan et al., 1997). In most cases, line-of-sight propagation is used, which places limitations on the precise locations where communication equipment can be located.

5.2. TYPES OF WIRELESS NETWORKS

An ad hoc wireless network, also known as a peer-to-peer network, is made up of numerous computers, each of which has a wireless networking interface card. This type of network is also known as a mesh network (Chen et al., 2019). Direct communication is feasible between any computer and any other computer that possesses wireless technology, provided both computers are in the same physical location. Because of this, they are able to share files and printers; however, it is possible that they will not be able to access resources on a wired Network unless one of the computers uses specialized software to act as a bridge to the wired LAN. Although they are able to share files and printers, they may not be able to access resources on a wired Network. The phenomenon in question is referred to as "bridging" (Shen & Zeng, 2008).

A wireless network may make use of an AP, which is also known as a base station in some contexts. Within this particular network, the AP serves as a central point of communication for wireless personal computers. It is possible to connect the wireless LAN to a conventional LAN in order to provide wireless PCs with access to LAN resources such as file servers and pre-existing Internet connectivity (Sakarindr & Ansari, 2007).

A wireless connection between a client computer and an AP can only be maintained within a specific range for each AP. Manufacturers often list indoor and outdoor ranges to give a good approximation of dependable performance, even if the distance varies depending on the situation. Also, it should be understood that performance may suffer when working at the range's limitations because the system adjusts as the connection quality degrades.

The typical interior ranges are between 150 and 300 feet; however, they may be less if the building's structure interferes with radio signals. Although longer ranges are feasible, performance will suffer as distance increases.

The manufacturer determines the individual AP capacity. The recommended maximum for some hardware entry points is 10, whereas the maximum supported by much more premium APs is 100 wireless connections (Kumar & Gambhir, 2014). Performance and dependability will suffer if you use more computers than is advised.

User restrictions may also be imposed through software APs; however, this depends on the software and the host computer's processing power.

5.2.1. Wireless PAN

WPANs communicate with other devices in a region that is typically within the reach of a person and are fairly modest in size. [3] When a headset is attached to a laptop, for instance, the laptop gives forth inaudible emissions of infrared light, which illustrates a WPAN that is offered by Bluetooth wireless. In addition to this, ZigBee is compatible with WPAN applications (Biswas et al., 2015). In 2010, Wi-Fi PANs (personal area networks) started to become the industry standard as product designers began incorporating Wi-Fi into an increasing number of consumer electronic devices. The "virtual Wi-Fi" features of Windows 7 and the "My Wi-Fi" feature of Intel have helped to simplify the process of setting up and configuring Wi-Fi PANs (Shakkottai et al., 2003) (Figure 5.2).

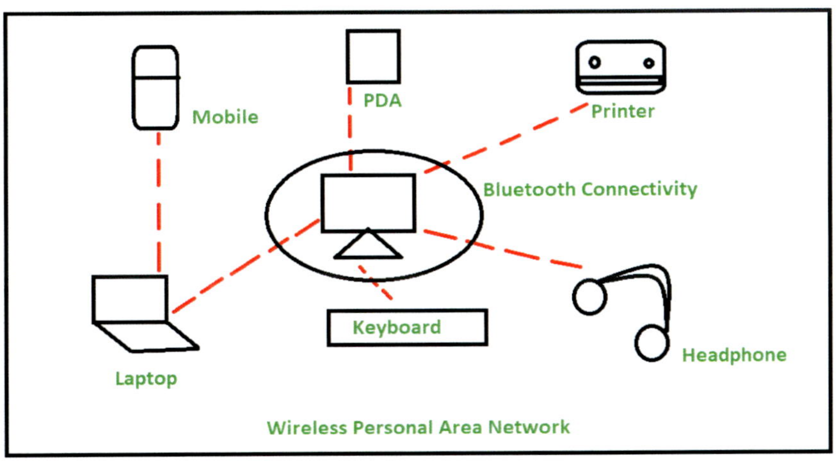

Figure 5.2. Illustration of the WPANs communication.

Source: Geeks for Geeks, Creative Commons License.

5.2.2. Wireless LAN

A wireless local area network, more often known as a WLAN, is a type of network that connects several devices over a relatively short distance using a wireless distribution mechanism. WLANs typically offer an AP through which users can connect to the Internet (Dekleva et al., 2007). Spread spectrum and OFDM (orthogonal frequency division multiplexing) are two technologies that let users to move freely within a limited-service area while maintaining their connection to the network.

TIPS

Secure your wireless network with strong passwords, MAC address filtering, and encryption to prevent unauthorized access and data theft.

Products sold under the Wi-Fi brand are guaranteed to meet the requirements of the IEEE 802.11 WLAN standard. Fixed wireless technology establishes point-to-point communications between computer networks or other electronic devices located at two separate remote locations by sending dedicated microwave or modified laser light beams through line-of-sight pathways (Andrews et al., 2010). It is commonly used in urban areas to connect devices located in two or even more buildings without the usage of a cable connection.

5.2.3. Wireless WAN

Wide areas are generally covered by wireless wide-area networks, such as between cities or towns close to one another or between a city and a suburb.

Figure 5.3. Schematic of the wireless WAN.

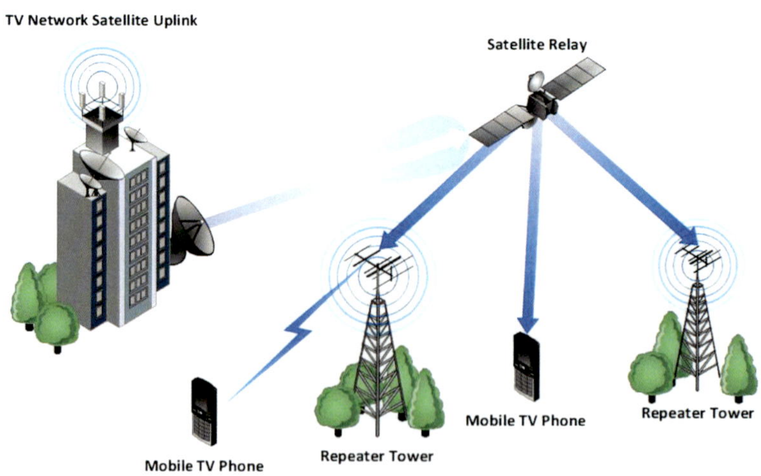

Source: Concept Draw, Creative Commons License.

These systems can be utilized as a community internet access system or to connect commercial branch offices. Instead of the antenna arrays used with smaller networks, the transmitter and receiver between APs are typically point-to-point microwave communications employing conical dishes on the 2.4 GHz band (Varshney & Jain, 2001). Ground station gateways, APs, and wireless bridging relays are common system components. Mesh systems are another design in which each AP also serves as a relay. They can function as stand-alone systems with renewable energy sources like solar or wind power (Figure 5.3).

5.2.4. Cellular Network

A cellular network, also called a mobile network, is a radio channel that is dispersed over sections of land cells is called and is linked to at least one fixed transceiver, often known to as a base station or cell site (Ko et al., 2010). Another name for a cellular network is a mobile network. Every cell in a cell connection will often use distinctive radio signals from its immediate neighbors in order to avoid interfering with one another.

When connected to one another, these cells provide radio coverage for a substantial portion of the earth's landmass. Because of this, it is feasible for a large number of portable transceivers to connect with one another, with stationary transceivers, and with telephones through base stations, irrespective of the fact that certain transceivers are moving through a large number of cells while they are transmitting (Chen et al., 2017).

The first generation of cellular telephone networks were only intended to support voice conversations. Nevertheless, with the proliferation of smartphones, these networks now also routinely convey data in addition to voice calls:

5.2.4.1. Global System for Mobile Communications (GSM)

Switching, base station, and operation and support are the three main systems that make up the GSM network (Maraiya et al., 2011). The mobile phone links to the rule base station, which links to the management and support station. From there, it connects to the switchboard, where the call is routed to its destination. The vast majority of mobile phones use the GSM protocol, which is the most widely used one (Figure 5.4).

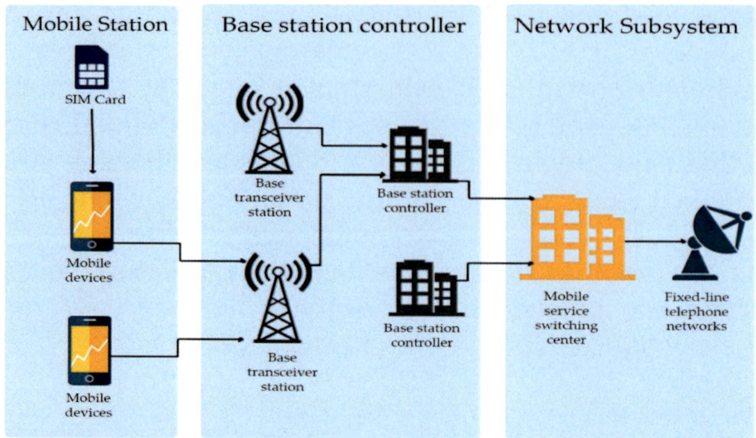

Figure 5.4. Illustration of the working of a GSM network.

Source: Spice Works, Creative Commons License.

5.2.4.2. Personal Communications Service (PCS)

Mobile phones in South Asia and North America can use the PCS radio band (Khan & Pathan, 2013). Interestingly, Sprint was the first provider to establish a PCS.

5.2.4.3. D-AMPS

Due to technological advancements, Virtual Advanced Mobile Phone Service, an enhanced version of AMPS, is being phased out. Older systems are being replaced by more recent GSM networks.

5.2.5. Global Area Network

Did you Know?

Global area network (GAN) is a telecommunications network that extends coverage to allow mobile devices to roam beyond the boundaries of a single wireless network.

A network that supports mobile across various wireless LANs, cellular coverage areas, etc., is called a GAN (global area network). The transfer of includes technologies from one local service area to the next is the main difficulty in mobile communications. This is a series of terrestrial wireless LANs under IEEE Project 802 (Sharma & Dhir, 2014).

5.2.6. Space Network

Space networks allow spacecraft to communicate with one another, typically close to the Earth (Shuaib et al., 2006). NASA's Space Network is one instance of this.

5.3. WLAN STANDARDS

The usage of radio frequencies and data transmission-related underpinning technology is necessary for wireless networking gear. The Institute of Electrical and Electronic Engineers established the 802.11 standards, the most frequently adopted (IEEE). This is a specification that covers every facet of radio frequency wireless networking (Pahlavan et al., 1997).

IEEE adopted the comprehensive set of specifications known as 802.11 in 1999. The following three signal transmission techniques underlie the operation of the technologies covered by the 802.11 standards:

5.3.1. DSSS

For the direct sequence ***s***pread ***s***pectrum, use the acronym. The other sort of spread spectrum radio is frequency-hopping spread spectrum, and DSSS is one of them. In DSSS, a data signal is paired with a greater rate of the data bit sequence, or chipped code, at the sending station to divide the user data into segments based on a spreading ratio (Ge et al., 2004). With every bit broadcast, the chipping code creates a redundant bit pattern, increasing the signal's resilience to interference. Due to the redundancy of the transmission, even if one or more bits in the pattern are broken during transmission, the original data can still be recovered.

5.3.2. OFDM

For large-scale digital data transmission over a radio wave, also known as orthogonal frequency division multiplexing. For OFDM to function, the radio signal must be divided into numerous small communities simultaneously delivered to the receiver at various frequencies. Crosstalk, a disturbance brought on by electromagnetic interference (EMI), is lessened using OFDM in signal transmissions. There are currently three IEEE 802.11 standards: 802.11b, 802.11a, and 802.11g.

5.3.3. 802.11 b

The 802.11b technology, also referred to as 802.11 high-rate or Wi-Fi ('wireless fidelity'), was authorized by the IEEE in 1999 and is presently the most widely used technology by makers of wireless devices. The 802.11b specification states that chip sets would transmit digital signals at 11 Mbps (megabits per second) across an unlicensed spectrum section at roughly 2.4 GHz using a modulation technique called CCK (complementary code keying) (Sidhu et al., 2007). The 802.11b standard, considered innovative at the time, paved the way for a new generation of products that finally allowed an Ethernet connection to be wire-free. However, the speed was still only one-tenth that of its wired counterparts. DSSS is the operating system for 802.11b.

Several corporations have backed the 802.11b standard, including Microsoft, Cisco, Alcatel, Agere Systems, and the other 120 WECA members (Wireless Ethernet Compatibility Alliance). Supporting businesses released several 802.11b-based products that, despite ongoing general wireless security issues, have been well-received by users (Park & Dicoi, 2003).

5.3.4. 802.11 a

The 802.11a standard was approved at the same time as 802.11b. Because 802.11a uses the OFDM method for signal transmission, 802.11b devices cannot be used with it. The 802.11a standard uses the 5GHz frequency range and provides a speed of 54 Mbps (Van Nee et al., 1999).

The standard has changed significantly since its debut in 1999 due to the public's skewed focus and the decreased number of supporting businesses. Intel and 3Com announced the launch of a line of products based on 802.11a in September 2001. Smaller businesses released several niche-specific support items.

5.3.5. 802.11 g

KEYWORD

Technology is the application of knowledge for achieving practical goals in a reproducible way.

The overarching Working Group of the IEEE that supervised the creation of 802.11 delegated various duties to many specialty groups, each with the goal of advancing the technology even further. This was done so that the 802.11 standards might be improved. The purpose of 802.11g was to increase the data transfer to "turbo" frequencies of 54 Mbps while yet preserving interoperability with older specifications (Yeh et al., 2003). Consumers, as well as enterprise users, sellers, investors, and pretty much everyone else who invested in previous versions of the technology, would be able to gain an understanding of how the market will eventually develop by using this method.

Yet, the path toward the following generation was fraught with difficulties as it went. After a proposal put forth by National Instruments was eliminated from contention in May, Task Group G, which is comprised of approximately 175 people, split into two distinct camps as a result of this development. Despite the fact they had been operating on this proposal for years, this proposal was ultimately rejected. They ensured that their modulation method, which is known as Packet Binary Convolution Coding (PBCC), became an acceptable alternative to the CCK schema in order to guarantee complete backward capability. They went so far as to spend $300 million on the acquisition of a business (Alantro Communications) that was instrumental in the creation of PBCC (Siddiqui et al., 2015).

In the end, on November 16, 2001, the IEEE voted to accept the new 802.11g standard, which claims to give a bandwidth of 20–54 MBps in the 2.4GHz band. This decision came after protracted deliberations.

5.4. DIFFERENT USES OF WIRELESS NETWORKS

Cellular phones, which are a part of common wireless networks and enable simple personal conversations, are some examples of usage. Intercontinental network systems are another instance that employs radio satellites for global communication. Wireless networks are also used by emergency services like the police to communicate effectively (Li et al., 2003). Wireless networks are used by people and businesses to transfer and share data quickly, whether they are in tiny office buildings or all over the world.

Remember

A satellite radio service works by transmitting its signal from a ground-based station to one or more satellites orbiting Earth.

5.4.1. General

Wireless networks provide many uses for users at home and in business (Bui et al., 2013). "At the moment, the industry embraces a variety of wireless technologies. Each mobile technology is described by a guideline that details certain operations at the OSI Model's Physical and Data Connection levels. These standards vary, among other things, in the signaling techniques they specify, the geographic bounds, and the frequency usages. Due to these variations, some technologies may be more appropriate for use in residential networks than others in networks for bigger enterprises."

5.4.2. Performance

Each standard has a different geographic coverage area, so depending on what one wants to achieve with a wireless network, one standard may be preferable to another (Niknam et al., 2022). Applications like speech and video are satisfied by the performance of Wi-Fi communication. The adoption of this technology also allows for future developments, such as the transition from 2G to 3G and, most recently, 4G, or the fourth generation of mobile communications standards. As the widespread use of wireless networking, network hardware, and software configurations become more sophisticated, resulting in an increased ability to send and receive faster and larger volumes of data (Iwata et al., 1999).

5.4.3. Space

Another aspect of wireless networking is space. When trying to communicate across a bridge or river, in a warehouse on the opposing side of the premises, or between two buildings that are distinct but function as one, wireless networks have many advantages. Users of wireless networks can specify a specific area where the connection can communicate with other devices. In addition to freeing up space, homes with less wire clutter have more space (Tang & Baker, 2000). This technique provides an alternative to establishing physical network media, which can be costly and include TPs, coaxes, and fiber-optic cables (Figure 5.5).

Figure 5.5. Illustration of the use of wireless networking in space.

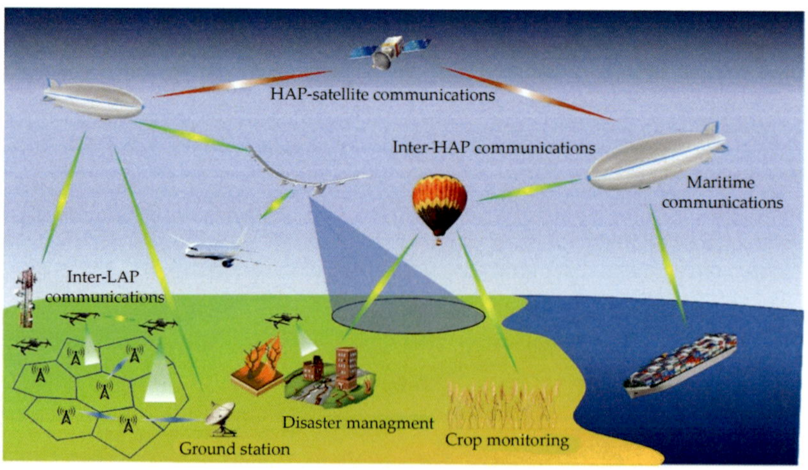

Source: Francesco et al., Creative Commons License.

5.4.4. Home

Wireless technology gives homes a more effective way to share high-speed internet connections, printers, and scanners than ethernet. WLANs make it easier for networked devices to move around while also cutting down on the expense and difficulty of installing cable media physically (Solis et al., 2006). Wireless networks are simple to set up and require a single AP linked via a router directly to the Internet (Bruno, 2007).

5.4.5. Time Savings

The most significant and obvious benefit of using WLAN is the amount of time that may be saved. According to the findings of a study conducted by the Wireless Industry's Information Source, a user of a wireless LAN can save up to eight hours per week when compared to a user of a traditional LAN. The amount of money that users save on a weekly basis might range anywhere from $30 to $750 (Lin et al., 2010). It is fascinating to note that the greatest time savings can be achieved by catching up on e-mails and retrieving data from the local area network (LAN) without having to engage in conversation with other employees. An example of this would be a nurse who is stationed at a specific level of a hospital and is required to view a patient's medical records. It is possible that she will utilize a wireless device so that she may obtain the information on her own, without having to call the receptionist or another aide.

KEYWORD

A **local area network (LAN)** is a network contained within a small geographic area, usually within the same building.

5.4.6. Flexibility and Quality of Work

Some of the unquantifiable "soft" benefits that influence WLAN adoption are quality and flexibility. Users using wireless LANs can connect to the LAN from several locations both within and outside of their facilities (Haas et al., 2017). Thanks to the extensive coverage, users have the freedom to stay connected to the network and be mobile simultaneously. The degree of flexibility will, of course, depend on the diversity of places where wireless APs are located, but users of wireless LANs are aware of the increased productivity and convenience provided by being able to connect to the network from a range of locations.

The advantages in work quality that wireless LAN users highlight are mostly the result of increased precision. Data can now be sent directly from multiple locations utilizing a wireless LAN rather than having to be manually entered at a later time.

5.5. ELECTROMAGNETIC INTERFERENCE (EMI) IN WIRELESS NETWORKS

Wireless networks commonly experience EMI in comparison to wired ones. Other networks or equipment that produce radio waves within or near the radio bands used for communication may be the source. The signal may suffer from interference, and the system may malfunction (Figure 5.6).

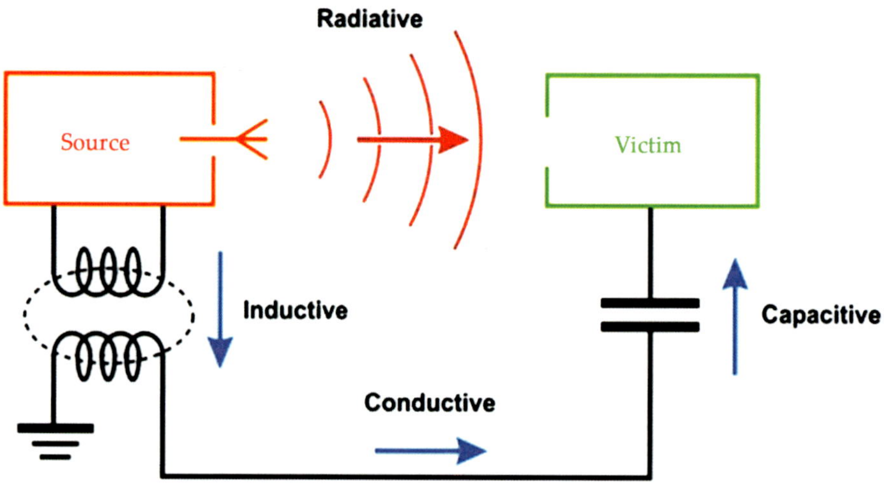

Figure 5.6. Example diagram showing electromagnetic interference to highlight inductive, conductive, capacitive, and radiative EMI in a system.

Source: Colin Zauner, Creative Commons License.

5.5.1. Absorption and Reflection

Electromagnetic waves can be absorbed by some materials, preventing them from reaching the receiver, although they can also be reflected, especially by metallic or conductive materials (Liao et al., 2017). Dead zones with no reception may result from this. Modern homes' aluminum foiled thermal insulation can easily lower inside mobile signal levels by 10 dB, which usually results in complaints about trouble receiving long-distance rural cell signals.

5.5.2. Multipath Fading

Due to reflections, the signal might travel two or more separate paths during multipath fading, which can cause the signal to cancel out in some places and become stronger in others (upgrade) (Komine & Nakagawa, 2003).

5.5.3. Hidden Node Problem

In some types of networks, the hidden node problem arises when a network is accessible from a mobile AP yet hidden by other nodes corresponding with that AP. This makes media access control challenging.

5.5.4. Shared Resource Problem

Every node within the range of a wireless transmitter shares a finite amount of spectrum. The distribution of bandwidth becomes complicated when numerous users are involved (Batur et al., 2008). Users frequently are unaware that advertised capacities are shared by all users and not just them; therefore, the actual individual user rate is much lower. The capacity constraint is becoming more and more likely as demand rises. Over-provisioning may not always need updating to newer technologies; instead, user-in-the-loop (UIL) may be an alternative.

5.5.5. Network

The total network bandwidth is affected by the dispersion of the medium (a more dispersed medium typically has a better total frequency band since it minimizes interference), the number of frequencies available, the noise level of those frequencies, the number of aerials used, the use of a directional antenna, the use of power control by nodes, and other factors (Çiftçi et al., 2022).

Due to the use of directional aerials and the flexibility to reuse radio frequencies in non-adjacent cells, cellular wireless networks typically have good capacity. Also, by utilizing low-power transmitters, it is possible to create very small cells, which are employed in cities to provide network capacity that scales linearly with population density.

KEYWORD

Network bandwidth is a measure of the data transfer rate or capacity of a given network.

5.5.6. Safety

Even though the power of wireless signals rapidly diminishes with distance according to the inverse square law, wireless APs are routinely situated in close proximity to people. Wi-Fi is more likely to cause lower radio frequency (RF) exposures than mobile phones, as reported by the Health Protection Agency (HPA) of the United Kingdom. In addition, it came to the conclusion that there was "no reason why schools and other organizations should not use Wi-Fi equipment" (Loyka, 2004). In October 2007, on behalf of the United Kingdom government, the HPA launched a new "systematic" examination of the effects that Wi-Fi networks had in order to assuage concerns that had been raised in the media in recent times up until that point. According to Dr. Michael Clark of HPA, the published study on mobile phones and masts does not form a case against Wi-Fi.

5.5.7. Security Concerns

Wireless communications raise potential security risks because an attacker does not need physical access to an existing wired network in order to view data transfers (Stenumgaard, 2006). This is in contrast to wired networks. Nevertheless, straightforward analyzers and short-wave receivers, among other devices, are unable to even detect 802.11 wireless signals, let alone decipher them. Because of this, there is a common misunderstanding that it is not possible to eavesdrop on wireless conversations. Eavesdropping is still possible, but it requires the use of specific equipment in order to do it.

KEYWORD

Wireless communications is the transmission of voice and data without cable or wires.

To protect against potential vulnerabilities in network security, 802.11 wireless communications include a feature known as WEP (Wired Equivalent Privacy). WEP is a form of encryption that provides users with a level of privacy that is analogous to that provided by a conventional wired network (Kaur et al., 2011). If the wireless network contains data that needs to be protected, WEP should be used to ensure that the data is protected at levels comparable to those seen in traditional wired networks. This is because WEP ensures that the data is protected at levels similar to those seen in traditional wired networks. In recent months, a number of market companies have made secure wireless solutions available. On September 12, 2001, for instance, Harrison Communications presented its SecNet-11 to the public as a solution for use by the government and the military. The National Security Agency has already given its blessing to the implementation of this technology (Figure 5.7).

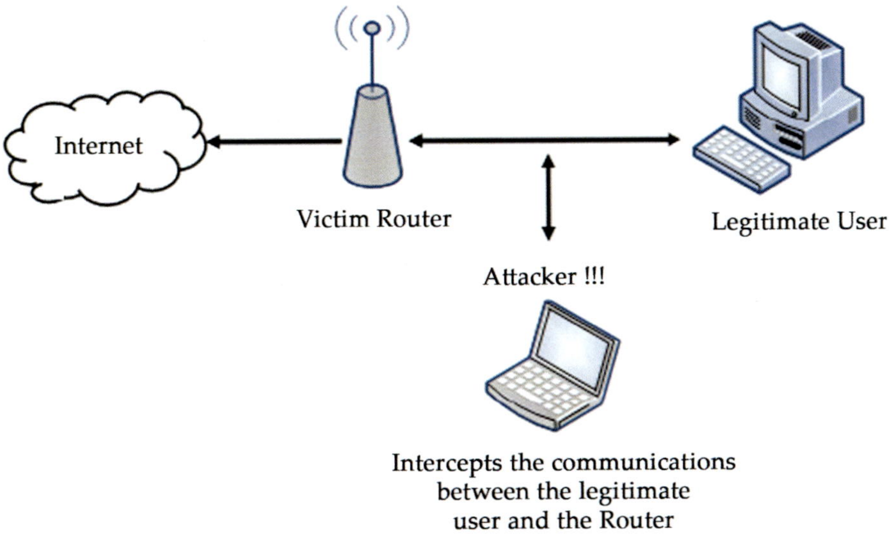

Figure 5.7. Schematic of the wired equivalent privacy.

Source: Ali M. Alsahlany, Creative Commons License.

ACTIVITY 5.1.

How have you implemented wireless networking in a large organization, and what measures have you taken to ensure the security of wireless devices and data?

5.5.8. Economic Impact

Whether deciding whether to build wireless LANs or not, most IT professionals are trying to determine whether the advantages will outweigh the disadvantages. The desire of end users to adopt the technology will be crucial to its success (Lapinsky & Easty, 2006). While more adaptability, efficiency, and accuracy are acknowledged as possible advantages, it is exceedingly challenging to estimate the cost savings from employing WLANs.

5.6. SUMMARY

A wide range of subjects relating to wireless technology is covered in the article on Wireless Networks. The chapter's learning goals cover wireless network types, WLAN standards, wireless network components, and electromagnetic fields in wireless networks. The chapter explains several wireless link types, including IR, RF, and microwave. It discusses the variations between these links and how they are used in wireless communication. Also, several wireless network types, such as wireless personal area networks (WPAN), wireless local area networks (WLAN), wireless metropolitan area networks (WMAN), and wireless wide area networks, are covered in the chapter (WWAN). Each network type's function and applications are described in detail in this chapter. The chapter also covers the IEEE 802.11a, 802.11b, 802.11g, 802.11n, and 802.11ac WLAN protocols. It describes the variations in speed, frequency, and range between various standards. There is also a discussion of the various components of wireless networks, including APs, routers, and adapters. The function of each component in establishing a wireless network and enabling wireless communication is discussed in detail in this chapter. The chapter concludes with an explanation of EMI, which can harm wireless networks. It talks about the effects of EMI on wireless communication and its sources, including radio waves, power lines, and electronic gadgets. Also, the chapter describes methods to lower EMI in wireless networks.

REVIEW QUESTIONS

1. Explain the different types of wireless networks.
2. What are the various types of wireless links? Describe each of them.
3. What are the different WLAN standards? How do they differ from each other?
4. What are the elements of a wireless network? Explain their functions.
5. What is electromagnetic interference? How can it affect wireless communication?
6. Explain how to reduce electromagnetic interference in wireless networks.
7. How can wireless networks be secured? Explain different security measures for wireless networks.
8. What is the role of Access Points (AP) in wireless networks?
9. How can you improve the performance of a wireless network?

MULTIPLE CHOICE QUESTIONS

1. Which of the following is not a type of wireless network?

a. WPAN

b. WLAN

c. WMAN

d. LAN

2. **Which of the following is the standard for wireless networking?**
   a. IEEE 802.3
   b. IEEE 802.11
   c. IEEE 802.1x
   d. IEEE 802.2
3. **Which type of wireless link uses radio waves to transmit data?**
   a. Infrared
   b. Microwave
   c. Radio Frequency
   d. None of the above
4. **Which of the following is an element of a wireless network?**
   a. Access Points (AP)
   b. Modem
   c. Ethernet cable
   d. All of the above
5. **Which of the following can cause electromagnetic interference in wireless networks?**
   a. Power lines
   b. Electronic devices
   c. Radio signals
   d. All of the above
6. **Which IEEE standard provides the highest speed for WLAN?**
   a. 802.11a
   b. 802.11b
   c. 802.11n
   d. 802.11ac
7. **Which type of wireless network is designed to provide internet access over a large geographical area?**
   a. WPAN
   b. WLAN
   c. WMAN
   d. WWAN

Answers to the Multiple-Choice Questions

1. (d); 2. (b); 3. (c); 4. (a); 5. (d) 6. (d) 7. (d)

REFERENCES

1. Andrews, J. G., Ganti, R. K., Haenggi, M., Jindal, N., & Weber, S., (2010). A primer on spatial modeling and analysis in wireless networks. *IEEE Communications Magazine, 48*(11), 156–163.
2. Balakrishnan, H., Padmanabhan, V. N., Seshan, S., & Katz, R. H., (1997). A comparison of mechanisms for improving TCP performance over wireless links. *IEEE/ACM Transactions on Networking, 5*(6), 756–769.
3. Batur, O. Z., Koca, M., & Dundar, G., (2008). Measurements of impulsive noise in broad-band wireless communication channels. In: 2008 *Ph.D. Research in Microelectronics and Electronics* (Vol. 1, pp. 233–236). IEEE.
4. Bernardos, C. J., De La Oliva, A., Serrano, P., Banchs, A., Contreras, L. M., Jin, H., & Zúñiga, J. C., (2014). An architecture for software defined wireless networking. *IEEE Wireless Communications, 21*(3), 52–61.
5. Biswas, S., Bicket, J., Wong, E., Musaloiu-e, R., Bhartia, A., & Aguayo, D., (2015). Large-scale measurements of wireless network behavior. In: *Proceedings of the 2015 ACM Conference on Special Interest Group on Data Communication* (Vol. 1, pp. 153–165).
6. Bruno, J., (2007). *Interference Reduction in Wireless Networks* (Vol. 1, pp. 5–9). Computing Research Topics, Computing Sciences Department, Villanova University.
7. Bui, D. H., Lee, K., Oh, S., Shin, I., Shin, H., Woo, H., & Ban, D., (2013). Greenbag: Energy-efficient bandwidth aggregation for real-time streaming in heterogeneous mobile wireless networks. In: *2013 IEEE 34th Real-Time Systems Symposium* (Vol. 1, pp. 57–67). IEEE.
8. Chen, M., Challita, U., Saad, W., Yin, C., & Debbah, M., (2017). *Machine Learning for Wireless Networks with Artificial Intelligence: A Tutorial on Neural Networks, 4*(1), 4–7.
9. Chen, M., Challita, U., Saad, W., Yin, C., & Debbah, M., (2019). Artificial neural networks-based machine learning for wireless networks: A tutorial. *IEEE Communications Surveys & Tutorials, 21*(4), 3039–3071.
10. Çiftçi, B., Gross, J., Augustin, T., Wang, X., Norrga, S., & Nee, H. P., (2022). Wireless communication in modular multilevel converters and electromagnetic interference characterization. *IEEE Access, 10*(1), 38189–38201.
11. Davis, C. C., Smolyaninov, I. I., & Milner, S. D., (2003). Flexible optical wireless links and networks. *IEEE Communications Magazine, 41*(3), 51–57.
12. Dekleva, S., Shim, J. P., Varshney, U., & Knoerzer, G., (2007). Evolution and emerging issues in mobile wireless networks. *Communications of the ACM, 50*(6), 38–43.
13. Ge, Y., Esselle, K. P., & Bird, T. S., (2004). E-shaped patch antennas for high-speed wireless networks. *IEEE Transactions on Antennas and Propagation, 52*(12), 3213–3219.

14. Haas, H., Chen, C., & O'Brien, D., (2017). A guide to wireless networking by light. *Progress in Quantum Electronics, 55,* 88–111.
15. Iwata, A., Chiang, C. C., Pei, G., Gerla, M., & Chen, T. W., (1999). Scalable routing strategies for ad hoc wireless networks. *IEEE Journal on Selected Areas in Communications, 17*(8), 1369–1379.
16. Kaur, M., Kakar, S., & Mandal, D., (2011). Electromagnetic interference. In: *2011 3rd International Conference on Electronics Computer Technology* (Vol. 4, pp. 1–5). IEEE.
17. Khan, S., & Pathan, A. K., (2013). *Wireless Networks and Security* (Vol. 10, pp. 369–402). Springer.
18. Ko, J., Lu, C., Srivastava, M. B., Stankovic, J. A., Terzis, A., & Welsh, M., (2010). Wireless sensor networks for healthcare. *Proceedings of the IEEE, 98*(11), 1947–1960.
19. Komine, T., & Nakagawa, M., (2003). Integrated system of white LED visible-light communication and power-line communication. *IEEE Transactions on Consumer Electronics, 49*(1), 71–79.
20. Kumar, U., & Gambhir, S., (2014). A literature review of security threats to wireless networks. *International Journal of Future Generation Communication and Networking, 7*(4), 25–34.
21. Lapinsky, S. E., & Easty, A. C., (2006). Electromagnetic interference in critical care. *Journal of Critical Care, 21*(3), 267–270.
22. Li, X. Y., Calinescu, G., Wan, P. J., & Wang, Y., (2003). Localized Delaunay triangulation with application in ad hoc wireless networks. *IEEE Transactions on Parallel and Distributed Systems, 14*(10), 1035–1047.
23. Liao, W., Shi, J., & Wang, J., (2017). Electromagnetic interference of wireless power transfer system on wearable electrocardiogram. *IET Microwaves, Antennas & Propagation, 11*(3), 330–335.
24. Lin, Y., Shao, L., Zhu, Z., Wang, Q., & Sabhikhi, R. K., (2010). Wireless network cloud: Architecture and system requirements. *IBM Journal of Research and Development, 54*(1), 1-4.
25. Loyka, S., (2004). Electromagnetic interference in wireless communications: Behavioral-level simulation approach. In: *IEEE 60th Vehicular Technology Conference, 2004; VTC2004-Fall 2004* (Vol. 6, pp. 3945–3949). IEEE.
26. Maraiya, K., Kant, K., & Gupta, N., (2011). Application based study on wireless sensor network. *International Journal of Computer Applications, 21*(8), 9–15.
27. Moscibroda, T., & Wattenhofer, R., (2006). The complexity of connectivity in wireless networks. In: *INFOCOM 2006: 25th Annual Joint Conference of the IEEE Computer and Communications Societies* (Vol. 1, pp. 5–8). Barcelona, Spain.
28. Niknam, S., Roy, A., Dhillon, H. S., Singh, S., Banerji, R., Reed, J. H., & Yoon, S., (2022). Intelligent O-RAN for beyond 5G and 6G wireless networks. In: *2022 IEEE Globecom Workshops (GC Wkshps)* (Vol. 1, pp. 215–220). IEEE.

29. Pahlavan, K., Zahedi, A., & Krishnamurthy, P., (1997). Wideband local access: Wireless LAN and wireless ATM. *IEEE Communications Magazine, 35*(11), 34–40.
30. Park, J. S., & Dicoi, D., (2003). WLAN security: Current and future. *IEEE Internet Computing, 7*(05), 60–65.
31. Sakarindr, P., & Ansari, N., (2007). Security services in group communications over wireless infrastructure, mobile ad hoc, and wireless sensor networks. *IEEE Wireless Communications, 14*(5), 8–20.
32. Shakkottai, S., Rappaport, T. S., & Karlsson, P. C., (2003). Cross-layer design for wireless networks. *IEEE Communications Magazine, 41*(10), 74–80.
33. Sharma, K., & Dhir, N., (2014). A study of wireless networks: WLANs, WPANs, WMANs, and WWANs with comparison. *International Journal of Computer Science and Information Technologies, 5*(6), 7810–7813.
34. Shen, W., & Zeng, Q. A., (2008). Cost-function-based network selection strategy in integrated wireless and mobile networks. *IEEE Transactions on Vehicular Technology, 57*(6), 3778–3788.
35. Shuaib, K., Boulmalf, M., Sallabi, F., & Lakas, A. A. L. A., (2006). Co-existence of Zigbee and WLAN-a performance study. In: *2006 IFIP International Conference on Wireless and Optical Communications Networks* (Vol. 1, p. 5). IEEE.
36. Siddiqui, F., Zeadally, S., & Salah, K., (2015). Gigabit wireless networking with IEEE 802.11 ac: Technical overview and challenges. *Journal of Networks, 10*(3), 164.
37. Sidhu, B., Singh, H., & Chhabra, A., (2007). Emerging wireless standards-Wi-Fi, Zigbee and WiMAX. *World Academy of Science, Engineering and Technology, 25*(2007), 308–313.
38. Solis, R., Borkar, V. S., & Kumar, P. R., (2006). A new distributed time synchronization protocol for multihop wireless networks. In: *Proceedings of the 45th IEEE Conference on Decision and Control* (Vol. 1, pp. 2734–2739). IEEE.
39. Stenumgaard, P. F., (2006). A simple impulsiveness correction factor for control of electromagnetic interference in dynamic wireless applications. *IEEE Communications Letters, 10*(3), 147–149.
40. Tang, D., & Baker, M., (2000). Analysis of a local-area wireless network. In: *Proceedings of the 6th Annual International Conference on Mobile Computing and Networking* (Vol. 1, pp. 1–10).
41. Van, N. R., Awater, G., Morikura, M., Takanashi, H., Webster, M., & Halford, K. W., (1999). New high-rate wireless LAN standards. *IEEE Communications Magazine, 37*(12), 82–88.
42. Varshney, U., & Jain, R., (2001). Issues in emerging 4G wireless networks. *Computer, 34*(6), 94–96.
43. Xylomenos, G., Polyzos, G. C., Mahonen, P., & Saaranen, M., (2001). TCP performance issues over wireless links. *IEEE Communications Magazine, 39*(4), 52–58.

44. Yeh, J. H., Chen, J. C., & Lee, C. C., (2003). WLAN standards. *IEEE Potentials, 22*(4), 16–22.
45. Zamalloa, M. Z., & Krishnamachari, B., (2007). An analysis of unreliability and asymmetry in low-power wireless links. *ACM Transactions on Sensor Networks (TOSN), 3*(2), 7, 8.
46. Zhang, C., Patras, P., & Haddadi, H., (2019). Deep learning in mobile and wireless networking: A survey. *IEEE Communications Surveys & Tutorials, 21*(3), 2224–2287.

CHAPTER 6

EMERGING NETWORKING APPLICATIONS

UNIT INTRODUCTION

A network is, at its core, a distributed database system that enables networking programs to execute on many nodes and still has access to the same data objects (Parthasarathy et al., 2011). As a result of the rapid expansion of the Internet, many more complex networking services are becoming available. Some examples of these services are storage over IP, voice over IP, and video streaming. To successfully meet the requirements of these applications, the underlying network processor needs to have an efficient design.

Learning Objectives

At the end of this chapter, readers will be able to learn:

- Various emerging networking applications;
- Functionality, requirements, and general characteristics;
- Caches and memory access patterns in web caching;
- Parallelism in emerging network applications;
- Bottlenecks in emerging network applications;
- Concept of the processor architectures;
- Case study of the distributed video streaming over the internet.

Key Terms

- Algorithm
- Bottlenecks
- Cache
- Coherency
- Memory
- Parallelism
- Perfecting
- Processor
- Routing

6.1. FUNCTIONALITY AND REQUIREMENTS

As the introduction mentions, these networking apps' primary purpose is to transmit data, voice, or video through a network. Depending on how interactive they are, these programs will have different requirements. For instance, minimal jitter and loss rate are necessary for voice-over IP applications for communication to be appropriate. Buffering allows media streaming to withstand a modest latency, but low jitter and loss rate are still desired. On the contrary, because the protocol is built to accept these, typical TCP/IP routing has no strict restrictions on delay, jitter, or loss (Mijumbi et al., 2015). The network processors must be adaptable while delivering great performance to fulfill these objectives.

KEYWORD

A protocol is a standardized set of rules for formatting and processing data. Protocols enable computers to communicate with one another.

Additionally, the applications can be divided into two categories: data-plane tasks, which seem to be fundamental device processes and are in charge of processing, transferring, and accessing the packets, and control-plane tasks, which are less time-critical and responsible for maintaining device states (Han et al., 2015).

6.2. GENERAL CHARACTERISTICS

Lee et al., (1997) states networking applications often incorporate the following characteristics:

- High data-level parallelism;
- Manageable to multithreading.

Having several execution cores is favorable:

- Precise inputs: network packets;
- Specialized hardware is required to transfer packet data.

Its modular structure:

- Has a specified list of duties to be carried out;
- Can work with standardized organizations (Memik & Mangione-Smith, 2003).

We look at the properties of networking applications in this chapter.

6.3. CACHES AND MEMORY ACCESS PATTERNS IN WEB CACHING

Now we go into great detail about web caching behavior and memory access patterns. The concept of employing proxy servers for caching originated via the use of firewalls in businesses to filter user inquiries and responses. Users inside one organization are likely to access the same collection of documents. Hence cached pages on the server are likely to receive hits (Figure 6.1).

Figure 6.1. Illustration of the web caching.

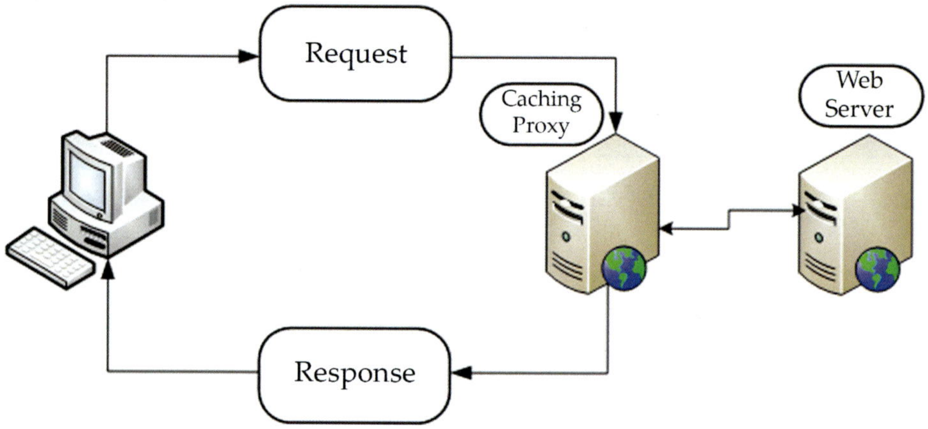

Source: Acunetix, Creative Commons License.

Following are the advantages:

- reduce bandwidth utilization;
- reduce accessibility to the users;
- reduce the strain on the remote web servers (Barishs & Obraczka, 2000);
- increases the document's accessibility and cached.

Following are the disadvantages:

- Access to outdated data;
- Additional processing as a result of a cache miss;
- A bottleneck would result from a single proxy cache;
- Quick access, transparency, scalability, effectiveness, flexibility, consistency, load balancing, ability to handle heterogeneity, and simplicity are desirable characteristics of a WWW caching system (Pallis et al., 2008).

6.3.1. Caching Architectures

Many caching architectures are listed in subsections.

Remember

Boost performance by organizing data in a hierarchical cache architecture.

6.3.1.1. Hierarchical

Caches at several levels, including institutional, bottom, regional, and national

Following are the advantages:

- The time it takes to connect to the network decreases whenever a copy is stored on an intermediary node (Karakostas & Serpanos, 2002).

Following are the disadvantages:

- Each level can create delays;
- Higher-level caches might cause snags and have protracted querying times;
- Many copies are kept at various cache levels.

6.3.1.2. Distributed

Caches are at the lowest level, with shared data among various stocks. Following are the advantages:

- Minimizing transmission delays as the majority of traffic moves via less congested areas;
- It improved dispersed bandwidth utilization at lower network levels of the hierarchy;
- Greater bandwidth utilization (Jin & Bestavros, 2001).

6.3.1.3. Hybrid

As in a distributed caching architecture, a hierarchy of caches works together at each level. Larger numbers imply greater relative popularity of the document. It is how network congestion is measured (Venketesh & Venkatesan, 2009):

1. **Connection Time:** It depends on how many network connections are required to access the necessary document. Polarizing documents Very extended connection times are experienced by both schemes. Hierarchical caches offer faster connection times and are moderately popular.

Very popular papers: The two methods are similar. It demonstrates how a hybrid stock with four collaborating CPUs outperforms the other two strategies (Chang & Sohi, 2006).

2. **Transmission Time:** These are the transmission times under conditions of extremely congested networks. When documents are transmitted over lower tiers of the network, distributed routing has faster transmission times. The hybrid design performs better than both the other approaches.
3. **Total Latency:** Depending on the size of the document, either the connection time or the transmission time will have a greater impact on the overall latency (Jiang & Zhang, 2003). The connection time is more significant than the transmission time for small document sizes, while the transmission time is more significant for larger documents. Depending on the document sizes, the ideal number of cooperating caches differs. In this case, it is 16 (Figure 6.2).

Figure 6.2. Illustration of the network latency.

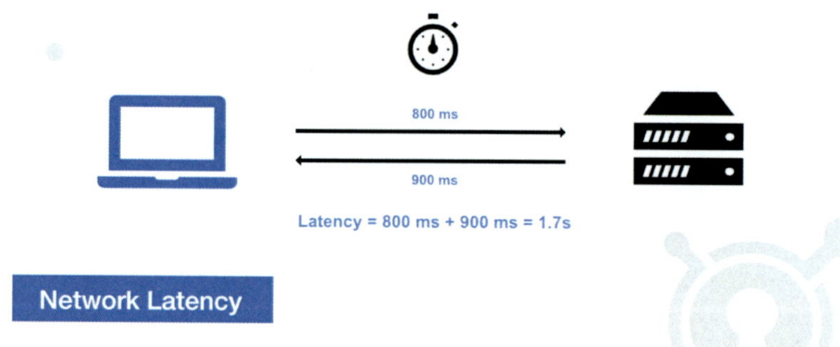

Source: Key CDN, Creative Commons License.

6.3.2. Cache Resolution/Routing

The most difficult part of using these methods is locating the cache with the requested content as rapidly as possible. Hierarchical addressing makes it impossible to employ route aggregation, which makes scaling this problem difficult. Traditional routing protocols can use route aggregation, but hierarchical addressing cannot. Also, cached materials must be updated regularly. Cache-based routing tables or hash functions could be used to accomplish this task. (Will we share details here?)

6.3.3. Prefetching

Two distinct types of preloading are distinguishable from one another. The information used to identify which objects should be preloaded was the basis for generating both the local and server-predicted preloads. When executing a local preload, the agent (like a browser client or proxy) uses local data (a reference schema) to decide which objects should be loaded (Lu & Shen, 2007).

In server-based prefetching, the server decides which items to prefetch based not only on its content knowledge of the objects that have been requested but also on reference patterns provided by numerous clients (Cidon et al., 2015) (Figure 6.3).

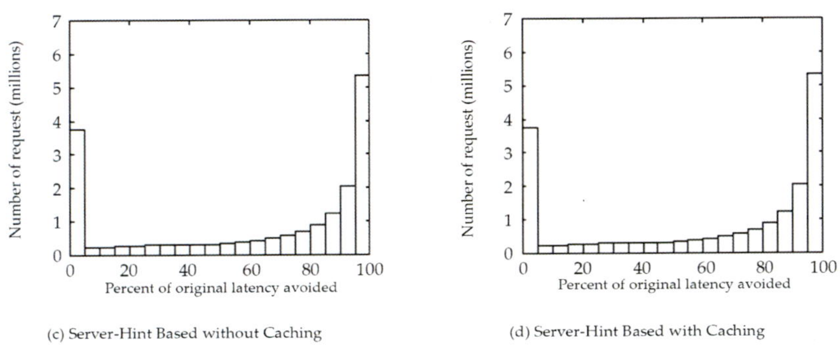

Figure 6.3. Graphs of the bimodal distribution.

Source: Janani Ravi, Creative Commons License.

The above graphs display a bimodal distribution in which we can observe either little to no reduction in latency (peak at about 0%) or significant reductions in latency (peaks between 95% and 100%). Therefore, a web request can notice a big latency decrease or little or no deduction for such models.

6.3.4. Cache Placement/ Replacement

These policies try to reduce several cost indicators, such as the byte hit rate, the hit rate, the average latency, and the total cost. They can be broken down into the following categories:

1. Traditional relief strategies and their direct extensions-least used Pitkow/Rector which evicts objects in LRU order but if all have been accessed on the same day then the largest one is removed (Chen et al., 2003).

2. Crucial-grounded eviction programs Evict objects dropped on size, LRU-MIN prefers lower things, LRU thresholds act like LRUs, except objects larger than a certain size are no way cached, smallest quiescence first eviction attestation is smallest download quiescence attestation and further.
3. Cost Based Replacement Policies-GreedyDual-Size associates a cost with each object and evicts the one with lowest cost/size, Hybrid associates a utility with each object and evicts one with least utility to reduce total latency and others. (Liu et al., 2020).

TIPS

Maintain cache coherency by ensuring all processors accessing the same memory location have the same view of the data, which can be achieved through hardware protocols or software algorithms.

6.3.5. Cache Coherency

The cache consistency mechanism provides two types of consistency: strong cache consistency and weak cache consistency.

6.3.5.1. Strong Cache Consistency

Client validation entails the proxy inquiring at regular intervals to determine whether or not the page has been modified (Kelly, 2002). The server issued an incorrect page change request, resulting in server invalidation.

6.3.5.2. Weak Cache Consistency

Adaptive TTL – adjusts the lifetime of a document based on observations of its lifetime. Piggyback invalidation – the validation or acknowledgment request is supplemented with a proxy request or a client response, respectively (Shi et al., 1997).

Predicting user access, load balancing, proxy placement, dynamic data caching, and analyzing network traffic patterns are other techniques to improve network caching systems.

6.4. PARALLELISM

Taking advantage of the fact that the host computer has more than one processor is one strategy for improving the efficiency of the network protocol subsystem. Many different network protocols have incorporated parallelism strategies at some point. The methods used here are classified by units of concurrency or in which processing elements are executed in parallel.

6.4.1. Layer Parallelism

In layer parallelism, a unit of concurrent is defined as each protocol layer. Some layers are solely responsible for managing particular aspects of the system, and interprocess communication is used to convey messages from one protocol to another.

- **Advantage:** Easy to understand and maintains a clear distinction between different protocol borders (Carvalho et al., 2018).
- **Disadvantage:** The array of layers in the stack is the only limiting factor for concurrent processing, and there is a significant amount of context switching and synchronization between layers.

6.4.2. Connection Level Parallelism

With connection-level parallelism, the connections are the basic building block for concurrent activity (Zheng et al., 2022). Using several associations, each processed in parallel increases speed.

- **Advantage:** Simplicity while making use of the naturally occurring concurrent nature of the connections
- **Disadvantage:** No parallelism is achievable inside a single connection

6.4.3. Functional Parallelism

The operations of the protocol layer constitute a unit of concurrency. The functions inside a single protocol layer, such as the generation of checksums and ACKs, are disassembled into their component pieces and assigned to a single processing unit. These functions include the age of checksums and ACKs (Miao, 2018) (Figure 6.4).

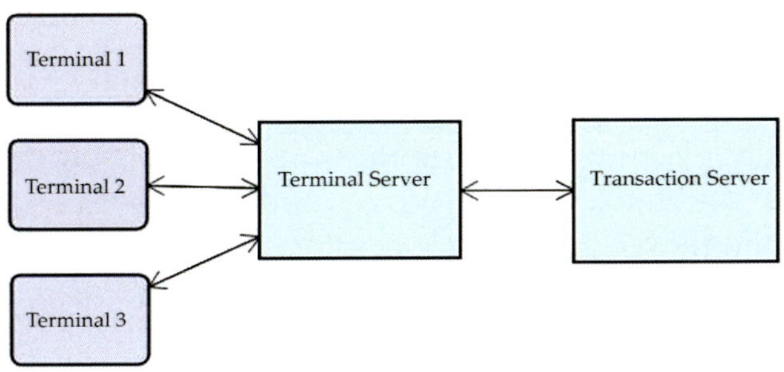

Figure 6.4. Schematic of the functional parallelism.

Source: University of Missouri, Creative Commons License.

- **Advantage:** Granular and capable of improving both the overall throughput and the delay experienced by a particular message
- **Disadvantage:** It is that coordination within a protocol layer is required, and the degree of concurrency that can be achieved between the functions included in that layer relies on the amount of synchronization that can take place.

6.4.4. Data Level Parallelism

The unit of concurrency is the data itself. Processing units are all tasked with performing identical operations, but they do so with unique components of the same message (Zhang et al., 2022).

- **Advantage:** The most granular, with the potential for the biggest increase in throughput and latency.
- **Disadvantage:** Synchronization of the various processing parts is required, which can be costly.

TIPS

In computer network ing, latency is an expression of how much time it takes for a data packet to travel from one designated point to another.

6.4.5. Packet Level Parallelism

- **Advantage:** Because packets are handled regardless of the connectivity they are linked with or the layer in which they are presented, a simultaneous speedup can be achieved for both single and many connections (Boral, 1988).
- **Disadvantage:** It is necessary to lock the shared state.

6.5. BOTTLENECKS

The following is a list of some of the bottlenecks that were discovered by real-time application publications:

1. The primary bottleneck is the cost of providing real-time performance while maintaining inter-process communication.
2. The cost of switching can also be a bottleneck if it is costly. While transmitting data to an outgoing network, you must frequently move contexts between the user's applications and the operating system.
3. The delay caused by memory access (Patounas et al., 2020)

6.6. CASE STUDY: DISTRIBUTED VIDEO STREAMING OVER THE INTERNET

1. Because of the difficulties associated with high data rates, delay, and loss sensitivity, there are better choices than the TCP protocol for video streaming.
2. The method described in this study makes it possible to create multimedia content accessible from various sources, allowing the receiver to select the "best" sender based on the bit rate, the amount of data lost, and the amount of time it takes to receive the data (Baranasuriya et al., 2015).

6.6.1. Receiver Side: Rate Allocation Algorithm

1. It is up to the receiver to supply control information that divides the sending rates among all the senders according to an anticipated loss rate and the amount of bandwidth now available.
2. When there is an unexpected change in the bandwidth available, allocating it is only carried out a few times to make room for additional data.
3. The estimation algorithm has a high TLP because the bandwidth of each sender may be computed on its own; this allows the program to provide an accurate estimate of the total bandwidth.
4. Despite this, the utilization of predicted bandwidth information must be carried out in one node to determine whether or not a change should be made in the allocated transmission rate (Sattari et al., 2022). It will likely be done in sequential order, and the increased number of sources will make the task more difficult to compute. The encouraging news is that this phase is carried out infrequently only when there has been a significant change in the predicted bandwidths.

6.6.2. Sender Side: Packet Partition Algorithm

1. Each of the numerous senders remembers when the most recent control information was read and uses that to choose when to send a packet.

2. A sender j will only send a packet k if it is expected that the arrival time of the packet at the receiver from source j will be the longest.
3. This estimation is reliable across all senders since it relies entirely on the control packet delivered by the receiver (Wei et al., 2022).
4. Because the estimated difference between each source can be determined independently, each node must carry out its copy of the procedure to compute the expected difference for all senders. This results in a significant amount of double and triple lost packets.

Did you get it?

Processor architectures are typically classified into two types, Reduced Instruction Set Computing (RISC) and Complex Instruction Set Computing (CISC), with each having its own strengths and weaknesses.

6.7. PROCESSOR ARCHITECTURES

Cabling is no longer the limiting factor in network capacity since rapid technological innovation has increased the theoretical bandwidth of networks to the point that it is no longer the bottleneck. The network nodes responsible for intercepting and forwarding data flow are where the backup can be found. Specialized processors have been implemented to manage the data flow through these nodes. The proper name for these chips is Network Processors (Crowley et al., 2003).

The expansion of network technology has resulted in a rise in the significance of the Network Interface (NI) function, which enables one computer system to communicate via message passing with other computer systems connected to the same network. Using programmable microprocessors on network interfaces (PNI) configured with domain-specific software is becoming increasingly popular to meet the functionality and performance needs of currently available and upcoming network applications (Brand et al., 2022).

ACTIVITY 6.1.

How are you staying up-to-date on emerging networking applications, and what steps have you taken to evaluate their potential value and impact on your organization?

To analyze the various network designs, we need to determine what kinds of workloads the processor must be able to support, what degree of performance is necessary, and what kind of architecture can give that level of performance. The first six programs have a comparatively tiny amount of data stored within the protocol headers of their respective packets; however, the processing requirements for these services are not impacted by the overall size of the packages (Chen et al., 2020). Despite this, many applications keep their state tables stored in complex data structures and inspecting them on a per-packet basis is necessary. The last three applications require significant computing power to process data packets at the same rate as the network link.

6.8. SUMMARY

- This chapter provides an in-depth understanding of various emerging networking applications, such as distributed video streaming, cloud computing, and IoT. It covers the functionality, requirements, and general characteristics of these applications. The chapter also delves into the concept of web caching, including caches and memory access patterns. The discussion on parallelism in emerging network applications highlights the importance of parallel processing in enhancing application performance. Additionally, the chapter identifies common bottlenecks in emerging network applications, such as network congestion and processing delays. Furthermore, the chapter explains the concept of processor architectures and how they impact networking applications. A case study of distributed video streaming over the internet is presented to illustrate the practical applications of the concepts discussed throughout the chapter. Overall, this chapter provides readers with a comprehensive understanding of emerging networking applications and the various factors that impact their performance.

REVIEW QUESTIONS

1. What are some examples of emerging networking applications?
2. What are the general characteristics of emerging networking applications?
3. How do caches and memory access patterns affect web caching?
4. What is parallelism in the context of emerging network applications?
5. What are some common bottlenecks in emerging network applications?
6. How do processor architectures impact networking applications?

MULTIPLE CHOICE QUESTIONS

1. What is the focus of this chapter?

a. Processor architectures
b. Emerging networking applications
c. Distributed video streaming
d. Web caching

2. What does the chapter cover regarding web caching?

a. Caches and memory access patterns
b. Functionality and requirements
c. Processor architectures
d. Parallelism

3. **What is the case study presented in this chapter?**
   a. Distributed video streaming over the internet
   b. Web caching
   c. Processor architectures
   d. Emerging networking applications
4. **What is covered in this chapter regarding emerging network applications?**
   a. Functionality and requirements
   b. Bottlenecks
   c. Parallelism
   d. All of the above
5. **What is the concept covered in this chapter regarding processor architectures?**
   a. Functionality and requirements
   b. Parallelism
   c. Caches and memory access patterns
   d. General characteristics

Answers to the Multiple-Choice Questions

1. (b); 2. (a); 3. (a); 4. (d); 5. (d)

REFERENCES

1. Baranasuriya, N., Navda, V., Padmanabhan, V. N., & Gilbert, S., (2015). QProbe: Locating the bottleneck in cellular communication. In: *Proceedings of the 11th ACM Conference on Emerging Networking Experiments and Technologies* (Vol. 1, pp. 1–7).
2. Barish, G., & Obraczka, K., (2000). World wide web caching: Trends and techniques. *IEEE Communications Magazine, 38*(5), 178–184.
3. Boral, H., (1988). Parallelism in bubba. In: *Proceedings International Symposium on Databases in Parallel and Distributed Systems* (Vol. 1, pp. 68, 69). IEEE Computer Society.
4. Brand, M., Hannig, F., Keszocze, O., & Teich, J., (2022). Precision-and accuracy-reconfigurable processor architectures: An overview. *IEEE Transactions on Circuits and Systems II: Express Briefs, 2*(1), 7–9.
5. Carvalho, G. H., Woungang, I., Anpalagan, A., & Jaseemuddin, M., (2018). Analysis of joint parallelism in wireless and cloud domains on mobile edge computing over 5G systems. *Journal of Communications and Networks, 20*(6), 565–577.
6. Chang, J., & Sohi, G. S., (2006). Cooperative caching for chip multiprocessors. *ACM SIGARCH Computer Architecture News, 34*(2), 264–276.

7. Chen, Y., Xie, Y., Song, L., Chen, F., & Tang, T., (2020). A survey of accelerator architectures for deep neural networks. *Engineering, 6*(3), 264–274.
8. Chen, Z., Zhou, Y., & Li, K., (2003). Eviction-based cache placement for storage caches. In: *USENIX Annual Technical Conference, General Track* (Vol. 1, pp. 269–281).
9. Cidon, A., Eisenman, A., Alizadeh, M., & Katti, S., (2015). Dynacache: Dynamic cloud caching. In: *HotStorage, 2*(1), 3–6.
10. Crowley, P., Franklin, M. A., Hadimioglu, H., & Onufryk, P. Z., (2003). *Network Processor Design: Issues and Practices* (Vol. 1, pp. 5–9). Morgan Kaufmann.
11. Dwivedi, V. P., Joshi, C. K., Laurent, T., Bengio, Y., & Bresson, X., (2020). *Benchmarking Graph Neural Networks, 3*(1), 6–8.
12. Franke, H., Xenidis, J., Basso, C., Bass, B. M., Woodward, S. S., Brown, J. D., & Johnson, C. L., (2010). Introduction to the wire-speed processor and architecture. *IBM Journal of Research and Development, 54*(1), 1-3.
13. Guthaus, M. R., Ringenberg, J. S., Ernst, D., Austin, T. M., Mudge, T., & Brown, R. B., (2001). MiBench: A free, commercially representative embedded benchmark suite. In: *Proceedings of the Fourth Annual IEEE International Workshop on Workload Characterization; WWC-4 (Cat. No. 01EX538)* (Vol. 1, pp. 3–14). IEEE.
14. Han, B., Gopalakrishnan, V., Ji, L., & Lee, S., (2015). Network function virtualization: Challenges and opportunities for innovations. *IEEE Communications Magazine, 53*(2), 90–97.
15. Jiang, S., & Zhang, X., (2003). Efficient distributed disk caching in data grid management. In: *2003 Proceedings IEEE International Conference on Cluster Computing* (Vol. 1, pp. 446–451). IEEE.
16. Jin, S., & Bestavros, A., (2001). GreedyDual* Web caching algorithm: Exploiting the two sources of temporal locality in web request streams. *Computer Communications, 24*(2), 174–183.
17. Jin, Z., & Cheng, A. C., (2008). Implantbench: Characterizing and projecting representative benchmarks for emerging bioimplantable computing. *IEEE Micro, 28*(4), 71–91.
18. Kang, M., Lim, S., Gonugondla, S., & Shanbhag, N. R., (2018). An in-memory VLSI architecture for convolutional neural networks. *IEEE Journal on Emerging and Selected Topics in Circuits and Systems, 8*(3), 494–505.
19. Karakostas, G., & Serpanos, D. N., (2002). Exploitation of different types of locality for web caches. In: *Proceedings ISCC 2002 Seventh International Symposium on Computers and Communications* (Vol. 1, pp. 207–212). IEEE.
20. Kelly, T., (2002). Thin-client web access patterns: Measurements from a cache-busting proxy. *Computer Communications, 25*(4), 357–366.
21. Lee, C., Potkonjak, M., & Mangione-Smith, W. H., (1997). Mediabench: A tool for evaluating and synthesizing multimedia and communications systems. In: *Proceedings of 30th Annual International Symposium on Microarchitecture* (Vol. 1, pp. 330–335). IEEE.

22. Lin, Y., Shao, L., Zhu, Z., Wang, Q., & Sabhikhi, R. K., (2010). Wireless network cloud: Architecture and system requirements. *IBM Journal of Research and Development, 54*(1), 1-4.
23. Liu, E., Hashemi, M., Swersky, K., Ranganathan, P., & Ahn, J., (2020). An imitation learning approach for cache replacement. In: *International Conference on Machine Learning* (Vol. 1, pp. 6237–6247). PMLR.
24. Lu, P., & Shen, K., (2007). Virtual machine memory access tracing with hypervisor exclusive cache. In: *Usenix Annual Technical Conference* (Vol. 1, pp. 29–43).
25. Memik, G., Mangione-Smith, W. H., & Hu, W., (2001). Netbench: A benchmarking suite for network processors. In: *IEEE/ACM International Conference on Computer Aided Design. ICCAD 2001; IEEE/ACM Digest of Technical Papers (Cat. No. 01CH37281)* (Vol. 1, pp. 39–42). IEEE.
26. Miao, J. T., (2018). Parallelism and evolution in transnational policy transfer networks: The case of SINO-Singapore Suzhou industrial park (SIP). *Regional Studies, 52*(9), 1191–1200.
27. Mijumbi, R., Serrat, J., Gorricho, J. L., Bouten, N., De Turck, F., & Boutaba, R., (2015). Network function virtualization: State-of-the-art and research challenges. *IEEE Communications Surveys & Tutorials, 18*(1), 236–262.
28. Nanda, A. K., Shing, H., Tzen, T. H., & Ni, L. M., (1991). Resource contention in shared-memory multiprocessors: A parameterized performance degradation model. *Journal of Parallel and Distributed Computing, 12*(4), 313–328.
29. Pallis, G., Vakali, A., & Pokorny, J., (2008). A clustering-based prefetching scheme on a web cache environment. *Computers & Electrical Engineering, 34*(4), 309–323.
30. Parthasarathy, S., Ruan, Y., & Satuluri, V., (2011). Community discovery in social networks: Applications, methods and emerging trends. *Social Network Data Analytics, 2*(1), 79–113.
31. Patounas, G., Foukas, X., Elmokashfi, A., & Marina, M. K., (2020). Characterization and identification of cloudified mobile network performance bottlenecks. *IEEE Transactions on Network and Service Management, 17*(4), 2567–2583.
32. Sattari, F., Farooqi, A. H., Qadir, Z., Raza, B., Nazari, H., & Almutiry, M., (2022). A hybrid deep learning approach for bottleneck detection in IoT. *IEEE Access, 10*(1), 77039–77053.
33. Shi, Y., Watson, E., & Chen, Y. S., (1997). Model-driven simulation of world-wide-web cache policies. In: *Proceedings of the 29th Conference on Winter Simulation* (Vol. 1, pp. 1045–1052).
34. Tsimpourlas, F., Petoumenos, P., Xu, M., Cummins, C., Hazelwood, K., Rajan, A., & Leather, H., (2023). *BenchDirect: A Directed Language Model for Compiler Benchmarks, 2*(1), 4–8.
35. Venketesh, P., & Venkatesan, R., (2009). A survey on applications of neural networks and evolutionary techniques in web caching. *IETE Technical Review, 26*(3), 171–180.

36. Wei, L., Chen, P., Mei, Y., & Wang, Y., (2022). Turn-level network traffic bottleneck identification using vehicle trajectory data. *Transportation Research Part C: Emerging Technologies, 140*(1), 103–707.

37. Yi, K., & Gaudiot, J. L., (2006). Features of future network processor architectures. In: *IEEE John Vincent Atanasoff 2006 International Symposium on Modern Computing (JVA'06)* (Vol. 1, pp. 69–76). IEEE.

38. Zhang, S., Diao, L., Wu, C., Wang, S., & Lin, W., (2022). Accelerating large-scale distributed neural network training with SPMD parallelism. In: *Proceedings of the 13th Symposium on Cloud Computing* (Vol. 1, pp. 403–418).

39. Zheng, D., Shen, G., Cao, X., & Mukherjee, B., (2022). Towards optimal parallelism-aware service chaining and embedding. *IEEE Transactions on Network and Service Management, 19*(3), 2063–2077.

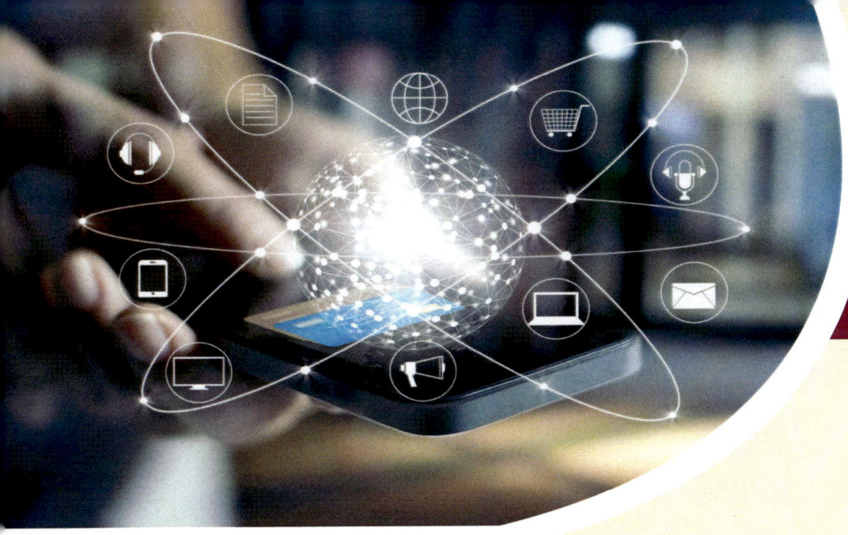

CHAPTER 7

NETWORK PERFORMANCE AND OPTIMIZATION

UNIT INTRODUCTION

Because we live in a digital world, it is necessary for individuals and businesses alike to make use of networks in order to interact and exchange information. Whether it's for sending e-mails, transferring data or accessing the internet, the performance of the network plays an essential part in ensuring that these tasks proceed without hiccups and in the most time-effective manner possible. Network performance optimization is becoming increasingly crucial as networks continue to grow more sophisticated and data intensive (Alsamhi et al., 2019). This is done to ensure that the network is able to handle the load and provide a high-quality user experience.

Performance and optimization of a network are essential for a number of different reasons. To begin, a network that does not operate well can have a negative influence on productivity and cause users to become frustrated, which in turn results in lost time and income for enterprises. Second, a network that does not perform well can also result in privacy vulnerabilities, which can put the availability, integrity, and confidentiality of data at risk (Chen & Yao, 2001). In today's highly competitive workplace, companies that are able to deliver faster and more dependable network performance have an advantage over their competitors.

Network performance is to deliver data consistently, swiftly, and efficiently. It takes into account a number of different aspects, including throughput, bandwidth, latency, error rates, and packet loss. On the other side, the term "network optimization" is the process of improving the performance of a network by decreasing its latency, increasing its throughput, and limiting the number of packets lost and the error rates (Kleinrock & Kamoun, 1977). This can be performed through numerous strategies, including deduplication, traffic shaping, load balancing, and compression. The optimization of a network is a never-ending process that involves constant monitoring and fine-tuning in order to guarantee that the network will continue to function at its optimum level.

Learning Objectives

At the end of this chapter, readers will be able to learn:

- Different factors that affect the performance of the network;
- Methods and tools for measuring the performance of the network;
- Various network optimization techniques;
- Tuning and troubleshooting of the performance;
- Future direction in network optimization and performance.

Key Terms

- Caching
- Compression
- Duplication
- Error rates
- Jitter
- Latency
- Network
- Optimization
- Packet loss
- Performance
- Quality of service
- Traffic

7.1. FACTORS AFFECTING THE PERFORMANCE OF NETWORK

The performance of a network is affected by a number of elements, each of which has the potential to have an effect on the quantity and velocity of data transmission. The following are a few of the major aspects that influence the performance of the network.

Remember

Throughput measures data transmission, while bandwidth defines the maximum data transfer rate.

7.1.1. Throughput and Bandwidth

The quantity of information that may be sent via a network in a specific amount of time is referred to as the connection's bandwidth. The exact amount of information that is transmitted through the network in a specific amount of time is referred to as the throughput, and it is measured in bits per second (bps). The greater the bandwidth, the greater the amount of data that can be carried at once, which ultimately leads to a faster pace of data transfer (Sesay et al., 2004). There are a number of factors that might influence throughput, including packet loss, network congestion, and latency (Figure 7.1).

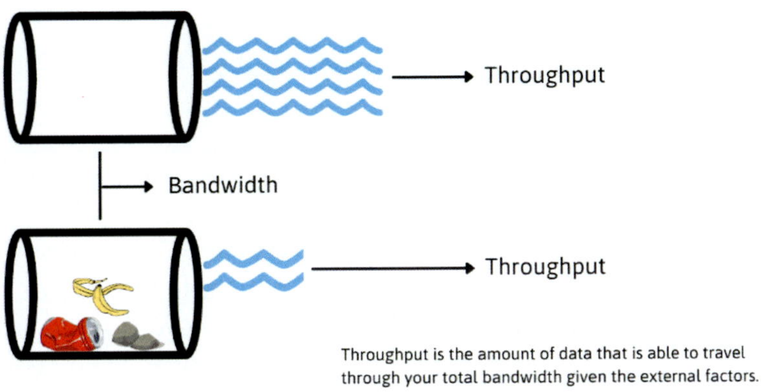

Figure 7.1. Illustration of throughput and bandwidth in performance of network.

Source: Diego Coutinho, Creative Commons License.

7.1.2. Jitter and Latency

The amount of time that elapses between the sending of a data packet from one computer (device) to another and the receipt of a response is referred to as latency. On the opposite hand, jitter refers to variations in latency that occur over the course of time. Specially for real-time applications like VoIP(voice-over-IP) calls, video conferencing, and online gaming, high levels of jitter and latency can delay in the transfer of data and results in slow network performance (Yang et al., 2021) (Figure 7.2).

Figure 7.2. Graph showing the jitter and latency in network performance.

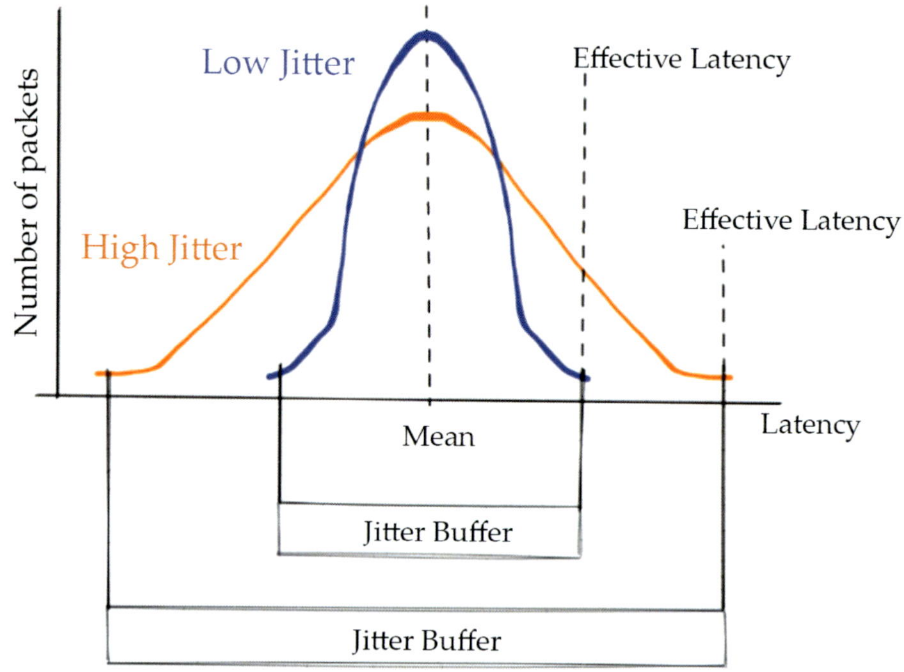

Source: Atatus, Creative Commons License.

7.1.3. ERROR RATES AND PACKET LOSS

It is possible for data packets to be lost or destroyed during transmission, which can lead to gaps in the stream of data. This is referred to as "packet loss." Congestion on the network, a malfunction in the hardware, or flaws in the software could all be to blame (Andrews et al., 2010). When there is a high packet loss rate, the performance of the network may suffer, which may result in delays and poor data transmission quality. In a similar vein, excessive error rates can hinder the functioning of a network and ultimately result in the corruption or loss of data.

7.1.4. Queuing and Congestion

Congestion on a network happens when there is an excessive amount of devices or applications vying for limited network resources.

This results in delays and a general slowdown in the performance of the network. If there are an excessive number of packets queuing to be transmitted, a phenomenon known as "queuing" can take place. This can result in delays and a reduction in the rate at which data can be transferred. Queuing and Congestion can both be controlled using strategies like quality of service (QoS), traffic shaping, and load balancing, which are designed to prioritize traffic and guarantee that network performance is at its highest possible level (Perkins et al., 2002).

7.2. MEASURING THE PERFORMANCE OF NETWORK

There are a variety of measures that may be utilized in order to assess the performance of a network. The following are a few of the most significant ones:

1. Bandwidth: It describes the quantity of data which can be sent over a network in a specific length of time (Petrova et al., 2007). This term refers to the bandwidth of the network. Bps or Mbps are the standard units of measurement for it.
2. Latency: It is the time required for a data packet to transit from one location in a network to another location in that same network. ms (Milliseconds) or S (microseconds) are the standard units of measurement for it.
3. Packet Loss: It is the percentage of data packets that are either lost or thrown away while the transmission is taking place. Congestion on the network, faults during transmission, or other causes could all be to blame for this issue (Huaizhou et al., 2013).
4. Jitter: It refers to the fluctuation in the amount of time that elapses before a packet is delivered. It is often measured in milliseconds (ms), and there are a number of potential causes, including network congestion, which might contribute to it.
5. Throughput: It is the exact amount of information that is sent through the network in a specific amount of time. This term refers to the throughput of the network. Bps or Mbps are the standard units of measurement for it.

7.2.1. Tools for Measuring the Performance of a Network

There are a number of tools available to choose from when measuring the performance of a network. The following are some of the ones that are used most frequently:

1. **Ping:** It is a command-line program that transmits a short data packet to a destination IP address and monitors the time it requires for the answer to come back. 2 (Sonntag et al., 2013). Traceroute is another command-line application that traces the path that data takes through a network. It is possible to use it to measure the delay as well as the packet loss.
2. **Traceroute:** It traces the route that a data packet goes from its source to its final destination. It does this by following the path that the packet travels. It is possible to use it to determine which devices on the network are contributing to packet loss or latency.
3. **Network Analyzers:** These record and examine the data on a network. They are useful for determining issues such as network congestion, lost packets, and other problems (Wac et al., 2005).
4. **Bandwidth:** Its testers measure the real bandwidth that is available over a network connection. They can be utilized to determine bandwidth limits in addition to other problems.

TIPS

Congestion is often related to latency, throughput, and bandwidth.

7.2.2. Analyzing Network Performance Data

After the data on the performance of the network has been gathered, it needs to be examined in order to determine whether or not there are any problems and whether or not there are any potential solutions. The following are some of the most important processes in the process of examining network performance data:

1. **Identify the Main Reason for Any Issues:** This may involve looking at the topology of the network, the configuration of the devices connected to the network, or the behavior of the traffic on the network (Jeremiah Ekah et al., 2022).
2. **Evaluate the Effect of the Issues:** This may absolutely look at the metrics that were covered before, such as throughput, latency, and packet loss, to evaluate how the challenges are affecting the performance of the network.

3. **Develop Solutions:** On the basis of the study, potential solutions to any problems that have been found can be established. This may require making modifications to the configuration of the network, upgrading the hardware, or updating the software.
4. **Testing the Solution:** After remedies have been devised, they must be thoroughly evaluated to determine whether or not they are successful and whether or not they result in any new complications (Panait et al., 2015).

In general, monitoring the performance of a network is a vital responsibility for network operators and other professionals working in the information technology field. It is simple to determine and resolve issues with network performance if one makes use of the appropriate metrics and tools and performs a rigorous analysis of the data. This will ensure that the network is working at its optimal level.

7.3. NETWORK OPTIMIZATION TECHNIQUES

The performance of a network, its efficiency, and its dependability can all be improved by the application of various optimization approaches. The following represent a few of the most often-used strategies.

7.3.1. Quality of Service (QoS)

The Quality of Service (QoS) is a collection of methods that prioritize network traffic depending on the significance of the traffic or the type of traffic (Sendra Compte et al., 2011). This ensures that vital traffic, such as video or speech, is given precedence over less critical traffic, including checking e-mail or browsing the web. Voice and video are examples of important traffic (Figure 7.3).

Figure 7.3. Quality of service and its factors.

Source: Cybersecurity Glossary, Creative Commons License.

7.3.2. Policing and Traffic Shaping

KEYWORD

Network traffic is the amount of data moving across a computer network at any given time.

Techniques known as traffic shaping and traffic policing are utilized in order to manage the traffic of the network by regulating the amount of data that is transmitted (Mohammed et al., 2020). Traffic shaping can make network traffic smoother by managing the packet flow, whereas traffic policing can restrict the quantity of traffic that can reach a network. Both of these techniques are used to manage traffic.

7.3.3. Traffic Routing and Load Balancing

The goal of load balancing is to maximize performance while minimizing the effects of overloading on the system. This is accomplished by distributing network traffic among a number of servers or network lines (Diallo et al., 2013). The process of traffic routing involves determining the most efficient path for traffic of the network depending on a variety of criteria, including the amount of available bandwidth, the amount of latency, and the total cost.

7.3.4. Network Caching

The technique of storing data that is frequently retrieved in a local database is referred to as caching. Caching can reduce latency and increase network performance by lowering the amount of information that has to be obtained from a remote server (Yetgin et al., 2017). Caching works by minimizing the amount of information that requires to be retrieved.

7.3.5. Deduplication and Compression

By eliminating redundant information, compression is able to shrink the amount of data packets, whereas deduplication gets rid of material that has already been stored. Compression and deduplication are two techniques that, when combined, can improve the performance of a network and cut down on the amount of bandwidth it uses. This is accomplished by lowering the quantity of data that must be sent over the network (Singh & Sharma, 2016). In general, the application of various strategies for network optimization plays a significant part in guaranteeing that a network is quick, dependable, and efficient. IT and Network administrators' experts can enhance the efficiency of their networks and offer their customers a more satisfying experience by putting these strategies into practice. This will also benefit their customers (Figure 7.4).

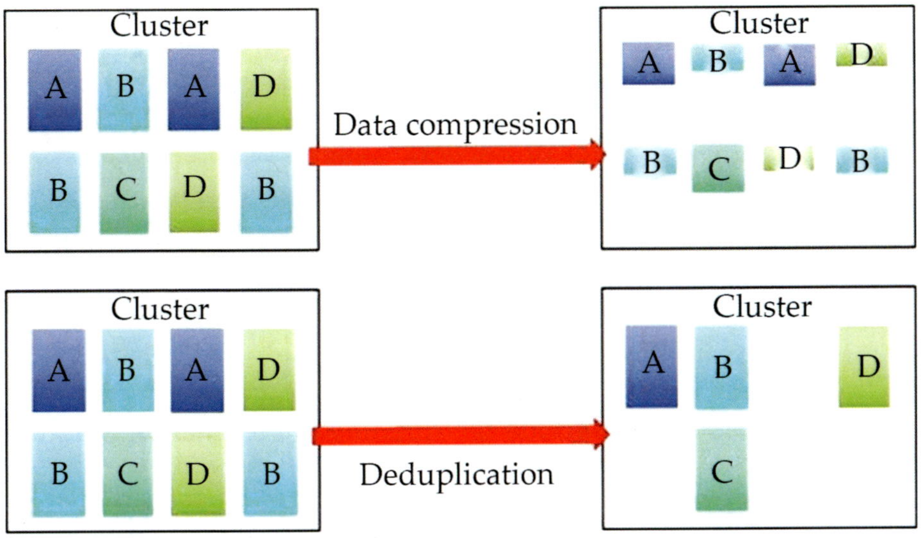

Figure 7.4. Illustration of the duplication and compression of data.

Source: Ruay-Shiung Chang et al. Creative Commons License.

7.4. PERFORMANCE TROUBLESHOOTING AND TUNING

Troubleshooting and performance optimization are two jobs that are absolutely necessary for network managers and IT experts. The following is a list of important stages and tactics for recognizing and resolving issues related to network performance:

1. **Identifying Difficulties with Network Performance:** The first stage in performance troubleshooting and tuning is to determine the root issues that are influencing network performance (Al Aghbari et al., 2020). This can be accomplished by conducting a network performance audit. This may involve monitoring network equipment, collecting performance data, and analyzing network traffic.
2. **Methods for Enhancing the Performance of the Network:** After it has been determined what the problems are, there are a number of methods that may be utilized to enhance the performance of the network. A few of the most often-used tactics are as follows:

3. **Upgrading Hardware:** Doing hardware upgrades, which may include upgrading network servers, switches, or routers in order to increase overall performance (Wang et al., 2005).
4. **Enhancing Network Configurations:** Involve modifying network settings in order to increase performance. For example, load balancing, QoS parameters, or traffic shaping are all examples of network settings.
5. **Streamlining Traffic of the Network:** Involve minimizing the amount of unneeded network traffic, such as by banning spam or restricting the amount of streaming video that can take place (Balakrishnan et al., 1995).
6. **Network Caching Implementation:** Involve putting in place caching servers in order to cache data that is frequently accessed and reduce the quantity of information that must be sent over the network.
7. **Troubleshooting Techniques for Identifying and Fixing Performance Problems:** In the event that the aforementioned strategies do not improve the performance of the network, troubleshooting methods can be used to discover and fix performance problems. The following are some of the most often-used troubleshooting techniques:
8. **Packet Capture and Analysis:** This process involves utilizing network analysts to capture and analyze network traffic in order to understand the issues including packet loss, delay, or congestion on the network.
9. **Ping and Traceroute:** These are command-line applications that can be used to verify the connectivity of a network and determine the cause of any connectivity problems that may occur (Mismar et al., 2019).
10. **Monitoring Network Devices:** This entails monitoring network gadgets like servers, routers, and switches in order to identify problems such as high CPU consumption, memory usage, or disc usage.
11. **Log Analysis:** This entails studying the device logs to determine if there are any mistakes or problems that could be influencing the performance of the network (Huaizhou et al., 2013).

KEYWORD

Troubleshooting is a systematic approach to solving a problem.

IT professionals and Network administrators can enhance the performance, stability, and effectiveness of their networks by following the tactics and procedures that are outlined below. This will result in a better customer experience for the administrators' customers.

7.5. NETWORK SECURITY CONSIDERATIONS

While constructing and operating a network, it is essential to strike a balance between performance and security in order to get optimal results. Network security is an essential component of network administration. The following is a list of important things to keep in mind while trying to strike a balance between performance and security, as well as some tactics for managing a high-performance network and common security risks and vulnerabilities:

Did you get it?

Balancing security and performance are critical in network performance, as overly aggressive security measures can impede performance and result in poor user experience.

7.5.1. Balancing Security and Performance

Because security measures can occasionally have an influence on network performance, it is vital to strike a balance between the demand for high performance and the requirement for adequate security. This can involve choosing the appropriate security protocols for the particular network and making sure that such measures do not have a detrimental influence on the performance of the network (Parsons et al., 2014). The following are some examples of striking a balance between performance and security:

- Selecting appropriate encryption protocols and technologies to secure traffic of the network while also reducing their influence on network performance
- Reducing the likelihood of security flaws by restricting access to vital network resources to users who have been given permission to do so (Perrig et al., 2004).
- Choosing network security mechanisms that have a low influence on the performance of the network, including IPS (intrusion prevention systems) that make use of hardware acceleration.

7.5.2. Strategies for Securing a High-Performance Network

It is essential to put in place a variety of different network security measures in order to ensure the safety of a high-performance network. Listed below are various approaches that can be taken to ensure the safety of a high-performance network:

- Putting in place firewalls to restrict who can access which network resources and to prohibit traffic from untrusted sources (Blilat et al., 2012).
- Employing systems that identify and prevent intrusions to monitor traffic of the network for potential security risks.
- Establishing virtual private networks, sometimes known as VPNs, as a means of providing protected distant access to the network (McGee et al., 2012).
- Putting in place access control systems and user authentication so that network resources can be accessed only by authorized users.
- Doing routine software and hardware updates on all network devices in order to keep them safe against any newly discovered vulnerabilities (Lim et al., 2010).

7.5.3. Common Network Security Vulnerabilities and Threats

There are various potential weaknesses and threats to the security of a network, including the following:

- Malware, which includes Trojans, viruses, and worms is software that has the potential to compromise security and infect devices of the network.
- Attacks using social engineering and phishing, in which an attempt is made to deceive individuals into disclosing sensitive information (Azzabi et al., 2017).
- Distributed denial-of-service (DDoS) and denial-of-service (DoS) attacks, which include flooding the network with traffic in order to overwhelm network resources and interfere with normal network operations.
- Threats from within, which occur when people with authorized access privileges abuse their privileges to jeopardize network security.
- Unsecured software or devices, which could be manipulated by attackers to get access to the network; these vulnerabilities allow attackers to acquire network access (Gupta et al., 2020) (Figure 7.5).

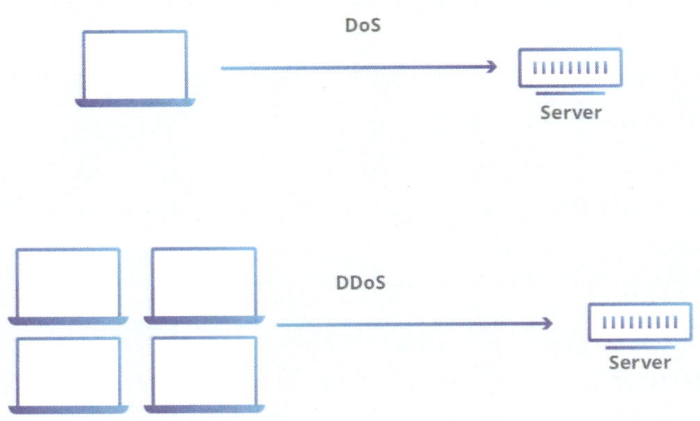

Figure 7.5. Illustration of the distributed denial-of-service (DDoS) and denial-of-service (DoS) attacks.

Source: Cloud Flare, Creative Commons License.

IT professionals and Network administrators can secure their networks while preserving high performance by first gaining an understanding of these network protective measures, then putting appropriate security measures into place, and finally monitoring the network on a regular basis for potential security threats.

7.6. FUTURE DIRECTIONS IN NETWORK OPTIMIZATION AND PERFORMANCE

Network optimization and performance will continue to develop in tandem with the progression of technological capabilities. The following is a list of some new technologies and trends, difficulties and possibilities, research directions, and open issues in the field:

7.6.1. Emerging Trends and Technologies

There are a number of developing technologies and trends that are likely to have an impact on the performance and optimization of networks, including the following:

- **5G Networks:** 5G technology will deliver faster speeds, reduced latency, and improved dependability, which will make it possible to develop use cases and new applications.
- **Edge Computing:** This entails data processing closer to its source, which can increase network speed and minimize latency. Edge computing is also known as fog computing (Noshy et al., 2018).

- **Machine Learning (ML) and Artificial Intelligence (AI):** Both AI and ML can be put to use to evaluate network data and improve network performance in real time.
- **IoT (Internet of Things):** The proliferation of IoT will cause an increase in the amount of data produced and will place an extra burden on the performance of the network (Baktir et al., 2017).

7.6.2. Challenges in Network Optimization and Performance

In spite of the numerous advancements made in network optimization and performance, the sector is still fraught with a great deal of difficulty as well as opportunity. The following are some of the most important opportunities and challenges:

- **Security:** As networks continue to get more complicated and interconnected, the number of security risks will continue to rise, which will make it harder to get the most out of them and optimize their performance (Samaan & Karmouch, 2009).
- **Scalability:** Networks need to have the ability to manage growing amount of traffic and data as more users and devices join to the network.
- **Automation:** It is something that can assist in optimizing the performance of a network, but it needs proper planning and implementation (Assunção et al., 2015).
- **Computing on the Cloud:** Cloud computing offers many opportunities for enhancing performance of the network, but it also raises issues such as worries about data privacy and security.

KEYWORD

Data privacy is a discipline intended to keep data safe against improper access, theft or loss.

7.6.3. Research Directions and Open Problems in the Field

Within the realm of performance of the network and optimization, there are a great deal of unsolved issues and potential new lines of inquiry. Among the most important aspects of research are the following:

- The creation of innovative algorithms and methods for enhancing the performance of networks and cutting down on latency (Gills & Buyya, 2018).

- The development of innovative architectures of the network that are safe, scalable, and efficient all at the same time.
- Doing research into how new technologies, such as internet of things (IoT) 5G, edge computing, and artificial intelligence (AI), affect the overall performance and optimization of networks.
- Creating innovative methods for evaluating and visually representing network performance data in order to find and fix performance issues.
- Doing research on how application performance and user experience are influenced by network performance and optimization (Golden et al., 1981).

IT professionals and Network administrators can continue to optimize network performance and deliver a better customer experience for their customers by tackling the difficulties described above, exploring emerging trends and technologies, and undertaking research in the sector.

ACTIVITY 7.1.

Can you describe a situation in which you were tasked with improving network performance, and what steps did you take to identify and address the underlying issues?

7.7. SUMMARY

- This chapter focuses on various factors that can affect the performance of a network, including network architecture, protocols, and hardware. The chapter also explores different methods and tools for measuring network performance and various optimization techniques, including load balancing, traffic shaping, and caching. Additionally, the chapter covers tuning and troubleshooting network performance issues and future directions in network optimization and performance. Finally, the chapter discusses the implications of network performance for organizations and professionals who work with networks.

REVIEW QUESTIONS

1. What are some factors that can affect network performance, and how do they impact the network?
2. What are some methods and tools for measuring network performance, and how can they be used to improve performance?
3. What are some network optimization techniques, and how can they improve network performance?
4. Why is tuning and troubleshooting network performance issues important, and what are some common issues that can arise?
5. What is the future direction in network optimization and performance, and how can organizations and professionals prepare for it?

MULTIPLE CHOICE QUESTIONS

1. What are some factors that can affect network performance?

a. Network architecture
b. Protocols
c. Hardware
d. All of the above

2. What is a common network optimization technique?

a. Caching
b. Deleting files
c. Restarting the network
d. None of the above

3. What is the purpose of tuning and troubleshooting network performance issues?

a. To maintain network security

b. To improve network speed and reliability
c. To increase network bandwidth
d. All of the above

4. What is the future direction in network optimization and performance?

a. Increased use of outdated hardware
b. Decreased focus on security measures
c. More reliance on artificial intelligence and machine learning
d. None of the above

5. What are the implications of network performance for organizations and professionals who work with networks?

a. Increased productivity
b. Improved customer satisfaction
c. Decreased revenue
d. All of the above

6. What is the purpose of measuring network performance?

a. To identify performance issues
b. To create more performance issues
c. To increase security
d. None of the above

Answers to Multiple Choice Questions

1. (d); 2. (a); 3. (b); 4. (c); 5. (d); 6. (a)

REFERENCES

1. Al Aghbari, Z., Khedr, A. M., Osamy, W., Arif, I., & Agrawal, D. P., (2020). Routing in wireless sensor networks using optimization techniques: A survey. *Wireless Personal Communications, 111*(1), 2407–2434.
2. Alsamhi, S. H., Ma, O., Ansari, M. S., & Gupta, S. K., (2019). Collaboration of drone and Internet of public safety things in smart cities: An overview of QoS and network performance optimization. *Drones, 3*(1), 13–15.
3. Andrews, J. G., Ganti, R. K., Haenggi, M., Jindal, N., & Weber, S., (2010). A primer on spatial modeling and analysis in wireless networks. *IEEE Communications Magazine, 48*(11), 156–163.
4. Assunção, M. D., Calheiros, R. N., Bianchi, S., Netto, M. A., & Buyya, R., (2015). Big data computing and clouds: Trends and future directions. *Journal of Parallel and Distributed Computing, 79*, 3–15.

5. Azzabi, T., Farhat, H., & Sahli, N., (2017). A survey on wireless sensor networks security issues and military specificities. In: *2017 International Conference on Advanced Systems and Electric Technologies (IC_ASET)* (Vol. 1, pp. 66–72). IEEE.
6. Baktir, A. C., Ozgovde, A., & Ersoy, C., (2017). How can edge computing benefit from software-defined networking: A survey, use cases, and future directions. *IEEE Communications Surveys & Tutorials, 19*(4), 2359–2391.
7. Balakrishnan, H., Seshan, S., & Katz, R. H., (1995). Improving reliable transport and handoff performance in cellular wireless networks. *Wireless Networks, 1*, 469–481.
8. Blilat, A., Bouayad, A., Chaoui, N. E. H., & El Ghazi, M., (2012). Wireless sensor network: Security challenges. In: *2012 National Days of Network Security and Systems* (Vol. 1, pp. 68–72). IEEE.
9. Chen, H., & Yao, D. D., (2001). *Fundamentals of Queueing Networks: Performance, Asymptotics, and Optimization* (Vol. 4, pp. 5–9). New York: Springer.
10. Diallo, O., Rodrigues, J. J., Sene, M., & Lloret, J., (2013). Distributed database management techniques for wireless sensor networks. *IEEE Transactions on Parallel and Distributed Systems, 26*(2), 604–620.
11. Gill, S. S., & Buyya, R., (2018). A taxonomy and future directions for sustainable cloud computing: 360 degree view. *ACM Computing Surveys (CSUR), 51*(5), 1–33.
12. Golden, B., Ball, M., & Bodin, L., (1981). Current and future research directions in network optimization. *Computers & Operations Research, 8*(2), 71–81.
13. Gupta, B. B., Perez, G. M., Agrawal, D. P., & Gupta, D., (2020). *Handbook of Computer Networks and Cyber Security, 10*, 369–402. Springer.
14. Huaizhou, S. H. I., Prasad, R. V., Onur, E., & Niemegeers, I. G. M. M., (2013). Fairness in wireless networks: Issues, measures and challenges. *IEEE Communications Surveys & Tutorials, 16*(1), 5–24.
15. Jeremiah, E. U., Iloke, J., Obi, E., & Ewona, I., (2022). Measurement and performance analysis of signal-to-interference ratio in wireless networks. *Asian Journal of Advanced Research and Reports, 16*(3), 22–31.
16. Kleinrock, L., & Kamoun, F., (1977). Hierarchical routing for large networks performance evaluation and optimization. *Computer Networks (1976), 1*(3), 155–174.
17. Lim, S., Oh, T. H., Choi, Y. B., & Lakshman, T., (2010). Security issues on wireless body area network for remote healthcare monitoring. In: *2010 IEEE International Conference on Sensor Networks, Ubiquitous, and Trustworthy Computing* (Vol. 1, pp. 327–332). IEEE.
18. McGee, A. R., Coutière, M., & Palamara, M. E., (2012). Public safety network security considerations. *Bell Labs Technical Journal, 17*(3), 79–86.
19. Mismar, F. B., Choi, J., & Evans, B. L., (2019). A framework for automated cellular network tuning with reinforcement learning. *IEEE Transactions on Communications, 67*(10), 7152–7167.

20. Mohammed, A. S., Basha, S., Asha, P. N., & Venkatachalam, K., (2020). FCO—Fuzzy constraints applied cluster optimization technique for wireless Ad Hoc networks. *Computer Communications, 154*(1), 501–508.
21. Noshy, M., Ibrahim, A., & Ali, H. A., (2018). Optimization of live virtual machine migration in cloud computing: A survey and future directions. *Journal of Network and Computer Applications, 110*(1), 1–10.
22. Panait, C., & Dragomir, D., (2015). Measuring the performance and energy consumption of AES in wireless sensor networks. In: *2015 Federated Conference on Computer Science and Information Systems (FedCSIS)* (Vol. 1, pp. 1261–1266). IEEE.
23. Parsons, K., McCormac, A., Pattinson, M., Butavicius, M., & Jerram, C., (2014). A study of information security awareness in Australian government organizations. *Information Management & Computer Security, 22*(4), 334–345.
24. Perkins, D. D., Hughes, H. D., & Owen, C. B., (2002). Factors affecting the performance of ad hoc networks. In: *2002 IEEE International Conference on Communications. Conference Proceedings. ICC 2002 (Cat. No. 02CH37333)* (Vol. 4, pp. 2048–2052). IEEE.
25. Perrig, A., Stankovic, J., & Wagner, D., (2004). Security in wireless sensor networks. *Communications of the ACM, 47*(6), 53–57.
26. Petrova, M., Wu, L., Mahonen, P., & Riihijarvi, J., (2007). Interference measurements on performance degradation between colocated IEEE 802.11 g/n and IEEE 802.15. 4 networks. In: *Sixth International Conference on Networking (ICN'07)* (Vol. 1, p. 93). IEEE.
27. Samaan, N., & Karmouch, A., (2009). Towards autonomic network management: An analysis of current and future research directions. *IEEE Communications Surveys & Tutorials, 11*(3), 22–36.
28. Sendra, C. S., Lloret, J., García, P. M., & Toledo, A. J. F., (2011). Power saving and energy optimization techniques for wireless sensor networks. *Journal of Communications, 6*(6), 439–459.
29. Sesay, S., Yang, Z., & He, J., (2004). A survey on mobile ad hoc wireless network. *Information Technology Journal, 3*(2), 168–175.
30. Singh, S., & Sharma, R. M., (2016). Optimization techniques in wireless sensor networks. In: *Proceedings of the Second International Conference on Information and Communication Technology for Competitive Strategies* (Vol. 1, pp. 1–7).
31. Sonntag, S., Manner, J., & Schulte, L., (2013). Netradar-measuring the wireless world. In: *2013 11th International Symposium and Workshops on Modeling and Optimization in Mobile, Ad Hoc and Wireless Networks (WiOpt)* (pp. 29–34). IEEE.
32. Wac, K. E., Bults, R., Van, H. A., Konstantas, D., & Nicola, V. F., (2005). Measurements-based performance evaluation of 3G wireless networks supporting m-health services. In: *Multimedia Computing and Networking 2005* (Vol. 5680, pp. 176–187). SPIE.

33. Wang, W., Liew, S. C., & Li, V. O., (2005). Solutions to performance problems in VoIP over a 802.11 wireless LAN. *IEEE Transactions on Vehicular Technology, 54*(1), 366–384.
34. Yang, Z., Ghubaish, A., Unal, D., & Jain, R., (2021). Factors affecting the performance of sub-1 GHz IoT wireless networks. *Wireless Communications and Mobile Computing, 2021, 1*, 1–13.
35. Yetgin, H., Cheung, K. T. K., El-Hajjar, M., & Hanzo, L. H., (2017). A survey of network lifetime maximization techniques in wireless sensor networks. *IEEE Communications Surveys & Tutorials, 19*(2), 828–854.

CHAPTER 8

FUTURE OF COMPUTER NETWORKING

UNIT INTRODUCTION

For the purpose of sharing data and other resources, computers can be joined to form a network. To connect computers together, an OSI (open system interconnection) model is used.

Several protocols are established at every layer of the OSI model, where they specify how two entities are to communicate with one another via the network (Jovanovic, 2011). Applications for computer networks include file and data transfer, instant messaging, electronic commerce, VoIP (voice over internet protocol), and resource sharing (using protocols like TCP/IP1, UDP, HTTP, and FTP).

These days, networks are utilized in a wide variety of settings. It has come to our attention that the field of digital networking is undergoing a great deal of innovation, with the primary objective being the improvement of network safety. Edge computing, the IoT, artificial intelligence (AI), cloud networking, orchestration, SDN (Software Defined Network) Technology, Intent-based learning, 4D Network, 5G, IPv6, automation, and many other developments are among the latest trends in the world of networking that are revolutionizing the digital world (Hakiri et al., 2014). Other developments include many others. These technologies are currently under development in order to make communication more effective and secure. In this study, we do a literature assessment on latest trend and advancements in the field of computer networks. Our focus is on the field of computer networking.

Learning Objectives

At the end of this chapter, readers will be able to learn:

- Basics of edge computing;
- Fundamentals of cloud networking;
- Concepts of software defined WAN (SD-WAN) and software defined networking (SDN);
- Concepts of cloud automation and cloud orchestration;
- Basics of the intent-based networking;
- 5G and its applications;
- 4D networking and its components.

Key Terms

- Architecture
- Automation
- Cloud networking
- Data
- Edge computing
- Intent
- Network
- Orchestration
- Plane

8.1. EDGE COMPUTING

Edge computing is a fragmented style of processing of data that has been designed specifically with the goal of managing the information produced by IoT devices (Varghese et al., 2016). The phrase "edge computing" relates to this form of data processing. The major function of edge computing is to provide data to cloud services, where it can be processed, stored, and transferred. This has been the edge computing model since its inception. After the surplus of useless data has been culled down to just the essential data, that information is then sent throughout the network. The concept of "edge computing" refers to the computing infrastructure that is positioned so that it is physically close to the sites at which data is generated (Yu et al., 2017). Some examples of industrial machinery include wind turbines, MR (magnetic resonance) scanners, and submarine explosion preventers. Industrial controllers, such as time series databases and SCADA systems, are also examples of industrial machinery. These systems aggregate data from a variety of pieces of equipment and sensors (Figure 8.1).

Remember

Reduce latency and improve performance with edge computing by processing data closer to the source.

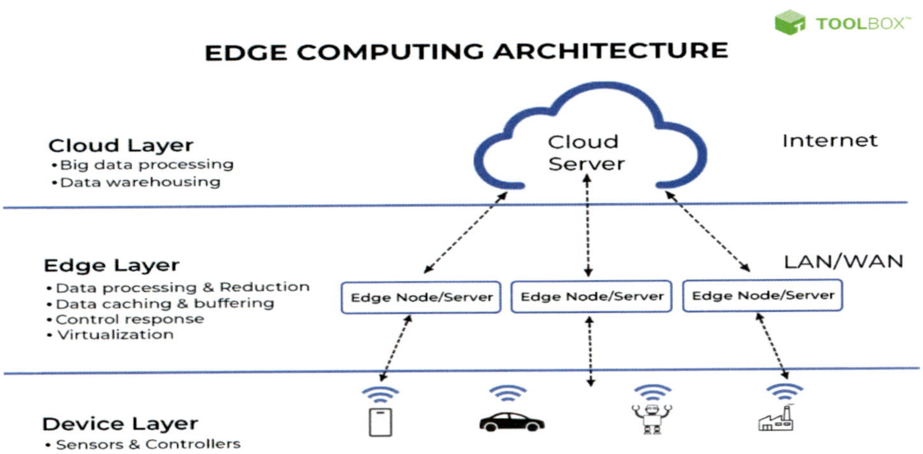

Figure 8.1. Schematic of the edge computing architecture.

Source: Remya Mohanan, Creative Commons License.

Computing systems at the edge of the network are becoming increasingly powerful in terms of their ability to compute, store, and analyze data (Hassan et al., 2019). They are more valuable since they have applications in different types of industrial organizations. Edge computing refers to the capability of performing analytics and processing locally on the device itself. Edge computing opens up new avenues for exploration in IoT applications and machine learning endeavors (Chen & Ran, 2019). Some examples of these kinds of endeavors include facial recognition, object detection, and language processing. It is anticipated that investments made in edge infrastructure would account for 18% of total expenditures on IoT infrastructure by the year 2020. The following is a list of the causes that are driving edge computing:

- Faster processing;
- Cloud adoption increase;
- Increasing pressure on the networks (Abbas et al., 2017).

The industrial machines generate an enormous amount of data, which necessitates the development of an architecture that meets certain requirements. These requirements include speed, the ability to operate in remote contexts, and the ability to save bandwidth, storage space, time, and money by reducing the amount of data that must be transmitted. The following are some of the primary drivers that have made edge computing a much more practicable reality in today's world:

- A significant drop in the prices of both computing power and sensors.
- Increased computational capacity in devices with a reduced physical footprint (including sensor hub or gateway)
- Large volume of data (Shi et al., 2016)
- Artificial intelligence and data analysis the following situations will cause edge computing to become extremely important:
- Unreliable internet access in outlying areas
- Limited bandwidth and the expensive cost that comes along with sending information to the cloud.
- Low latency, including interaction between actuation and machine insights in a closed loop.
- Access to historical data in order to perform real-time analytics.
- Obligations imposed by regulations or concerns about online safety (Mao et al., 2017).

8.2. CLOUD NETWORKING

Cloud computing is a technology that is expanding at a quick rate, and according to the most recent study from Gartner, it is anticipated that cloud computing services will expand at a rate of 17.3% in the year 2019. Also, it is anticipated that by the year 2022, cloud services would be utilized by 90% of all businesses. This is the case since these sophisticated technologies provide a variety of benefits, which are listed above. Cloud services are affordable, offer the flexibility to access data anywhere at any time with the assistance of a reliable internet connection, guarantee the safety of the data, and have a wide variety of additional applications. Cloud networking refers to the practice of obtaining or making use of shared services and networks provided by a cloud-based provider (Mechtri et al., 2013). Cloud computing entails nothing more than the sharing of computer resources, whereas cloud networking refers to the act of sharing network resources within an existing shared network. Virtual routers, firewalls, bandwidth, and software for network management are only a few examples of the various types of network resources (Luong et al., 2017) (Figure 8.2).

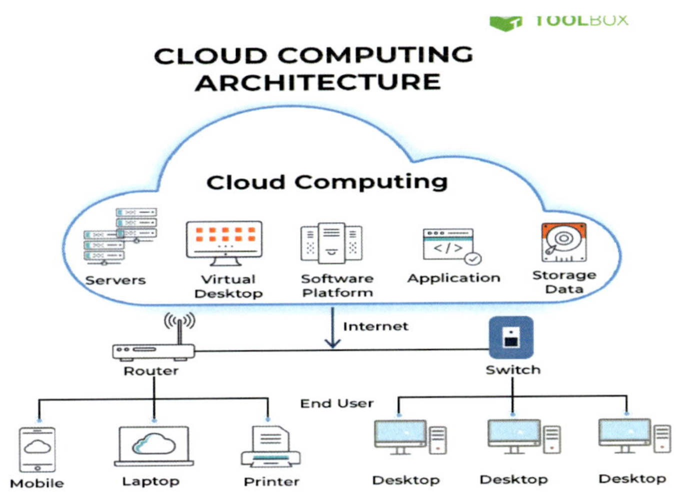

Figure 8.2. Illustration of the cloud computing.

Source: Prajakta Patil, Creative Commons License.

There are many distinct varieties of cloud computing services, and they can be broken down into the following three categories:

8.2.1. Infrastructure as a Service (IaaS)

The necessary infrastructure, including Servers, OS (Operating Systems), Networks, Virtual Machines, and Storage, is made available on a rental basis through this service. In this type of service, enterprises make use of the infrastructure of a service provider while running their own platforms and applications. Access to the vendor's computer resources, such as servers, storage, and networking, is contingent on the user making a simple rental payment to the vendor (Bitar et al., 2013). This service is used by Microsoft Azure and Amazon Web Service, which are two of the top cloud service providers.

8.2.2. Platform as a Service (PaaS)

The creation of software, its testing, and its ongoing maintenance all make use of this service. PaaS is identical to IaaS, with the exception that it also offers supplementary resources, such as BI and DBMS service. In this scenario, the service provider grants users accessibility to a cloud-based infrastructure in which they are able to construct and distribute applications. This is indicated by the name of the service. The service provider is responsible for supplying the underlying infrastructure (Lee et al., 2014). This service has an advantage over IaaS in that it not only gives users access to the computer resources they need, but it also includes a set of prebuilt tools that can be used to design, tweak, and test their very own apps. Cloud providers Apprenda and Red Hat are examples of those who utilize this technique.

8.2.3. Software as a Service (SaaS)

Users are capable of connecting to the applications or programs through the World Wide Web (WWW) by subscribing to this service, and accessing the applications can be done either through the web or through the vendor APIs. Users of this service do not need to worry about managing, installing, or upgrading software because they can just access the program through a remote network in the cloud. SaaS is utilized by Google Apps and Salesforce.

KEYWORD

A **program** is a set of instructions that a computer uses to perform a specific function.

There are several cloud service providers throughout the world, some of the most notable of which include Kamatera, Amazon Web Services (AWS), Google Cloud Platform, Phoenix NAP, Microsoft Azure, and Adobe, to name just a few of the available options. Recent research suggests that AWS has established itself as the industry's leading cloud provider. It has gained increased popularity as a result of features like mobile friendliness, security, and serverless cloud operations, all of which are thought to improve the productivity of any firm (Schoo et al., 2010). Hybrid and multi-cloud solutions, artificial intelligence (AI) frameworks, backup and disaster recovering, serverless computing, data containers, and cloud security are some of the trends that are expected to emerge in the field of cloud computing in 2019. Consumers required enhanced clouds because the public cloud provides very few options; one such cloud is the hybrid cloud, which is a combination of on-premises, third-party, and private cloud. Since the public cloud offers very few options, users required enhanced clouds. While using serverless computing, the client is not required to purchase or rent services in advance, nor is the customer required to configure these services. The provision of the platform, its setup, and a wide variety of effective features for working with data and building applications is the responsibility of the Cloud. This particular cloud service is of the PaaS variety.

TIPS

Streamline network management and improve performance by implementing SD-WAN technology, which centralizes control and can dynamically route traffic over multiple connections.

In recent years, there has been a significant uptick in interest in AI. AI is utilized in settings that involve a large amount of automation and demand speedier outputs. AI can't exist without Machine Learning, which in turn relies on Artificial Neural Networks (Benson et al., 2011). AI can assist to cut costs in a wide range of ways, including minimizing the duplication of work and taking over some labor-intensive operations that would otherwise need to be performed by humans, including copying or extracting data. The preceding idea argues that cloud has a great deal of applications and advantages, and that it is an absolute blessing for the development of new technologies.

8.3. SOFTWARE DEFINED WAN (SD-WAN)

It was estimated that the global SD-WAN market will be worth $676.9 million in 2017, and it is anticipated to experience a CAGR (compound annual growth rate) of 54.1% during the period of 2018–2023. The need for cost-effective WAN management solutions, the increasing implementation of cloud technologies, the requirement for simpler network architecture, and the requirement for end-to-end network visibility and security are all factors that are driving the expansion of the market globally (El Kamel & Youssef, 2020). This elucidates the need for advanced technologies such as cloud computing, SD-WAN, SDN, and a great number of other technologies, and SD-WAN is a prime example of a technology that is successfully pushing the market for other technologies.

The phrase "software-defined method to controlling the WAN or wide-area network," is how CISCO summarizes its explanation of what "SD-WAN" is and what it does. When we delve deeper into the theory of SD-WAN, we see that there are actually several components at play (Rajagopalan, 2020). The term "software-defined wide area network" (SD-WAN) refers to a type of virtual wide area network architecture that enables businesses to securely connect customers to applications by utilizing any combo of transport services, such as MPLS (Multiprotocol Label Switching), LTE, and broadband internet services. A network that spans a significant portion of a larger geographic region is referred to as a WAN (wide area network) (Yang et al., 2019). LAN (Local area networks) and metropolitan area networks are two of the smaller networks that can be connected to a wide area network (WAN) (MANs). TCP/IP is the protocol that is utilized for a WAN, and it is used in conjunction with various devices like routers, switches, firewalls, and modems.

The traditional wide area networks (WANs) that are premised on conventional routers are really not cloud friendly. In contrast to the traditional router-centric architecture of WAN, the SD-WAN is designed to support applications that are hosted in on-premises data centers, public or private clouds, and SaaS solutions including Salesfore.com, Workday, Office365, and Dropbox, all while delivering the top levels of application performance, which enhances the user experience. This is why SD-WAN came into existence and supplanted conventional Backhauling of traffic was another issue that plagued older wide area networks (WANs). Backhauling only adds latency or delay, which is detrimental to application performance and results in a negative user experience as well as a loss of productivity in situations where users want their calculations to be completed quickly, such as in corporate settings. By utilizing SD-WAN, all of these issues were resolved (Majdoub et al., 2020).

KEYWORD

Backhaul (or backhauling) is the connection between an access node and the core network.

8.4. SOFTWARE DEFINED NETWORKING (SDN)

The global Software – defined networking Market is expected to increase in value from $8.8 billion in 2018 to $29.1 billion by 2023, representing a CAGR of 26.8% between 2018 and 2023 (Karakus & Durresi, 2017). With the capacity to allow network invention, SDN is quickly growing into one of the most promising and lucrative networking technologies, capable of solving the majority of long-standing networking issues. Through the use of a control plane, multiple devices can be managed centrally in a software-defined network (Figure 8.3).

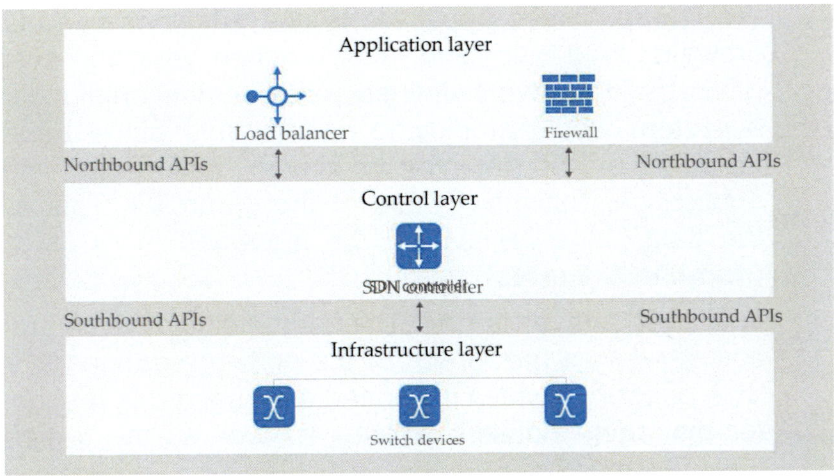

Figure 8.3. Components and architecture of SDN.

Source: Howard, Creative Commons License.

The data plane and control plane are two distinct but equally important components of a network, and SDN is notable for its novel approach to this separation. Ethernet switches are used to do this by decoupling the hardware that regulates the packets flow. The data plane is the section of the network responsible for transporting data sent by end users. It is also known as the forwarding aircraft, user plane, carrier plane, or bearer plane. The three primary elements of a telecommunications architecture are the information plane, the control plane, as well as the management (Benzekki et al., 2016). In a network, the data plane carries the traffic for which the network was designed. The management plane and control plane support this function. The term "data plane" is used to describe the set of operations and procedures responsible for transmitting data between interfaces. The phrase "control plane" describes the set of operations that decides which course to take (Shin et al., 2016). Such protocols include routing, spanning tree, link-state discovery protocol (ldp), and others. Control and monitoring of devices fall under the purview of the management plane.

8.4.1. SDN-Architecture

The control layer, the application layer, and the infrastructure layer are the three components that are typically included in a representation of a standard SDN architecture.

i. The application layer is where common network programmers and functions that companies make use of are stored. These applications and functions can include firewalls, load balancing, and intrusion detection systems (IDS). In a software-defined network, the appliance that a system would employ to handle data plane behavior, including a load balancer or firewall, is replaced with an application that makes use of the controller. This allows the data plane behavior to be managed more efficiently (Karakus & Durresi, 2017).

ii. The control layer is the SDN controller that is centralized and serves as the "brain" of the software-defined system. This controller, which is housed on a server, is responsible for managing network policies as well as the traffic flow over the network.

iii. The infrastructure layer consists of the network's physical switches and is the lowest level of the three layers (Shin et al., 2012).

These three levels are connected to one another through the use of northbound and southbound APIs (application programming interfaces) respectively.

8.4.2. Adaptive SDN

KEYWORD

A **network topology** is the physical and logical arrangement of nodes and connections in a network.

Software-defined networking makes use of an operation mode is referred to as adaptive or dynamic. In this mode, a switch sends a route request for a packet to a controller which lacks a specific route. This mode is sometimes called "adaptive" or "dynamic." This technique is distinct from routing that is adaptive, which sends route requests through algorithms and routers depending on the network topology rather than through a controller (Gelberger et al., 2013). Adaptive routing uses the network topology to determine which routes should be used.

8.5. CLOUD AUTOMATION AND ORCHESTRATION

It is anticipated that by the end of 2025, the global market for cloud orchestration would have surpassed 20 billion USD, having been valued at an estimated almost 6,970 million USD in 2017. Throughout the period covered by the projection, it is anticipated that total sales revenue would have a CAGR of 14.6%. (2017–2025). This suggests that in the years to come, it is anticipated that medium and small businesses would be the top cloud adopters of orchestration services and platforms. This is particularly the case for small and medium businesses. To say the least, the term "cloud automation" refers to the deployment and administration tasks that IT teams are able to carry out without the need for human intervention. Since it organizes, synchronizes, and manages the workflow of automated processes, cloud orchestration is intrinsically connected to cloud automation. Utilizing computer programming technology to control the interactions and interconnections of workloads running on public and private infrastructure of cloud is what is referred to as cloud orchestration. Cloud orchestration is often utilized in order to provision, deploy, or start servers, assign, and acquire storage space, manage networking, construct virtual machines (VMs), and obtain access to particular software that is hosted on cloud services (Bringhenti et al., 2019). This is achieved through the cloud's orchestration of its three most important and interconnected aspects: workload, resource, and service orchestration. Permission checks that are necessary for compliance and security can be integrated into an orchestration platform (Figure 8.4).

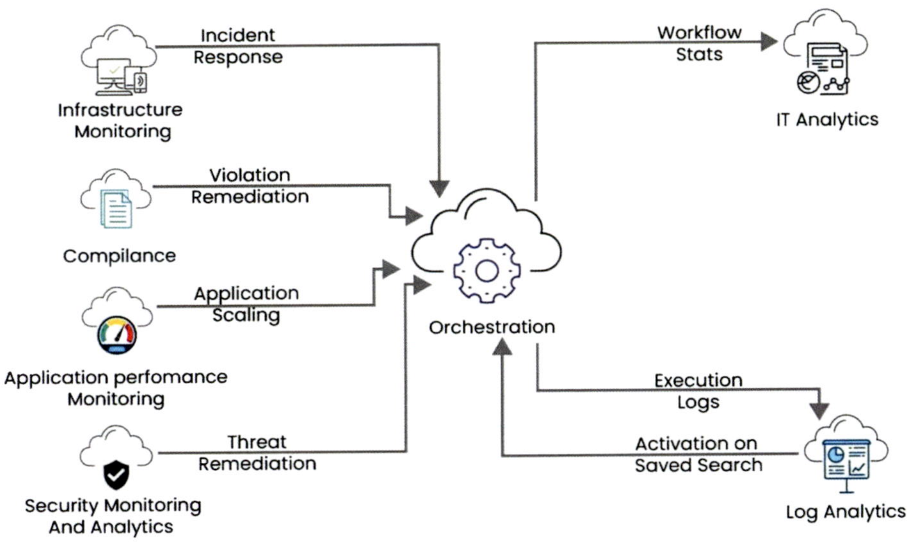

Figure 8.4. Illustration of the cloud automation vs. cloud orchestration.

Source: Ismile Technologies, Creative Commons License.

Since 2006, when infrastructure as a service (IaaS) and platform as a service (PaaS) multi-cloud deployments proceeded on to become gigantic in scale, cloud orchestration has gained prominence (Wu, 2020). As a result, management of an infrastructure of a cloud is becoming an enormous task for in-house IT professionals. In this situation, cloud orchestration plays a very essential role, as its tools may be utilized to facilitate deployment and maintenance, and they can also provide more insight into cloud processes and resources. The purpose of orchestration software is to bring together all the cloud's resources, which it does by first providing a way to link and then automating the delivery of the many services that businesses need. Orchestration combines a wide variety of jobs and characteristics into a single process, which can significantly minimize the amount of work that needs to be done by staff (Sarkar et al., 2022). They include high availability, scaling, dependency management, failure recovery, and many more. In addition, orchestration offers visibility into both resources and processes, something that standard cloud automation does not. Amazon Web Cloud Service and Cisco Cloud Center are just two of the companies that provide cloud orchestration as services and products, respectively.

Because automation is a component of orchestration, it follows that orchestration is responsible for providing coordination across and among numerous automated operations. In order to automate the deployment process, scripts are being employed. Scripts offer a versatile method for writing commands in the form of a file that may be run in a short amount of time. Chef and Puppet are two prominent open-source automation technologies. Both are available for download. The Chef concept is a procedural model since it defines in detail how to install and integrate the various components of a cloud application (Liu et al., 2011). The "cookbooks" and "recipes" that Chef generates are built in an approachable manner for computer programmers. Each step of the deployment procedure can be explained independently, and the process of creating a repetitive application deployment can be accomplished by putting together these individual recipes (Svorobej et al., 2020). Because each step of an operation can be outlined in a recipe, nothing is able to be manually deployed that Chef is unable to take over and do automatically. Puppet was developed by people working in operations, who are more accustomed to articulating what they want rather than the specific procedures that must be taken to get it. Chef, on the other hand, is designed to be user-friendly for programmers. The models in Puppet can facilitate deployment descriptions in the same way as a high-level computer programming language can. In addition, due to the fact that an end-state approach can be utilized to represent any stage in the application lifecycle management (ALM) process (ALM). In general, this is the approach that is taken while implementing cloud automation. Cloud orchestration and automation are complementary

KEYWORD

Automation is the use of technology to perform tasks with where human input is minimized.

processes, with each relying on the other for its own success. It would not make any sense to build automated tasks that are unable to be a portion of a process of cloud orchestration, nor would it make sense to establish an orchestration process that does not call any automated tasks (Azodolmolky et al., 2013). Neither of these things makes any sense.

8.6. INTENT-BASED NETWORKING

Intent-Based Networking is the field of network technology that is experiencing the most rapid growth right now (Wei et al., 2020). It automates network administration by utilizing AI and machine learning. IBN aims forward establishing self-managing systems. The majority of today's networks are operated and controlled by hand. The switches and dozens of other devices that enable enterprise networks are programmed using scripts that network administrators generate. These scripts contain every detail necessary to complete a given task, and network managers interact with them using a command line interface. Giving orders to the network based on your desired outcome (intent) instead of what it is supposed to do is what is meant by "intent-based networking." The purpose of these directives is to achieve the expected goal. Without the need for engineers to individually modify each network device, the intent is automatically translated and sent to all of the network's devices. The IBN requires fewer inputs, all of which are done so using a graphical user interface (GUI) that is easy to use (Zeydan & Turk, 2020) (Figure 8.5).

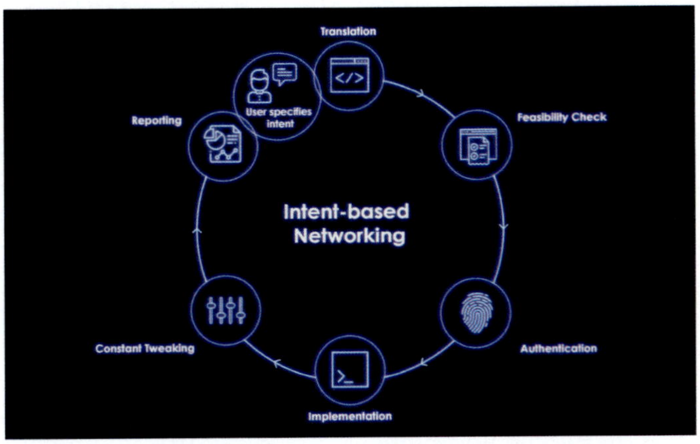

Figure 8.5. Schematic of the internet-based networking.

Source: Manage Engine, Creative Commons License.

Did you get it?

Intent Based Networking (IBN) automates network management by using artificial intelligence and machine learning to translate high-level business objectives into network configurations.

An intent-based network is an adaptable system that uses AI to learn from prior experiences and responds to the issue of what ought to be done in a specific circumstance (Velasco et al., 2021). This type of system is known as an adaptive learning system. It's possible that the response to the scenario at hand is an automatic one, triggered by some kind of system occurrence. If the system was provided with an occurrence or a desired event, it would be able to determine how to respond correctly without the need for human intervention. Data centers, public clouds, and the IoT are some of the places where intent-based networking can be applied. IBN is also in its early phases of development due to the fact that AI is still in its developmental stage (Riftadi & Kuipers, 2019). As the world continues to progress towards AI, IBN will likely be operational in the majority of networks in the not-too-distant future.

8.7. 5G AND ITS APPLICATIONS

The following are some of the requirements that must be met in order to develop the 5th generation of network technology (Table 8.1):

- Increasing interest in utilizing wireless broadband services.
- Wireless networks that are faster.
- Networks that have a large capacity (Gupta et al., 2019).
  - The internet of things (Smart Devices)
  - Networks that have a low latency
- Reliable networks.
- In order to construct 5G Networks, the following subfields of technology are required:
  - Radio access technology;
  - Antennas;
  - Network Slicing (Gao et al., 2017);
  - Spectrum utilization (air interface design).

Table 8.1. Parameter Values

SL. No.	Parameter	Value
1.	Air link's latency	<1 ms
2.	Latency device to core (end-to-end)	<10 ms

3.	Connection density	100X contrast with LTE
4.	Density of use across an area	1 $Tbits/s/km^2$
5.	Spectral efficiency of the system	10 bit/s/Hz/cell
6.	Peak throughput per connection (downlink)	10 Gbit/s
7.	Efficiency of energy	>90% advancement over LTE

Source: Ajay Kumar, Creative Commons License.

5G is ahead of its time in the following respects:

- High enhanced peak bit rate;
- Greater data capacity per unit area;
- A high capacity that enables simultaneous and instantaneous communication for a greater number of devices (Baratè et al., 2019);
- Decrease the amount of power the battery needs;
- Improved connectivity regardless of the region of the world in which you find yourself;
- A larger variety of devices that are compatible with the platform;
- Reduced expenses associated with the development of infrastructure;
- Improved consistency and dependability of the communications (Sun & Du, 2017).

IoT (internet of things), smart farming, security and surveillance, shipping and logistics, fleet management, high speed network, smart cities, and autonomous driving, are all examples of potential applications for 5G technology (Piao et al., 2020).

Remember

Fleet management software allows businesses to monitor, track, and create detailed performance reports on vehicle fleets.

8.8. 4D NETWORK

Tesseract is a prototype of a system that permits direct control of several computer networks from within a single administrative umbrella (Choy et al., 2019). Tesseract is built on 4D Architecture, which divides the network control plane into decision, dissemination, discovery, and data planes. This architecture is the foundation for Tesseract. It offers two essential services, the dissemination service, which transmits control the information and data from the network decision component to the network's nodes, and the node configuration service, which offers an interface (gui) for the decision component to command the network nodes to carry out desired operations. Both of these services are provided so that direct control can be enabled. Tesseract decreases the likelihood of errors caused by humans by limiting the amount of manual node configuration that is required. In terms of intra-domain routing control, it can deal with up to one thousand nodes. The adaptability of Tesseract is demonstrated by the fact that it can be used for both the combined packet forwarding and policy-based filtering of IP networks as well as the link-cost driven forwarding of Ethernet packets (Vishnevskiy et al., 2020). A list of the planes that are used in 4D architecture are discussed in subsections.

8.8.1. Data Plane

This plane is responsible for operations in switches of the network and offers services including the forwarding of IPv4, IPv6, and Ethernet packets. The decisions made by the decision plane influence the state of the switches, which in turn influences the operations carried out by the data plane. A few examples of states that can be found in switches include the forwarding table or the forwarding information base, the queue management parameters, the mappings for network and tunnels address translation, the flow scheduling weights, and the packet filters.

KEYWORD

A **packet filter** is a method to decide to allow or drop each packet going through the firewall based on the header information.

8.8.2. Discovery Plane

Each switch is accountable for figuring out its own hardware capabilities as well as how it physically connects to the switches in its immediate vicinity (Guo et al., 2020). After that, the information that was received is transmitted to the decision element that is located in the decision plane via the logical connections that are maintained by the dissemination plane. Due to the need to maintain backward compatibility, end hosts do not take part in the discovery plane.

8.8.3. Dissemination Plane

This plane is responsible for maintaining the logical channels that are used to transfer control information between the decision plane and the network switches (Shi et al., 2020). The data paths and the dispersion paths are managed independently of one another so that the dissemination paths can function normally without the need for path reconfiguration or the effective paths establishment in the data plane. Management and Control information of today's networks are transmitted by data channels, and these data paths have to be recognized by routing protocols. This creates a cyclical reliance, which in turn generates more problems.

ACTIVITY 8.1.

How do you envision the future of computer networking, and what steps are you taking to prepare for emerging technologies and changing industry trends?

8.8.4. Decision Plane

It possesses a decision element that is logically centralized and is responsible for making all decisions that drive network control, including decisions on access control, security, and load balancing (Wu et al., 2019). The information that is gathered by that of the discovery plane is utilized by the decision element, which then issues orders to the switches based on these decisions using the information that was collected from the discovery plane. The decision element is able to better command the switches with the assistance of the configuration service of the node interface.

8.9. SUMMARY

- The effectiveness and safety of networks have both been improved by the technologies that have been explored. The goal of the global community is to make life simpler for everyone. The applications from these techniques and technologies are extremely widespread, and they are currently being utilized in each nook and cranny of the nation. IoT, AI, machine learning, and cloud computing are the technologies that are currently on trend. In addition, big data and the analytics that come with it have made new opportunities available in the field of computer networking. It is anticipated that the technologies described above will dominate the whole digital market, and the usage of these cutting-edge technologies is causing the world to become more intelligent.

REVIEW QUESTIONS

1. What is edge computing, and what are its advantages?
2. How does cloud networking differ from traditional networking?
3. What is the difference between SD-WAN and SDN?
4. What is intent-based networking, and how does it work?
5. How does 5G differ from previous generations of cellular networks?

MULTIPLE CHOICE QUESTIONS

1. What is the focus of this chapter?

a. Cloud networking fundamentals
b. Edge computing
c. Intent-based networking
d. 5G and its applications

2. What are the concepts covered in this chapter related to software-defined networking?

a. Software-defined WAN and Software-defined Networking
b. Cloud automation and cloud orchestration
c. Intent-based networking
d. All of the above

3. What are the components of 4D networking?

a. Domain-based routing, content-based routing, and mobility-based routing
b. Domain-based routing, content-based routing, mobility-based routing, and time-based routing
c. Domain-based routing and content-based routing

d. Domain-based routing and mobility-based routing

4. What is the concept covered in this chapter related to cloud networking?

a. Edge computing
b. SD-WAN
c. SDN
d. Cloud automation

5. What is the concept covered in this chapter related to networking automation?

a. Cloud automation and cloud orchestration
b. SD-WAN
c. 5G
d. Edge computing

Answers to Multiple Choice Questions

1. (b); 2. (a); 3. (b); 4. (c); 5. (a)

REFERENCES

1. Abbas, N., Zhang, Y., Taherkordi, A., & Skeie, T., (2017). Mobile edge computing: A survey. *IEEE Internet of Things Journal, 5*(1), 450–465.
2. Azodolmolky, S., Wieder, P., & Yahyapour, R., (2013). Cloud computing networking: Challenges and opportunities for innovations. *IEEE Communications Magazine, 51*(7), 54–62.
3. Baratè, A., Haus, G., Ludovico, L. A., Pagani, E., & Scarabottolo, N., (2019). *5G Technology and Its Applications to Music Education* (Vol. 1, pp. 2–4). International Association for Development of the Information Society.
4. Benson, T., Akella, A., Shaikh, A., & Sahu, S., (2011). CloudNaaS: A cloud networking platform for enterprise applications. In: *Proceedings of the 2nd ACM Symposium on Cloud Computing* (Vol. 1, pp. 1–13).
5. Benzekki, K., El Fergougui, A., & Elbelrhiti, E. A., (2016). Software-defined networking (SDN): A survey. *Security and Communication Networks, 9*(18), 5803–5833.
6. Bitar, N., Gringeri, S., & Xia, T. J., (2013). Technologies and protocols for data center and cloud networking. *IEEE Communications Magazine, 51*(9), 24–31.
7. Bringhenti, D., Marchetto, G., Sisto, R., Valenza, F., & Yusupov, J., (2019). Towards a fully automated and optimized network security functions orchestration. In: *2019 4th International Conference on Computing, Communications and Security (ICCCS)* (Vol. 1, pp. 1–7). IEEE.
8. Chen, J., & Ran, X., (2019). Deep learning with edge computing: A review. *Proceedings of the IEEE, 107*(8), 1655–1674.

9. Choy, C., Gwak, J., & Savarese, S., (2019). 4D spatio-temporal convNets: Minkowski convolutional neural networks. In: *Proceedings of the IEEE/CVF Conference on Computer Vision and Pattern Recognition* (Vol. 1, pp. 3075–3084).
10. El Kamel, A., & Youssef, H., (2020). Improving switch-to-controller assignment with load balancing in multi-controller software defined WAN (SD-WAN). *Journal of Network and Systems Management, 28*, 553–575.
11. Gao, L., Luan, T. H., Liu, B., Zhou, W., & Yu, S., (2017). Fog computing and its applications in 5G. *5G Mobile Communications, 1*, 571–593.
12. Gelberger, A., Yemini, N., & Giladi, R., (2013). Performance analysis of software-defined networking (SDN). In: *2013 IEEE 21st International Symposium on Modeling, Analysis and Simulation of Computer and Telecommunication Systems* (Vol. 1, pp. 389–393). IEEE.
13. Guo, Y., Bi, L., Ahn, E., Feng, D., Wang, Q., & Kim, J., (2020). A spatiotemporal volumetric interpolation network for 4D dynamic medical image. In: *Proceedings of the IEEE/CVF Conference on Computer Vision and Pattern Recognition* (Vol. 1, pp. 4726–4735).
14. Gupta, R., Tanwar, S., Tyagi, S., & Kumar, N., (2019). Tactile Internet and its applications in 5G era: A comprehensive review. *International Journal of Communication Systems, 32*(14), e3981.
15. Hakiri, A., Gokhale, A., Berthou, P., Schmidt, D. C., & Gayraud, T., (2014). Software-defined networking: Challenges and research opportunities for future Internet. *Computer Networks, 75*(1), 453–471.
16. Hassan, N., Yau, K. L. A., & Wu, C., (2019). Edge computing in 5G: A review. *IEEE Access, 7*(1), 127276–127289.
17. Jovanovic, M. M., (2011). Power conversion technologies for computer networking and telecom power systems-past present and future. In: *International Power Conversion & Drive Conference (IPCDC)* (Vol. 1, pp. 156–161). St. Petersburg, Russia.
18. Karakus, M., & Durresi, A., (2017). A survey: Control plane scalability issues and approaches in software-defined networking (SDN). *Computer Networks, 112*(1), 279–293.
19. Karakus, M., & Durresi, A., (2017). Quality of service (QoS) in software defined networking (SDN): A survey. *Journal of Network and Computer Applications, 80*(1), 200–218.
20. Lee, E., Lee, E. K., Gerla, M., & Oh, S. Y., (2014). Vehicular cloud networking: Architecture and design principles. *IEEE Communications Magazine, 52*(2), 148–155.
21. Liu, C., Loo, B. T., & Mao, Y., (2011). Declarative automated cloud resource orchestration. In: *Proceedings of the 2nd ACM Symposium on Cloud Computing* (Vol. 1, pp. 1–8).
22. Luong, N. C., Wang, P., Niyato, D., Wen, Y., & Han, Z., (2017). Resource management in cloud networking using economic analysis and pricing models: A survey. *IEEE*

Communications Surveys & Tutorials, 19(2), 954–1001.

23. Majdoub, M., El Kamel, A., & Youssef, H., (2020). DQR: An efficient deep Q-based routing approach in multi-controller software defined WAN (SD-WAN). *Journal of Interconnection Networks, 20*(04), 2150002.
24. Mao, Y., You, C., Zhang, J., Huang, K., & Letaief, K. B., (2017). A survey on mobile edge computing: The communication perspective. *IEEE Communications Surveys & Tutorials, 19*(4), 2322–2358.
25. Mechtri, M., Zeghlache, D., Zekri, E., & Marshall, I. J., (2013). Inter and intra cloud networking gateway as a service. In: *2013 IEEE 2nd International Conference on Cloud Networking (CloudNet)* (Vol. 1, pp. 156–163). IEEE.
26. Piao, H., Jin, Y., & Qu, L., (2020). A compact and straightforward self-decoupled MIMO antenna system for 5G applications. *IEEE Access, 8*(1), 129236–129245.
27. Rajagopalan, S., (2020). An overview of SD-WAN load balancing for WAN connections. In: *2020 4th International Conference on Electronics, Communication and Aerospace Technology (ICECA)* (Vol. 1, pp. 1–4). IEEE.
28. Riftadi, M., & Kuipers, F., (2019). P4i/o: Intent-based networking with p4. In: *2019 IEEE Conference on Network Softwarization (NetSoft)* (Vol. 1, pp. 438–443). IEEE.
29. Sarkar, S., Choudhary, G., Shandilya, S. K., Hussain, A., & Kim, H., (2022). Security of zero trust networks in cloud computing: A comparative review. *Sustainability, 14*(18), 11213.
30. Schoo, P., Fusenig, V., Souza, V., Melo, M., Murray, P., Debar, H., & Zeghlache, D., (2010). Challenges for cloud networking security. In: *MONAMI* (Vol. 1, pp. 298–313).
31. Shi, H., Lin, G., Wang, H., Hung, T. Y., & Wang, Z., (2020). SpSequenceNet: Semantic segmentation network on 4D point clouds. In: *Proceedings of the IEEE/CVF Conference on Computer Vision and Pattern Recognition* (Vol. 1, pp. 4574–4583).
32. Shi, W., Cao, J., Zhang, Q., Li, Y., & Xu, L., (2016). Edge computing: Vision and challenges. *IEEE Internet of Things Journal, 3*(5), 637–646.
33. Shin, M. K., Nam, K. H., & Kim, H. J., (2012). Software-defined networking (SDN): A reference architecture and open APIs. In: *2012 International Conference on ICT Convergence (ICTC)* (Vol. 1, pp. 360–361). IEEE.
34. Shin, S., Xu, L., Hong, S., & Gu, G., (2016). Enhancing network security through software defined networking (SDN). In: *2016 25th International Conference on Computer Communication and Networks (ICCCN)* (Vol. 1, pp. 1–9). IEEE.
35. Sun, L., & Du, Q., (2017). Physical layer security with its applications in 5G networks: A review. *China Communications, 14*(12), 1–14.
36. Svorobej, S., Bendechache, M., Griesinger, F., & Domaschka, J., (2020). Orchestration from the cloud to the edge. *The Cloud-to-Thing Continuum: Opportunities and Challenges in Cloud, Fog and Edge Computing, 1*, 61–77.
37. Varghese, B., Wang, N., Barbhuiya, S., Kilpatrick, P., & Nikolopoulos, D. S., (2016). Challenges and opportunities in edge computing. In: *2016 IEEE International*

Conference on Smart Cloud (SmartCloud) (Vol. 1, pp. 20–26). IEEE.

38. Velasco, L., Signorelli, M., De Dios, O. G., Papagianni, C., Bifulco, R., Olmos, J. J. V., & Ruiz, M., (2021). End-to-end intent-based networking. *IEEE Communications Magazine, 59*(10), 106–112.
39. Vishnevskiy, V., Walheim, J., & Kozerke, S., (2020). Deep variational network for rapid 4D flow MRI reconstruction. *Nature Machine Intelligence, 2*(4), 228–235.
40. Wei, Y., Peng, M., & Liu, Y., (2020). Intent-based networks for 6G: Insights and challenges. *Digital Communications and Networks, 6*(3), 270–280.
41. Wu, Y., (2020). Cloud-edge orchestration for the internet of things: Architecture and AI-powered data processing. *IEEE Internet of Things Journal, 8*(16), 12792–12805.
42. Wu, Z. J., Tian, S., & Ma, L., (2019). A 4D trajectory prediction model based on the BP neural network. *Journal of Intelligent Systems, 29*(1), 1545–1557.
43. Yang, Z., Cui, Y., Li, B., Liu, Y., & Xu, Y., (2019). Software-defined wide area network (SD-WAN): Architecture, advances and opportunities. In: *2019 28th International Conference on Computer Communication and Networks (ICCCN)* (Vol. 1, pp. 1–9). IEEE.
44. Yu, W., Liang, F., He, X., Hatcher, W. G., Lu, C., Lin, J., & Yang, X., (2017). A survey on the edge computing for the internet of things. *IEEE Access, 6*(1), 6900–6919.
45. Zeydan, E., & Turk, Y., (2020). Recent advances in intent-based networking: A survey. In: *2020 IEEE 91st Vehicular Technology Conference (VTC2020-Spring)* (Vol. 1, pp. 1–5). IEEE.

INDEX

A

Access point (AP) 50
Acknowledgment 180
Acquiring system knowledge 130
Adaptive learning system 224
Adaptive routing 220
Ad hoc wireless network 152
Administrative authority 4
Advanced Research Projects Agency Network (ARPANET) 7
Algorithm 174, 183
Allocated transmission rate 183
ALME (Abstraction layer management entity) 63
Amazon Web Services (AWS) 216
Anticipated transmission power 51
Antivirus software 116
Application layer 219
Application lifecycle management (ALM) 222
Application performance 218
Application program interface (API) 100
Application service provider (ASP) 108
Application software 97, 107
ARPA (Advanced Research Projects Agency) 7
Artificial intelligence (AI) 211, 216
Artificial Neural Networks 217
Attack-resistant networks 130
Automatic phoning 138
Automatic retransmission 52

B

Balancing security 201
Bandwidth utilization 176, 177
Big data 228
Bimodal distribution 179
Bomb-resistant network 7
Bottlenecks 173, 174, 186
Broad band internet 2
Buffering 175

C

Cable connection 154
Cache-based routing tables 178
Cache consistency mechanism 180
Cache data 200
Caching system 176
CAGR (Compound annual growth rate) 217
CCK (Complementary code keying) 158
CD-ROM (Compact disc read-only memory) 86
Cellular network 155
Cellular telephone networks 155
Central processing units (CPU) 76
Cirrus computer 74
CIX (Commercial internet exchange) 8
Client-server topology 13
Client validation 180

Closed circuit television (CCTV) 126
Cloud adoption 214
Cloud automation 212, 221, 222
Cloud computing 214, 229
Cloud friendly 218
Cloud networking 211, 212, 215, 228, 229, 230, 231
Cloud orchestration 212, 220, 221, 222, 223, 228, 229
Cloud service 216, 217
Cluster configuration 50
CMDU (Control message data units) 63
Coherency 174, 180
Command-line program 196
Communication standard 3, 12
Complex Instruction Set Computing (CISC) 184
Compression 192, 198
Computational capacity 214
Computational resources 4
Computer hardware 74, 77, 97, 98, 103, 107, 108
Computer networking 2
Computer network paradigm 135, 136
Computer networks 2, 33, 41
Computer pointing device 89
Computer Science 127, 145, 146
Computer system 73, 76, 83, 88, 89, 93, 97, 98, 99, 100, 101, 106, 107
Confidentiality service 140
Congestion 194, 195
Connection density 225
Connection-level parallelism 181
Connectivity problems 200
Connectivity subsystem 46
Control layer 219, 220
Control plane 218, 219, 225
Control unit (CU) 76
Conventional Backhauling 218
Conventional routers 218
CRC (Cyclic redundancy check) 51
Crucial-grounded eviction programs 180
Cryptographic techniques 130
Customer experience 201, 205

D

DAO (Destination advertisement object) 55
Data analysis 214
Data intensive 191
Data link layer 45, 56
Data link standard 49
Data packet 193, 195, 196
Data plane 219, 220, 226, 227
Data privacy 204
Data protection 126
Data security 130, 143
Data storage 76, 84, 85, 86, 87, 109
Data transfer rate 193
Data transmission 6, 28, 34, 193, 194
Data transmission-related underpinning technology 157
Decision element 226, 227
Deduplication 192, 198
Demilitarized zones (DMZs) 125
Denial of service (DoS) 132
Dependability 197, 203
Dependency management 222
Developmental adaptability 128
Dial-up connection 2, 34, 35, 36
Digital networking 211
Digital rights management (DRM) 106
Digital world 191
Direct access techniques 88
Direct communication 152
Distinctive channel access 52
Distributed caching architecture 177
Distributed database system 173
Distributed denial-of-service (DDoS) 202
Distributed routing 178
Distributed video streaming 173, 185, 186
DODAG (Destination-oriented directed acyclic graph) 54
DVD (Digital video disc) 86
Dynamic data caching 180
Dynamic website 11

E

Eavesdropping 133

Edge computing 203, 211, 212, 213, 228, 229, 230, 231
Edge computing model 213
Electromagnetic interference (EMI) 157
Electromagnetic waves 162
Electronic commerce 211
Encryption procedure 140
Encryption protocols 201
End-to-end network visibility 217
End-User License Agreements 97
EPROM (Erasable programmable read-only memory) 92
Error rates 192
Escrowed Encryption Standard 127
Estimation algorithm 183
Ethernet packets 226
Eviction attestation 180

F

Fiber-optic cables 160
Fleet management 225
Fog computing 203
FTP (File Transfer Protocol) 13, 20

G

Geographic region 218
Global area network (GAN) 156
Global positioning system (GPS) 137
Graphical user interface (GUI) 223
Graphics software 112
GSM protocol 155

H

Half-duplex dependable wireless connectivity 52
Hardware acceleration 201
Hardware failure 116
Hash functions 178
Heterogeneity 176
Hierarchical addressing 178
High CPU consumption 200
High data-level parallelism 175
High-level computer programming language 222
High-performance network 201
High-quality user experience 191
High-speed connection 1
HTML (Hypertext markup language) 10
Human intervention 221, 224
Hybrid design 178
Hybrid stock 178

I

Identical operations 182
IEEE (Institute of Electrical and Electronics Engineers) 44
IETF (Internet Engineering Task Force) 44
Immune system 141
Industrial machinery 213
Informal communication 20
Infrastructure as a service (IaaS) 221
Infrastructure layer 219, 220
Instantaneous communications 20
Instant messaging 211
Integrity service 141
Intent-based learning 211
Intent Based Networking (IBN) 224
Internet connectivity 152
Internet Engineering Task Force (IETF) 131
Internet of things (IoT) 205
Internet protocol (IP) 140
Internet Protocol Security architecture 131
Internet Protocol Suite 131
Internet technologies 2, 33, 37, 38, 41
Interpersonal message 4
Intra-domain routing control 226
Intrusion detection 129, 131, 135, 144
Intrusion detection systems (IDS) 220
IoT (internet of things) 225
IPS (Intrusion prevention systems) 201
IP spoofing 133
ISM (Industrial Scientific Medical) 51
ITU (International Telecommunication Union) 44

J

Jeopardize network security 202

L

Labor-intensive operations 217
Language processing 214
LAN (Local area networks) 218
Latency device 224
Layer parallelism 181
link-state discovery protocol (ldp) 219
Load balancing 176, 180
Local Area Ethernet Networks 7
Local Area Network (LAN) 5
Logical Link Control and Adaptation Standard (L2CAP) 57
Long-distance computation 19
Lucrative networking technologies 218

M

M2M (Machine-to-machine) 43
MAC (Medium Access Control) 44
MAC standards 44, 63, 66
Magnetic ink character recognition (MICR) 92
Magnetic tape 83
Malfunction 162
Malicious intent 138
Malware 202
Management plane 219
Management standards 44
Media streaming 175
Medium-sized businesses (SMBs) 108
Memory devices 78
Mesh systems 155
Modern screen technology 91
MPLS (Multiprotocol Label Switching) 218
MR (Magnetic resonance) 213
Multiprocessing 80
Multithreading 175

N

National Control Protocol (NCP) 8
Network administration 201
Network administrator 198, 200, 203, 205
Network architecture 129
Network bandwidth 163, 207
Network communication 136
Network congestion 116, 193, 195, 196
Network design 128, 129
Networking capability 98
Network Interface (NI) 184
Network latency 178
Network management 215, 217, 224
Network optimization 191, 192, 198, 203, 204, 206, 207, 208
Network performance 191
Network performance data 196, 205
Network processor 173, 189
Network protection 126, 129
Network protocol subsystem 180
Network safety 211
Network security 126, 128, 129, 131, 135, 141, 142, 143, 144, 145, 146, 147, 201
Network security mechanisms 201
Network Slicing 224
Network speed 203, 207
Network standards 44
Network topology 220
Network traffic 197, 198, 199, 200
Network virtualization 81
NIC (Network Interface Card) 30
Node configuration service 226

O

OCR (Optical character recognition) 91
OFDMA (Orthogonal Frequency Division Numerous Access) 53
OFDM (Orthogonal frequency division multiplexing) 154
OMG (Object Management Group) 61
Online gaming 194
Online purchasing 9
Online safety 214
Open Systems Interface (OSI) 128
Operating system (OS 98, 99, 102
Orchestration 212, 222, 231

Orchestration platform 221
Organic light-emitting diode (OLED) 94
OSI model 211
OSI (Open system interconnection) 211
OS (Operating Systems) 215
Outdated data 176
Overwhelm network 202

P

Packet Binary Convolution Coding (PBCC) 159
Packet data 175
Packet flow 198
Packet loss 191, 193, 194, 196, 200
Packet verification 52
PANs (Personal area networks) 153
Parallel computing 81
Parallelism 173, 174, 181, 182, 185, 186, 188
Parallel processing 81, 82
Peer-to-peer network 50
Pentium chip 9
Performance troubleshooting 199
Persistent storage 83
Personal information managers (PIMs) 112
Phishing 133
Physical network media 160
Platform as a service (PaaS) 221
Point of access (POA) 138
Point-to-point microwave 155
Polarizing documents 177
Population density 163
Presentation software 116
Private network 2
Processing power 73, 82, 103
Programmable microprocessors on network interfaces (PNI) 184
Protocol layer 181, 182
Proxy placement 180
Proxy servers 176
Pseudo security 127

Q

Quality of Service (QoS) 197

R

Radio access technology 224
Radio communication technology 151
Radio frequency wireless networking 157
Radio transmission 151
Random access memory 79
RAN (Radio access network) 53
Rapid expansion 173
Rapid technological innovation 184
Read-only memory (ROM) 79
Real-time analytics 214
Real-time performance 182
Reduced Instruction Set Computing (RISC) 184
Redundant information 198
Remote computation 21
Remote service 4
Renewable energy 155
Repetitive application deployment 222
Resource sharing 211
RFID (Radio frequency identification) 92
Rigorous analysis 197
Route aggregation 178
Router firewall 127
Routing 174, 178
Routing layer 46, 54
Routing protocols 178
Routing standards 44

S

Safeguarding software 136
SAN (Storage area network) 85
Satellite internet 2, 34, 35, 36
Scalability 176
SDN (Software-defined networking) 45
Secondary storage 83, 88, 121
Security engineering 134
Security management 129, 145
Security threats 203
Self-managing systems 223
Self-replicating programs 132
Sequential access 83
Sequential order 183

Server-based prefetching 179
Server invalidation 180
Serverless computing 216, 217
Seven-layer ecosystem 45
Signal transmission techniques 157
SIG (Special Interest Group) 54
Single processing unit 181
Single proxy cache 176
Slow network performance 194
SOA (Services-oriented architecture) 45
Social engineering 202
Software as a service (SaaS) 108
Software-defined network 218, 220
Software-defined wide area network\" (SD-WAN) 218
Solid-state storage (SSD) 87
Space network 150
Spanning tree 219
Spectrum utilization 224
Speech recognition 138
Spreadsheet software 115
Stand-alone systems 155
Static website 11
Strong cache consistency 180
Supply control information 183
Synchronization 181, 182
System memory 98

T

Tape cartridge 83
TDMA (Time Division Multiple Access) 49
TEDSs (Transducer electronic data sheets) 64
Telecommunications architecture 219
Telecommunications equipment 76
Terrestrial microwave communication 151
Time-effective manner 191
Total bandwidth 183
Traffic policing 198
Traffic shaping 192, 195, 198, 200, 206
Transmission Control Protocol/Internet Protocol (TCP/IP) 1
Transparency 176
Transport layer standards 44
Troubleshooting 199, 200
Troubleshooting network performance 206
TSCH (Time-Slotted Channel Hopping) 56

U

ULE (Ultra Low Energy) 54
User experience 201, 205
User-in-the-loop (UIL) 163

V

Video conferencing 3, 24, 25
Virtual machines (VMs) 221
Virtual Private Network (VPN) 5
Virtual telephone conversations 3
Vital responsibility 197
Vital traffic 197
Voice-recognition technology 89
VoIP (voice over internet protocol) 211
Vulnerabilities 191, 201, 202

W

Weak cache consistency 180
Web caching 185, 186, 187
Web caching behavior 176
Web conferencing 2, 24, 25, 33, 34, 35, 36
Web page 10, 17
Web Server 13
Web services 1, 2
WECA members (Wireless Ethernet Compatibility Alliance) 158
WEP (Wired Equivalent Privacy) 164
Wide area network (WAN) 5, 218
Wi-Fi communication 160
Wireless bridging 155
Wireless broadband services 224
Wireless personal area networks (WPAN) 166
Wireless technology 53, 67, 68, 149, 152, 154, 166
Wireless transmission standard 51
Word processor 115
World Wide Web (WWW) 1, 9, 22, 216

Kolibri 360 GmbH
Ferdinand-Jühlke-Straße 7
99095 Erfurt, Deutschland
produktsicherheit@kolibri360.de